D0722628

Research Themes for Events

FSC
www.fsc.org
MIX
Paper from
responsible sources
FSC® C013604

Research Themes for Events

Edited by

Rebecca Finkel

Queen Margaret University

David McGillivray

University of the West of Scotland

Gayle McPherson

University of the West of Scotland

Peter Robinson

University of Wolverhampton

www.cabi.org

CABI is a trading name of CAB International

CABI	CABI
Nosworthy Way	38 Chauncey Street
Wallingford	Suite 1002
Oxfordshire OX10 8DE	Boston, MA 02111
UK	USA
Tel: +44 (0)1491 832111	T: +1 800 552 3083 (toll free)
Fax: +44 (0)1491 833508	T: +1 (0)617 395 4051
E-mail: info@cabi.org	E-mail: cabi-nao@cabi.org
Website: www.cabi.org	

© CAB International 2013. All rights reserved. No part of this publication may be reproduced in any form or by any means, electronically, mechanically, by photocopying, recording or otherwise, without the prior permission of the copyright owners.

A catalogue record for this book is available from the British Library, London, UK.

Library of Congress Cataloging-in-Publication Data

Finkel, Rebecca.
  Research themes for events / Rebecca Finkel, Queen Margaret University, David McGillivray, University of the West of Scotland, Gayle McPherson, University of the West of Scotland, Peter Robinson, University of Wolverhampton.
     pages cm
  ISBN 978-1-78064-252-9 (hbk)
  1. Special events--Research. I. Title.

  GT3405.F56 2013
  394.2072--dc23

                    2013024758

ISBN-13: 978 1 78064 252 9

Commissioning editor: Claire Parfitt
Editorial assistant: Emma McCann
Production editor: Lauren Povey

Typeset by Columns Design XML Ltd, Reading, UK.
Printed and bound in the UK by CPI Group (UK) Ltd, Croydon, CR0 4YY.

Contents

Contributors

Anna Borley, University of Northampton, Northampton Business School, Boughton Green Road, Northampton, NN2 7AL, UK. E-mail: anna.borley@northampton.ac.uk

Alan Clarke, University of Pannonia, Faculty of Economics, Tourism Department, 8200 Veszprém, Hungary. E-mail: alan.clarke@turizmus.uni-pannon.hu

Larry Dwyer, University of New South Wales, Australian School of Business, Sydney, NSW 2052, Australia. E-mail: l.dwyer@unsw.edu.au

Rebecca Finkel, Queen Margaret University, Edinburgh, Queen Margaret University Drive, Musselburgh, East Lothian, EH21 6UU, UK. E-mail: rfinkel@qmu.ac.uk

Malcolm Foley, University of the West of Scotland, Paisley Campus, PA1 2BE, UK. E-mail: malcolm.foley@uws.ac.uk

Matthew Frew, Bournemouth University, School of Tourism, Dorset House, Talbot Campus, Fern Barrow, Poole, Dorset, BH12 5BB, UK. E-mail: mfrew@bournemouth.ac.uk

Gemma Gelder, University of Wolverhampton, Walsall Campus, Gorway Road, Walsall, WS1 3BD, UK. E-mail: gemma.gelder@wlv.ac.uk

Andrea Giampiccoli, Durban University of Technology, Hospitality & Tourism, Durban, South Africa. E-mail: andrea.giampiccoli@gmail.com

Joe Goldblatt, Queen Margaret University, Edinburgh, Queen Margaret University Drive, East Lothian, EH21 6UU, UK. E-mail: jgoldblatt@qmu.ac.uk

Gordon Hunt, University of the West of Scotland, A220, School of Creative and Cultural Industries, Paisley Campus, PA1 2BE, UK. E-mail: gordon.hunt@uws.ac.uk

Leo Jago, University of Nottingham, University Boulevard, Nottingham, NG7 2RD, UK. E-mail: leo.jago@nottingham.ac.uk

Allan Jepson, Tourism, Hospitality and Event Management Group, Room M210, Hertfordshire Business School, University of Hertfordshire, de Havilland Campus, Hatfield, AL10 9AB, UK. E-mail: a.s.jepson@herts.ac.uk

Jennifer Jones, University of the West of Scotland, Paisley Campus, PA1 2BE, UK. E-mail: jennifer.jones@uws.ac.uk

Seungwon 'Shawn' Lee, George Mason University, Prince William Campus, Bull Run Hall 222, 10900 University Blvd, MS 4E5, Manassas, VA 20110, USA. E-mail: slz@gmu.edu

David McGillivray, University of the West of Scotland, A220, School of Creative and Cultural Industries, Paisley Campus, PA1 2BE, UK. E-mail: david.mcgillivray@uws.ac.uk

Gayle McPherson, University of the West of Scotland, A220, School of Creative and Cultural Industries, Paisley Campus, PA1 2BE, UK. E-mail: gayle.mcpherson@uws.ac.uk

Clare Mackay, Glasgow Caledonian University, 70 Cowcaddens Road, Glasgow, Lanarkshire, G4 0BA, UK. E-mail: clare_l_mackay@yahoo.co.uk

Kevin Markwell, Southern Cross University, School of Tourism & Hospitality Management, Lismore Campus, Military Road, East Lismore, NSW 2480, Australia. E-mail: kevin.markwell@scu.edu.au

Laura Misener, University of Western Ontario, Faculty of Health Sciences, 1151 Richmond Street, London, Ontario, Canada. E-mail: laura.misener@uwo.ca

John Nauright, School of Sport and Service Management, University of Brighton, Greynore Building, Darley Road, Eastbourne, BN20 7UR, UK and George Mason University, Academy of International Sport, 4400 University Drive, Fairfax, VA 22030, USA. E-mail: jnaurigh@gmu.edu

Peter Robinson, University of Wolverhampton, Walsall Campus, Gorway Road, Walsall, WS1 3BD, UK. E-mail: p.robinson@wlv.ac.uk

Gordon Waitt, University of Wollongong, School of Earth and Environmental Sciences, Wollongong, NSW 2522, Australia. E-mail: gwaitt@uow.edu.au

Debra Wale, University of Wolverhampton, Walsall Campus, Gorway Road, Walsall, WS1 3BD, UK. E-mail: d.wale@wlv.ac.uk

Acknowledgements

_____

The editors would like to thank everyone who made this book possible, especially the contributors, who continue to push the boundaries of research in this exciting and emerging field.

1 Introduction

Rebecca Finkel,[1]* David McGillivray,[2] Gayle McPherson[2] and Peter Robinson[3]

[1]Queen Margaret University, Edinburgh, UK; [2]University of the West of Scotland, Paisley, UK; [3]University of Wolverhampton, Walsall, UK

When conceptualizing this book, the editors made a point to identify the key themes of the prevailing research literature in events and recognized the need to highlight the seminal literature and theoretical frameworks underpinning primary research in this growing subject area (e.g. Richards and Palmer, 2010; Foley et al., 2011; Getz, 2012). Broadly, this is an events management book framed in a research context drawing social scientific approaches. It differs from other subject-specific books by not focusing on operations or management but rather on theoretical frameworks illustrated through case studies. The goal is to shine a brighter spotlight on research, bringing it to the forefront of the discussion in the events management field. This is neither a research methods text nor a business text but rather a text for the events researcher to use as a guide for comprehending what are the particular challenges of conducting primary research in this field. As events research encompasses cross-disciplinary perspectives, drawing from tourism, leisure, cultural studies, urban geography, sociology, marketing and other social science and management discourses, not all of the divergent themes that events researchers pursue could be included. The editors, therefore, purposefully selected the themes for this book to present a consistency and coherence that many edited books lack.

In order to avoid creating a collection of chapters loosely linking scholars' research interests, a more coherent narrative from one chapter to another is developed by connecting the theoretical contexts of each theme as the reader progresses. The book begins with an exploration of the social issues, impacts and developments in events research; it then moves on to analysing economic and management aspects surrounding research into the events industry, addresses issues of technology and tools and concludes with more political and policy-oriented chapters to highlight research into the main debates in the public sector and sphere. There are obviously discussions of social, economic and political elements in most of the chapters, as they do not exist in isolation, and each topic was selected to help readers fully understand the myriad of approaches and processes involved in undertaking this type of research. The chapters also develop similar sub-themes in order to examine some of the most relevant concepts in current events research and demonstrate how they can be applied to various topics within the field. These include analyses of: (i) holistic interpretations of sustainability; (ii) the complexity of authenticity; (iii) governance and policy influences; (iv) risk assessment and management; (v) public order and safety; (vi) liminality and transformational experiences; (vii) legacy and impacts, evaluation and measurement; and (viii) social inclusion, exclusion and accessibility. These were also selected because many scholars, students and

*rfinkel@qmu.ac.uk

© CAB International 2013. *Research Themes for Events*
(eds R. Finkel *et al.*)

practitioners frame their research around these concepts and construe meaning through these various lenses. The aim was to allow scholars to capture the approaches to research that have been utilized to either conceptualize practice or showcase issues of practice presented in the form of case studies. The book has its own methodological approach that demonstrates a coherence around the analysis of key issues and this is an important addition to the field of research in this area.

Each chapter is set out consistently to make it easy for students and readers to follow. Authors were asked to follow a certain set structure in order for them to present their work in a way that would be comprehensible and meaningful for the reader. Each chapter begins with an introduction of key theories and concepts and comprehensive review of the pertinent literature for the subject. Relevant primary research is then set out followed by a brief discussion of research methods if appropriate. There are different methodologies and methods employed throughout the book, which gives the reader an idea of the breadth and depth of the approaches to events research design and can help inform innovative thinking about how to advance new research projects. One case study is presented in each chapter to exemplify the main themes. Multifarious types of events, such as festivals and Olympic Games, as well as many genres of events, such as culture, music, sport, to name a few, have been included. Also, the case studies analyse events of different size and scope from community-based events to mega events in order to demonstrate the differing processes and approaches required for conceptualizing and researching a spectrum of events. Internationalization is an important factor in events worldwide and many of the chapters have an international focus or deal with issues that are internationally relevant through the case studies, which are diverse and have a focus on the developing as well as the developed world. Together, these case studies illustrate a contemporary landscape of events research and form a narrative of the international events environment. The chapters end with conclusions, implications for the events arena, recommendations for future research and questions for thought and discussion.

Outline of Chapters

Setting the tone for an examination of the more social aspects of researching events, Dr Allan Jepson and Dr Alan Clarke explore community festivals illustrated through a case study of the Derby Jubilee Festival. This chapter provides an overview of community festivals and seeks to provide a more inclusive definition of community festivals, which is firmly set within a local community context. Researching community festivals is an emergent, growing and vibrant sector of the tourism and leisure industries, which are seen to have significant economic, socio-cultural and political impacts on the destination area and host groups. This chapter seeks to develop community festivals research by arguing for a future research agenda beyond economic impact assessments.

The chapter by Dr Laura Misener focuses on the potential of sporting events to help build stronger communities and influence the development of community-level social capital. The purpose is to focus on the emergence of ways to utilize sporting events to affect communities in a positive manner and showcase how events can be leveraged for greater social benefits. By situating the discussion in relevant theoretical frameworks, this chapter identifies and examines the positive potential of the events processes as a way of building social capital, engaging communities and improving the overall social well-being of community members. A case study of the 'Playing for Keeps' strategy of the 2012 Ontario Summer Games and the 2015 Pan American Games in Toronto, Canada, is used to locate the analysis of key concepts related to leveraging positive social impact, social leveraging, community social capital and community engagement.

Events and festivals are increasingly being used as the social panacea for fractured communities and neighbourhoods. The apparent crisis in the lack of civic engagement in communities and cities has seen a growth in the use of events and festivals to encourage volunteers to ameliorate this problem. The chapter by Professor David McGillivray, Professor Gayle McPherson and Ms Clare Mackay examines theoretical understandings of the social and human case for events and the belief that they can work as the 'social glue' of communities by aiding capacity building and cementing a sense of place identity (whether a nation, a city or a neighbourhood). By presenting a case study of the 2010 Delhi Commonwealth Games, this chapter looks at how human capital, in the form of volunteering, meets social capital, through extended and sustainable networks and how this can generate useful and new knowledge for event organizers.

It can be argued that there are a myriad of reasons to attend, spectate and participate in an event, or to be an actor within the staging of an event. Such interaction depends on: (i) multiple needs and motives; (ii) the circumstances of the individual; (iii) the factors in society that influence those individuals; and (iv) the types of events that are available and accessible to those motivated to attend or participate. The chapter by Ms Gemma Gelder and Mr Peter Robinson builds upon research exploring event motivations and discusses the factors that influence decision making among audience and participants in events.

Events research often encompasses concepts relating to personal, lifestyle and cultural identities. In addition to this, special events and festivals have become increasingly important vehicles for the public manifestation of gay and lesbian identities, often framed within a discourse of 'pride'. These events are of critical interest not only because of the way they have been mobilized to achieve sexual diversity goals but also because of the social, cultural, economic and tourism impacts that they have on destination communities. The chapter by Dr Kevin Markwell and Dr Gordon Waitt explores the relationships between events and sexualities. Particular attention is given to introducing five key terms in the literature: (i) impacts; (ii) the body; (iii) sexuality; (iv) pride; and (v) the closet. The Sydney Gay and Lesbian Mardi Gras serves as a case study with which to illustrate conceptual and empirical understandings identified in the literature review. The chapter concludes by drawing out the ramifications of the discussion for festival and events management policies and practices.

While it is widely recognized that there are many reasons for a host destination to stage an event, one of the most important is the economic impact that events are seen to generate. The attraction of economic benefits for the host destination has underpinned the fierce competition that often takes place for the right to stage an event and helps explain the fact that governments are prepared to invest substantial sums providing the infrastructure needed to host the event and to subsidize its operation. Dr Leo Jago and Professor Larry Dwyer provide an historical overview of the way that the economic performance of events has been evaluated with commentary as to the theoretical and practical advantages and disadvantages of the different approaches. A case study based on the Auditor General's evaluation of the Melbourne Formula One Grand Prix is then presented to highlight issues in relation to some of the more advanced techniques used to assess the performance of a major event. Recommendations are then made as to the manner in which the performance of events should be evaluated in the future.

The professionalism and scale of the events management industry has grown in the past decade, as evidenced by the increase in investment in events of all types and sizes throughout the world. In his chapter, Professor Joe Goldblatt explores the developments and processes involved when researching the management of events. The case study of The Gathering 2009 in Edinburgh, Scotland, is used to highlight the key issues of events research as it pertains to the concept of managed phenomenon.

The trend towards a new phenomenon called 'sport event tourism' has led to policy makers and politicians trying to capitalize on their investment in hosting both mega events and also local events. Strategies are now formed around the return on investment that sports events can bring to towns, cities and nations. However, in their chapter Dr John Nauright, Dr Andrea Giampiccoli and Dr Seungwon 'Shawn' Lee discuss recurring sports events (RSEs) and their impact on policy decisions for governments and the tourism of an area. The ongoing, year-on-year benefits of RSEs are highlighted and they are critical of the many externally driven return-on-investment-type reports that have been commissioned by stakeholders with a key interest. They argue that a strategy based around recurring sporting and touristic interest is more likely to bring success in terms of visitor numbers and brand identity than one-off events that only briefly leave their mark.

By their nature, events are spectacular, experiential and capture the imagination of consumers. Today, multimedia has a symbiotic relationship with events, as it lies at the heart of the production, promotion and experiential performance of these modern spectacles. Dr Matt Frew explores the evolution of the relationship between media, spectacle and events by drawing on a case study of Glastonbury Music Festival. The chapter evaluates the emergence of mass media forms in the 19th century and their relationship with the major events of that period, including the Expos, World Fairs and the Olympic Games. It then examines the ways in which transformations in the media landscape have developed symbiotically with the changing purpose, shape and profile of what might be termed 'mediaevents', including the Olympics, the World Cup and major carnivals. Important within this discussion is how, with the sophisticated development of consumer capitalism, an uneasy relationship between traditional and new media has emerged.

Many local governments have invested in events, such as arts festivals, because they have the potential to assist in the promotion and support of cultural agendas, urban regeneration, tourism and place marketing. As inter-urban competition increases due to globalization processes, the role of events becomes increasingly important in conveying positive messages about the liveability of a place. Dr Rebecca Finkel analyses the political agendas associated with festival provision and evaluates the impacts such instrumental policies can have on event content, atmosphere and experience. Using the Cardiff Festival as a case study, the connections between place, people, policies and festivity are explored. Cardiff Council can be seen to be seeking to enhance its destination image by leveraging cultural events to position itself on a par with and even surpassing other British capital cities and European port cities in order to compete for tourists, investment and resources.

Professor David McGillivray and Ms Jennifer Jones take as their focus the increasingly prevalent narrative of resistance that accompanies sporting, cultural and political events. Because certain events represent the site for contestation over meaning and identity, these events have also been effectively employed historically to communicate political discontent, disagreement, dissent and protest. This chapter explores the two main ways of analysing the mobilization of resistance around events in the contemporary period. First, there are those events that have, as their raison d'être, the promotion of a political struggle (protest) for rights, for equality or for justice (e.g. gay rights parades, anti-capitalism protests). Second, there are those events organized around sporting or cultural themes but which act as a vehicle for protest and resistance to wider political, social and economic circumstances (e.g. the Olympic Games or carnival). This chapter analyses the contemporary significance of the second event type, drawing on case material from the authors' own research investigations into sporting and cultural events, focused especially on the Olympic Games. Finally, particular attention is paid to the increasingly influential role of 'new' media activism as a means of mobilizing resistance to the excesses associated with major sporting and cultural events.

In order to avoid commodification and to protect the authenticity, heritage and identity of their festivals, organizers are recognizing the need to re-establish the ethos and cultural values of these events. It is evident that there are still a number of festivals that hold true to their ethical and moral values within their ethos and culture. The chapter by Ms Anna Borley, Ms Debra Wale and Mr Peter Robinson analyses Glastonbury Music Festival as an example of a festival that has retained vestiges of its heritage in order to sustain the legacy of the 1960s' countercultural era when ecological values were emerging in importance with many pioneers of the Green Movement gaining traction at that time. By raising environmental awareness, the 'greening' of events educates a new generation of festival goers in sustainable practices and can have an impact on audience behaviour at events. This chapter suggests that, while festivals are effective forums for short-term change in behaviour through green education, securing a legacy of green cultural behaviour is problematic and needs further consideration and ongoing educational initiatives.

Professor Malcolm Foley and Mr Gordon Hunt take as their focus the contemporary issue of the use of technology in changing the way that sporting mega events are viewed and consumed. The role of technology in transforming the spectator relationship with sport is conceptualized and discussed before they present a case study of the Formula One World Championship. The shift from a purely live experience to an immersive multimedia environment is discussed in terms of Formula One's development as a truly global sport paralleled by advances in technology, broadcasting and social media. The ability of Formula One teams and media to engage fans interactively through social media channels is showcased and the issue of fan choices between different media environments is examined. The opportunity for fans to personalize their experience of the event and the boundary between the physical and virtual experience of Formula One as a mega event is at the centre of the discussion. The move from the passive spectator to the active and interactive spectator through their use of technology is presented and implications for the way sporting events are delivered and bought are explored.

Events, although temporary, are symbolic in nature and thus have the potential to reflect and represent the values and customs of communities and societies throughout the world. By including chapters that set out different research processes and approaches illustrated through diverse case studies, this book seeks to capture a snapshot of the major concepts and contexts employed to interpret, evaluate and analyse these experiential phenomena in an effort to make sense of their growing influence and impacts on all of our lives.

References

Foley, M., McGillivray, D. and McPherson, G. (2011) *Event Policy: From Theory to Strategy*. Routledge, London.

Getz, D. (2012) *Event Studies: Theory, Research and Policy for Planned Events*, 2nd edn. Butterworth-Heinemann, Oxford.

Richards, G. and Palmer, R. (2010) *Eventful Cities: Cultural Management and Urban Revitalisation*. Butterworth-Heinemann, Oxford.

2 Events and Community Development

Allan Jepson[1]* and Alan Clarke[2]

[1]*University of Hertfordshire, Hatfield, UK;* [2]*University of Pannonia, Veszprém, Hungary*

Introduction

Community festivals are recognized as a worldwide phenomenon (Chacko and Schaffer, 1993; Getz, 1997; Derrett, 2003; Gabr, 2004) with about 400 active festivals in Europe alone (Maurin, 2003). Arcodia and Whitford (2006) depicted festivals as an emergent, growing and vibrant sector of the tourism and leisure industries, which are seen to have significant economic, socio-cultural and political impacts on the destination area and host groups. Community festivals research has become skewed in many areas and has followed a positive pattern of benefits or impact research perhaps similar to the way in which tourism has evolved into a field of study.

This chapter is split into three distinct sections. The first section provides an overview of community festivals and seeks to provide a more inclusive definition of community festivals, which is firmly set within a local community context. The second section seeks to investigate the literature surrounding community festivals, while the third and final section of the chapter argues for a future research agenda within community festivals.

Defining Community Festivals

Community festivals can be considered as part of the new wave of alternative or special interest tourism as identified by Poon (1993).

This means that they contain certain unique elements that are not replicated or mass produced. Festivals can be seen as prime manifestations of the experience economy (Pine and Gilmore, 1999) as they entertain, educate, hold aesthetic value and provide the platform for escapism. Falassi (1987) saw festivals as 'a sacred or profane time of celebration marked by special observances' maintaining that the social functions of a festival are closely related to community values. Farber (1983, cited in Getz, 1991) investigated festivals and public celebrations and concluded that much could be learned about a community's symbolic, economic, political and social life. Falassi (1987) then added to Farber's notions of symbolism by commenting that both the social and the symbolic meanings were closely linked to a series of overt values that the local community see as essential to its ideology, worldview, social identity, history, and its physical survival, all of which the festivals celebrate. It is these very elements that constitute local culture and give each festival its uniqueness, which, it is suggested, is ultimately what visitors desire.

Mainstream definitions of festivals all tend to agree that the local community is vital to the success of any festival. Goldblatt (1997), for example, suggests that a festival's key characteristic is the sense of community created. Festivals and community events can assume many roles. For example, Dunstan (1994, cited in Derrett, 2003) observes that

* a.s.jepson@herts.ac.uk

© CAB International 2013. *Research Themes for Events*
(eds R. Finkel *et al.*)

festivals and cultural events provide a forum for cultural values and traditions and a shared purpose. One view echoed by previous festival research is that festivals provide a unique opportunity for community cultural development (Getz, 1997). Other studies (Getz and Frisby, 1988; Getz, 1991, 1997; Dunstan, 1994, cited in Derrett, 2003) also suggest festivals can be used as building blocks for communities, and promote ethnic understanding within society, and in doing so preserve and celebrate local traditions, history and culture, or be used as a strategy to extend a destination's life cycle (Chacko and Schaffer, 1993). Dugas and Schweitzer (1997, cited in Derrett, 2003) maintain that to develop a sense of community is hard work, long term, especially to build levels of connectedness, belonging and support.

Cultures and communities can be thought of as inseparable as they constantly evolve together; therefore a definition of a community festival should have reference to local cultures, including popular cultures. Inclusive culture provides a greater opportunity for the festival or event to include and recognize all ethnic groups within its boundaries. In this sense then festivals and community events are multifaceted, both as a result of the culture contained within them and also as a result of the multitude of relationships within local community groups (Quinn, 2006). The other and most crucial aspect is that if a community festival is to represent the 'way of life' of its communities then it needs to have community inclusivity within the planning and decision-making process, otherwise there is an inherent danger that the festival will not accurately represent the local community. Taking these aspects into consideration this chapter defines a community festival as:

> a themed and inclusive community event or series of events which have been created as the result of an inclusive community planning process to celebrate the particular way of life of people and groups in the local community with emphasis on particular space and time.

This definition is one that promotes equality between all stakeholders through the planning process and also helps to bring attention to preserving sensitive natural, cultural or social environments and, in particular, community values.

A Review of Literature Surrounding Community Festivals

The following section of the chapter will provide an overview of literature about community festivals, which has grown rapidly over the last decade. Many studies have laid claim to what festivals can do for local communities, and not what local communities can do for the festival and its programme of events. The majority of studies proclaim that festivals can: (i) create or reinforce or challenge local or regional cultural identity (Hall, 1992; Smith, 1993, cited in De Bres and Davis, 2001; Boyle, 1997, cited in De Bres and Davis, 2001; Davila, 1997, cited in De Bres and Davis, 2001; Waterman, 1998; De Bres and Davis, 2001); (ii) boost local pride and enhance prestige and image, creating a sense of place (Avery, 2000; Derrett, 2003); (iii) create a sense of community (Dugas and Schweitzer, 1997, cited in Derrett, 2003); and/or (iv) create a sense of well-being (Falassi, 1987; Adams and Goldbard, 2001, cited in Derrett, 2003). Falassi (1987) also commented that as 'well-being' is important in a symbolic and social way, festivals therefore have the opportunity to periodically renew the life stream of a community and give sanctions to its institutions and possibly in some cases prove their value to the local population. Adams and Goldbard (2001, cited in Derrett, 2003) give a similar perspective with regard to community well-being and tell us that people turn to their culture: (i) to self-define and mobilize; (ii) to assert their local values; and (iii) to present them to visitors in a positive sharing of values. However, it is thought a positive sharing of cultural values can only be achieved as a result of good festival organization, communication and management.

De Bres and Davis (2001) suggest that festivals can play a major role in challenging the perceptions of local identity or, as Hall (1992) proposes, can assist in the development or maintenance of community or regional identity. This is thought to be of great significance to smaller community festivals as it could enhance their cultural values and help to share them with other communities. Derrett (2003) assimilates this position in her research into community festivals and their sense of place, commenting that if directed in the right way, festivals can perform a very useful community service by enhancing both group and place identity, a perspective that is backed up by further festival research (Smith, 1993; Boyle, 1997; Davila, 1997, all cited in De Bres and Davis, 2001; Waterman, 1998). Derrett (2003) comments further that this sense of place should be celebrated through the festival as visitors see this as an outward manifestation of community identity and a strong identifier of community and its people. Clarke and Jepson (2011) argue this case further and maintain that community festivals and events too often manufacture historical context and culture to ensure a good fit with potential visitors especially if the programme of events is externally facing as well as internally facing. Therefore, it should be the case that cultural analysis takes place within the local community to ensure that any creation or reinforcement of cultural identity is built on solid cultural foundations, which will in turn ensure that the events have full community representation and support.

Community festivals are susceptible to a system of cultural production that aims to make the festival product as widely appealing as possible and in doing so can change it to a more homogenous or commodified product, which is then disconnected from the local communities it set out to serve (Saleh and Ryan, 1993). This was explored further by Ferris (1996, cited in Derrett, 2003) and Robinson *et al.* (2004) who gave the term 'placeless festivals' to ones that fell victim to a globalized marketplace and had become detached from place, space and cultural identity. Community identity is a facet of local culture, and that culture is thought to be the blood that flows through society. Wheatley and Kellner-Rogers (1998, cited in Derrett, 2003), for example, see festivals as providing the heart to a community as their celebratory nature enables residents to experience freedom, and the ability to connect to the cultural values and indeed the society in which they live rather than

seeing the fixed structure and rules surrounding the community.

Festivals also have the potential to enhance or improve a destination's development and economic regeneration through maximizing event marketing to both existing and prospective tourists (Getz, 1991), but with this potential comes problems. Getz's perspectives are also carried forward by academics who identify regional and central government involvement in festivals as a way of attracting both tourists and possibly new residents to economically neglected regions, to improve the economic and social life of the area (Ashworth and Voodg, 1990; Kearns and Philo, 1993; Paddison, 1993; Jarvis, 1994, cited in Jeong and Santos, 2004; Hall and Hubbard, 1996; Jeong and Santos, 2004). Connected to the improvement of the economic and social life of an area is prestige and image enhancement (Avery, 2000), which is often achieved through civic boosterism marketing campaigns, which can have a big impact on a destination as a pull factor with a view to attracting festival visitors (Hill, 1988; Janiskee, 1996, cited in De Bres and Davis, 2001; Brown, 1997, cited in De Bres and Davis, 2001; Waterman, 1998). It could be further suggested that developing local infrastructures should become a major priority for the public sector and its communities, especially if we are to create sustainable community festivals and events. It can also be further concluded that research in community festivals has so far ignored how festivals can have an impact on society and social change, and also have a real impact on the quality of life (Liburd and Derkzen, 2009) of those who live, work, learn and represent the local community of a place.

Sustainability is something that is being taken forward by the events industry with standards such as BS 8901 and the International Standard ISO 1401 being adopted and developed for mega events such as the 2012 Olympics (London 2012 Olympic Games, 2011). Putting this further into context is Hubbert's (1956) peak oil theory, which currently puts oil production at its highest rate of production and further predicts the decline in availability and depletion of oil, based on its 35-year exploration, discovery and refinement cycle. This becomes increasingly important if we bear in mind that the earth will be home to 8 billion people by 2025 (International Energy Agency, 2011). A final and sobering thought is that the aim of a capitalist economy is to ensure we all have the same standard of living and if we take the UK standard of living we would need three planet earths full of resources, and if we took an American standard of living we would need five planet earths. A major issue to developing sustainable community events is that there needs to be a paradigm shift from just compliance to consciousness. Developing local community-event infrastructures would greatly lower the carbon footprint and perhaps achieve what is currently just a concept of a sustainable festival. For example, it is a simple process to obtain supplier addresses and then plot the distance travelled to arrive at the local community festival and this would make it clear how 'local' the festival actually is. Therefore, local community festivals and their stakeholders should look to develop 'community webs' whereby local services can be used and integrated into the festival structure for the benefit of a more localized economy.

Community festivals and events tend to stay small scale until the organizers of the events begin to see them as a commodity from which economic benefits can be sought, and thus the tourism perspective is reached (Getz and Frisby, 1988; Chacko and Schaffer, 1993; Mules and Faulkner, 1996). After this stage popular events could then be integrated into tourism development and marketing strategies (Getz, 1989; Mules and Faulkner, 1996; Mehmetoglu, 2001). Zukin (1991, cited in Jeong and Santos, 2004) refers to the above as processes beyond commodification that act upon the festival, which could include consolidation of social control, with resistance to that control or demonstrations of community solidarity. Festivals, though, are typically not spontaneous (Jeong and Santos, 2004); moreover events are meticulously planned, controlled by festival directors and producers in order to produce what Henderson (1991) refers to as 'serious fun'.

In selecting venues, artists, themes and direction, festival producers and directors can be seen as the 'gate keepers' (Greenfeld, 1988;

Derrett, 2003) of festivals as they have absolute control over who goes to events, and which community traditions or values are displayed to visitors through a manipulation of marketing processes or festival strategy. It has already been identified that there is huge diversity in festivals in whether they are national, international, regional or local, and that research so far has supported them as tourist attractions even though they may not start out as such (Getz, 1991, 1997, 2002; Allen *et al.*, 2002, cited in Gabr, 2004).

Festivals can also be viewed as demonstrations of community power (Marston, 1989; Rinaldo, 2002, both cited in Jeong and Santos, 2004). For example, political hegemony could be exercised over less powerful ethnic groups by supplying the vast majority with nationalized celebrations to deflect attention away from these minority groups and their real issues. Jarvis (1994, cited in Jeong and Santos, 2004) comments that, historically, festivals were produced for political purposes or used as a mechanism of social control (Burke, 1978; Rydell, 1984; Ekman, 1991; Jarvis, 1994, all cited in Jeong and Santos, 2004). For instance it could help to provide a voice platform for those in marginalized or minority groups to speak out on issues and challenge the views of the established order.

The majority of academics have positioned their research on how festivals evolve and become successful (Getz and Frisby, 1988; Frisby and Getz, 1989; Walle, 1994; Sofield and Li, 1998; Sofield and Sivan, 2003; Richards and Ryan, 2004; Quinn, 2006). Lade and Jackson (2004), for example, tried to identify key success factors for festivals and concluded that festivals need to build on solid foundations, utilize a marketing orientation strategy, and have rules for local community engagement. A summary of the success factors identified through academic literature for local community festivals can be seen in Table 2.1.

Academics have now begun to investigate how festivals are constructed and much of the research agenda has focused on the festival and its numerous and often complicated stakeholder interactions and relationships (Larson and Wikstrom, 2001; Larson, 2002). This has led to an identification of stakeholder roles and

Table 2.1. Community festival success factors.

Success factor	Researcher
Festival created a sense of place	Arnold (2001), Derrett (2003), Robinson *et al.* (2004)
Festival demonstrated community involvement, inclusion and support	Getz (1997), Theodori and Luloff (1998, cited in Derrett, 2003), Derrett (2003), Jeong and Santos (2004), Lade and Jackson (2004)
Festival identified rules of inclusion for local community	Lade and Jackson (2004)
Festival achieved community well-being – livability, vitality, viability, sustainability	Cox (1995, cited in Arcodia and Whitford, 2006), Hancock *et al.* (1999)
Festival planning involved market scanning/ feasibility/research to form appropriate strategy	Lee *et al.* (2004), Mehmetoglu and Ellingson (2005)
Market orientation (planning and development process)	Getz and Frisby (1988), Mayfield and Crompton (1995), Getz (1997)
Festival satisfaction surveys 'pre-/post-/during'	Kotler and Levy (1969, cited in Lade and Jackson, 2004), Hall (1992), Mayfield and Crompton (1995), Lade and Jackson (2004)
Experienced employees with practical knowledge and marketing knowhow	Crompton and Lamb (1996)
Strong foundations/central theme/directional and measurable festival goals or objectives/strong leadership of the festival director and management team/annual feasibility studies/ good-quality facilities with emphasis on existing as well as purpose-built facilities	Lade and Jackson (2004)
Cultural diversity in a local community festival is only achieved if there is an inclusive local community planning process	Clarke and Jepson (2011)

responsibilities (Reid and Arcodia, 2002, cited in Andersson and Getz, 2008; Getz *et al.*, 2007), and also to an analysis of management (Andersson and Getz, 2007) and more profoundly why festivals could actually fail to deliver on their overarching aims, objectives or promises to the local community (Getz, 2002). Clarke and Jepson (2011) took this one stage further by exploring the festival planning process through relationships of power and hegemonic control, which manipulated the decisions of key stakeholders within a community festival. This study was unique as it is thought to be the first to be able to track decisions made during the planning process though to the consumption stages of a community festival.

From this section it can be seen that in defining community festivals and events many positive benefits have been discussed as a result of staging festivals, although it is important to recognize that these positive aspects are rarely challenged as they can influence priorities for public sector expenditure. It should further be understood that documented benefits of community festivals should be analysed in detail as they are not necessarily easily reached in practice and are often only reached over a period of time. This then sets another precedent for event management research: to embrace longitudinal research methodologies in order to fully understand the impact of community festivals and events.

Creating a Research Agenda for Community Festivals

The final section of this chapter will focus on six emergent themes and provide a research agenda in order to better understand community festivals and the impact they have within our communities. Community festivals can be analysed from a variety of different research methodologies and contain huge diversity, using a mix of research methods to capture data through all the community festivals' development stages: (i) planning; (ii) delivery; and (iii) consumption. This further justifies the use of flexible research methodologies that can adapt to the festivals' unique stages of development. The majority of festival research has yielded positive perspectives and stated that local communities can foster or build community pride (Wood, 2002, cited in Liburd and Derkzen, 2009), prestige or create image enhancement. It could be argued that building or boosting local pride should be a feature at every stage of the community festival from consultation and planning through to representation of the community at the festival and consumption of community culture within the festival. What this means is that the community and its location should be represented and promoted and not just the festival and its programme of events. Further studies suggest that festivals can provide members of a community with the means of escapism (Jago, 1998) and facilitate the exchange of information, goods and services within communities (Ryan, 1995).

Decision making: planning, production and power

The first major research theme is concerned with analysing the planning and production processes that are employed within a community festival's development. This is an area that is often overlooked, but it is the planning process itself and the resulting decisions that dramatically shape the festival and its evolution within the local community. Behind every festival and event decision-making process lies the existence of a multitude of stakeholder relationships; all of these relationships are connected through different cultures but all are influenced by power. So far few studies have engaged with power and decision-making debates. Clarke and Jepson (2011) in their research demonstrated how the values inscribed within exclusive ('culture as

high art forms and intellectual stimulation') rather than inclusive ('culture as a way of life') definitions of 'culture' can exclude participation from community festivals; furthermore, the study tracked culturally loaded decisions from planning forums to representations of cultural diversity and event consumption. Church and Coles (2007) argued that power and tourism cannot be separated as a result of the often complex decision processes and therefore research should engage with power discourses locally, regionally, nationally or internationally. It could be argued that the role of power in events and the decision-making process is even more important within an events context as it is often a small team of people within the public sector making decisions on behalf of local people.

One key question when investigating the event decision-making process is where the power actually comes from. Church and Coles (2007) argue that power does not simply exist but must be created through the relationships between stakeholders. This is an example of what Wallerstein (1994, cited in Robbins, 2000) referred to as the 'civilizing process' as this is where stakeholders align themselves within particular power structures. Westwood (2002, cited in Church and Coles, 2007) observed that the very environment where the decision-making processes take place can influence both the decision-making process and the stakeholders' involvement, the environment becomes a 'site of power'. Clarke and Jepson (2011) found that once power had been defined and reinforced through the civilizing process, people would readily obey a chain of command, which reinforces Weber's view that power is more easily exercised if it is linked to authority (Weber, 1986, cited in Church and Coles, 2007). Those in charge of making decisions can then become Ioannides's 'power brokers' (Ioannides, 1998, cited in Church and Coles, 2007).

Another way to refer to this power over other stakeholders is by bringing in the concept of 'hegemony' (Gramsci, 1976, cited in Church and Coles, 2007), which is the exercise of power, achieved by consensus as well as coercion, over one or more groups in the local communities. Researchers can also explore the way in which this power or hegemony is enacted; power can be seen in the constant surveillance of decision making or what Foucault (1978, cited in Church and Coles, 2007) described as 'disciplinary power'. Power can also be achieved by restricting stakeholder knowledge, in terms of both the organizations who perhaps contribute financially to the festivals, and the local communities themselves. As long as discipline is retained due to any number or all of the factors described above, then there will be very limited resistance to power, which in a wider context means that those with power and hierarchical control can assume complete control over the direction of the festival and its events.

Therefore, power has direct impacts over decision-making processes within a local community festival and could produce a non-inclusive community festival, where stakeholders, including local communities, feel unable to challenge the established order of the planning process. This means that: (i) community opinion may not be represented; (ii) local cultural identity is defined by the dominant social groupings; (iii) little or no democracy exists within the festival planning process because of the dominance of those with power over decisions; and (iv) there is very little space to organize resistance to challenge decisions made on behalf of the local communities.

This demonstrates that local community festivals can only achieve cultural diversity and inclusion where the local community is invited, heard and empowered within the festival planning process.

A community festival case study: the Derby Jubilee Festival

This case study forms part of a much wider doctoral study (Jepson, 2009) and draws primarily on research by Clarke and Jepson (2011), which explores the cultural relationships and planning processes that exist within local community festivals and events. Derby is a city in the East Midlands of the UK with a population of 246,900 people (Derby

City Council, 2001). It was a heritage market town, which developed through engineering within the railway and aero-engineering sectors. Within the population it has been identified that 87% are of white British origin. A community-wide festival was planned for the whole of the city. There is a danger of missing information, namely the diversity of the ethnic groupings in the city as, for example, the majority white population includes approximately 10% who describe themselves as Irish, Polish and Lithuanian within an umbrella count of 'white other'. Similarly, the non-white populations forming around 10% of the total include significant numbers of Asian or British Asians who can trace routes to Indian, Pakistani, Bangladeshi and other Asian communities. The UK census allows for some but not enough community identifiers, as can be seen with the idea of the Black or Black British communities, which includes African, Caribbean and other Black categories. There is also an active Chinese community in the city, although statistically they register less than 1% of the total population.

The festival was originally created to fill the void in a lack of any citywide festival or community event since the mid-1990s. The other more widely cited reasons for planning the festival were to include three notable anniversary celebrations: (i) HM Queen Elizabeth II's Golden Jubilee; (ii) 25 years as a city; and (iii) 75 years since the Church of England created the new Diocese of Derby and the church assumed cathedral status. The festival also offered an opportunity to promote local businesses in the city through which the festival captured the majority of its sponsorship.

The community festival in Derby was the creation of three principal planners (the Dean of Derby Cathedral, the Chair of Derby University Council and the Chief Executive of the Lord Mayor's Office, Derby City Council) who appointed a fourth member to their team (the External Festival Coordinator from Nottingham). They ran steering-group meetings held at Derby Council chambers to establish an order to planning the community festival and made decisions to ensure the festival objectives were met. The festival objectives were to:

- embrace all sections of the city's diverse multicultural community;
- provide an opportunity for people living and working in the city to celebrate and enjoy a wide range of events;
- highlight the existing quality of the city's events calendar;
- stimulate new events and activities specific to the Jubilee Festival;
- focus attention on the main festival period;
- raise the city's profile regionally and nationally;
- celebrate the multiculturalism and diversity of the city;
- integrate the principles of the city's marketing campaign; and
- celebrate partnerships between local organizations.

The original concept for the festival was one that was predominantly concerned with 'high culture', and classical music and choral groups influenced by Beethoven, Chopin, Haydn and Mozart, which was not a concept that the city had any previous history of staging. The team of four mentioned previously was therefore in charge of a community festival with no prior experience of staging cultural events and no heritage on which to base their festival around. So while the festival objectives listed above speak of openness and inclusion, there was a lack of know-how in achieving these goals for the benefit of the local community. Another vital point was the lack of ways and expertise in which to measure and evaluate the success of the festival objectives. A multi-methodological approach to data capture and analysis of the festival through techniques mentioned in previous sections of this chapter captured the existence of a multitude of stakeholder relationships, all of which were connected through different cultures, and all were influenced in some way by power. It was these very relationships and the lack of them that influenced how the Jubilee Festival was constructed, delivered and consumed. The community festival in Derby demonstrated how power could be created during the civilizing process (Wallerstein, 1994, cited in Robbins, 2000), could lead to the creation of four power brokers (Ioannides, 1998, cited in Church and

Coles, 2007) and reveal the way that stakeholder politics and power could become a representation of cultural decisions impacting on thousands of people within very diverse local communities.

This festival further highlighted Church and Coles' (2007) position that power does not exist but instead must be created, and it demonstrated that one of the major factors within this was the location and space where power was being defined, which may be more important if it is within a politically charged site such as the city council chambers. It also reinforces, that once established, power within the creation of community events can be identified as a group of people who adhere to a hierarchy of decision making and rules, especially if power is linked to authority (Weber, 1986, cited in Church and Coles, 2007). Power was also achieved by organizers through restricting knowledge or disciplinary power (Foucault, 1978, cited in Church and Coles, 2007) about the festival and its events. For example, invitations to attend a one-off meeting about the festival and its proposed programme of events were sent out to local communities in the English language only, and this was followed by not inviting local community groups to planning forums. In terms of the impact in the community, this accelerated the distrust for the city government, and led to almost all of the local community cultural groups ignoring the invitation to meet and discuss the proposed festival. The organizers failed to understand the diversity of the local populations within the city and concentrated instead on the 87% white population and the culture they were thought to enjoy. What this tells us is that the organizers also failed to understand and use a definition of inclusive culture, preferring instead to view culture as a process of intellectual development. The four decision makers in the Derby Jubilee Festival therefore achieved hegemony over all stakeholders involved within the festival by:

- restricting their knowledge, in terms of both the organizations which contributed financially and the local communities themselves;
- retaining discipline and governance (helped by the spatial dimensions of power held by the political venue of the forums); and

- limited the opportunity for any resistance to power.

As a result of this hegemony exerted by the four festival planners, very little community resistance was possible, leading to all the decisions being taken with no input from any of the local communities within the city. This power over decision making and hegemonic control produced as a result:

- a non-inclusive community festival;
- a community unable to challenge the established order of the planning process on decisions affecting the festival, which meant that community opinion was not demonstrated (Marston, 1989; Rinaldo, 2002, both cited in Jeong and Santos, 2004);
- local cultural identity being defined by the dominant social group (Saleh and Ryan, 1993); and
- little democracy existing within the festival planning process because the four organizers were consistently in charge of making festival planning and construction decisions, which meant other stakeholders were unable to hold any influence or have an effect on the decision-making processes.

Community values and valuing the community

There is a great need for policy makers, politicians and the local public sector to understand the community values associated with wards in their community. Over the last decade festival planners, whether full time or occasional, have tended to adopt a generic approach to understanding the communities for whom they will stage festivals. In doing so they have created community events that do not live up to local expectations in favour of following a political agenda linked to tourism marketing or urban regeneration. There is then a need to understand, measure and create a framework to categorize community values in order to understand the types of events that should become a feature of a community festival or event. In addition to this, studies have yet to show the value of a community and its cultures to its locality, region or nation's identity.

Community cultural preservation

Festivals, although cultural and 'living' products, are still susceptible to the production process and pressures of globalization, which can make events more prone to being copied and mass produced. This is leading to more events becoming homogenous with very little recognizable culture, as documented in the review of literature earlier in the chapter. The public sector has a duty to preserve and protect local cultural traditions and sustain them for future generations.

There are large gaps within event research as to how local cultural traditions are presented within a structured programme of events or festivals, and if local traditions are presented, how these cultures engage with a more modern and globalized world to ensure they are preserved and passed down through the local community. Community culture and its representation have not yet been fully explored within academic studies. It could, for example, be examined at all stages of a festival planning process to explore its evolution or how it may change or become commodified to ensure it fits within the festival theme or programme of events.

Creating inclusive cultural festivals

Another future research direction is the need to explore more deeply the development of practical guidelines for monitoring best practice and community inclusion within the festival planning process. Researching practical guidelines for organizers to implement in order to monitor the planning process of local cultural events should ensure that equality and democracy become end products of the planning process along with the inclusion of community voices. The ideology of the 'community' within local cultural events should also form an area of research enquiry, especially within the current climate of immigration and transitional economies. The perspective of the 'community' as a research direction can be realized through researching motivational dimensions, which became a prominent part of this research context to allow comparisons between organizers and visitors. In addition, this gave further insight into organizers' cultural motivations in light of the aim to create a local community festival. This research has established that there is a clear need to research and understand multicultural or ethnic minority cultural motivations if local cultural events are to realize the potential they have to become fully inclusive.

Further research should centre on the idea of 'community' and how communities are best included within the planning process that produce events for them. The creation of inclusive festivals should be the main priority for those involved in the creation of community events and therefore represents a comprehensive area of research for the future. This is because at the moment it could be strongly argued that community events are falling short in what they can achieve within society. The comprehensive definition put forward in the first section of this chapter should be tested within localities staging festivals and events, to examine the role of local communities within the planning and production process and in particular the role local communities play in making decisions affecting their festival. Research should be focused on how to engage local communities within the planning process and ensure they have a voice throughout the festival's key development stages. Without the creation of inclusive festivals then cultural diversity will not be a positive feature of the festival, therefore research on audience profiling should also form part of the future research agenda in local community festivals. A final area of enquiry could then be the role of marketing within community festivals, and an investigation as to whether inclusive marketing becomes a feature of an inclusive festival or vice versa.

To achieve success within the future research arena of community festivals and events, flexible and unique research method-ologies need to be employed, as they are more likely to capture data on a multicultural and multi-faceted event such as a community festival. Using a variety of research methods and data collection techniques will allow data capture that is easily applied to each stage of the festival's construction. The authors' doctoral studies, for example, utilized: (i) semi-structured interviews; (ii) semi-structured questionnaires; (iii) event observations; (iv) photography; and (v) observation of planning forums. All of these ended up not with 'triangulation' but with 'quintangulation' of primary data. It is often the case that the cultural relationships within community festivals manipulate and shape decisions within the planning process, which is why inclusion of the local community is so important.

This final section of the chapter has set the scene for further research in the area of community festivals with a particular focus on practical guidelines for monitoring best practice and community inclusion. Within the planning process the focus is on: (i) exploring cultural, multicultural or ethnic minority motivations; (ii) establishing a conceptual framework for staging locally inclusive cultural events or programmes of events; (iii) establishing 'community' ideology; (iv) analysing power relationships within festival construction and within local communities; and (v) testing multi-methodological approaches within community festival research.

Questions for Students

1. What roles does 'power' play within the local community festival planning and decision-making process?

2. Discuss the implications of not including the 'local community' within the festival planning process.

References

Andersson, T. and Getz, D. (2007) Resource dependency, costs and revenues of a street festival. *Tourism Economics* 13(1), 143–162.

Andersson, T. and Getz, D. (2008) Stakeholder management strategies of festivals. *Journal of Convention and Event Tourism* 9(3), 199–220.

Arcodia, C. and Whitford, M. (2006) Festival attendance and the development of social capital. *Journal of Convention and Event Tourism* 8(2), 1–18.

Arnold, N. (2001) Festival tourism: recognizing the challenges; linking multiple pathways between global villages of the new century. In: Faulkner, B., Laws, E. and Moscardo, G. (eds) (2001) *Tourism in the 21st Century: Lessons from Experience.* Continuum, London, pp. 130–162.

Ashworth, G. and Voodg, H. (1990) *Selling the City: Marketing Approaches in Public Sector Urban Planning.* Belhaven Press, London.

Avery, P.M. (2000) City cultures as the object of cultural tourism 2000. In: Robinson, M. (2000) *Developments in Urban and Rural Tourism.* Business Education Publishing, Sunderland, UK, pp. 1–35.

Burke, P. (1978) *Popular Culture in Early Modern Europe.* Temple Smith, London.

Chacko, H. and Schaffer, J. (1993) The evolution of a festival: Creole Christmas in New Orleans. *Tourism Management* 14(4), 475–482.

Church, A. and Coles, T. (2007) *Tourism, Power and Space.* Routledge, London.

Clarke, A. and Jepson, A. (2011) Power, hegemony and relationships in the festival planning and construction process. *International Journal of Festival and Event Management* 2(1), 7–19.

Crompton, T. and Lamb, C. (1996) *Marketing Government and Social Services.* Wiley, New York.

De Bres, K. and Davis, J. (2001) Celebrating group and place identity: a case study of a new regional festival. *Tourism Geographies* 3(3), 326–337.

Derby City Council (2001) Derby Census Profile 2001 (People 1). Available at: http://www.derby.gov.uk/NR/rdonlyres/A28DD98F-AD11-4620-A62D C973B7E8 9644/0/FF_derbypeople1.pdf (accessed 12 February 2007).

Derrett, R. (2003) Making sense of how festivals demonstrate a community's sense of place. *Event Management* 8, 49–58.

Falassi, A. (1987) *Time Out of Time: Essays on the Festival.* University of New Mexico, Albuquerque, New Mexico.

Frisby, W. and Getz, D. (1989) Festival management: a case study perspective. *Journal of Travel Research* 28(1), 7–11.

Gabr, H.S. (2004) Attitudes of residents and tourists towards the use of urban historic sites for festival events. *Event Management* 8, 231–242.

Getz, D. (1989) Special events: defining the product. *Tourism Management* 10(2), 125–137.

Getz, D. (1991) *Festivals, Special Events, and Tourism.* Van Nostrand Reinhold, New York.

Getz, D. (1997) *Event Management and Event Tourism.* Cognizant Communication Corp., New York.

Getz, D. (2002) Why festivals fail. *Event Management* 7, 209–219.

Getz, D. and Frisby, W. (1988) Evaluating management effectiveness in community-run festivals. *Journal of Travel Research* (summer), 22–27.

Getz, D., Andersson, T. and Larson, M. (2007) Managing festival stakeholders: concepts and case studies. *Event Management* 10(2/3), 103–122.

Goldblatt, J. (1997) *Special Events: Best Practices in Modern Events Management.* Van Nostrand Reinhold, New York.

Greenfeld, L. (1988) Professional ideologies and patterns of 'gatekeeping': evaluation and judgement within two art worlds. *Social Forces* 66, 903–925.

Hall, C.M. (1992) *Hallmark Tourist Events: Impact, Management and Planning.* Belhaven Press, London.

Hall, T. and Hubbard, P. (1996) The entrepreneurial city: new urban politics, new urban geographies? *Progress in Human Geography* 20, 153–174.

Hancock, T., Labonte, R. and Edwards, R. (1999) Indicators that count! Measuring population health at the community level. *Canadian Journal of Public Health* 90(1), 22–26.

Henderson, G. (1991) *Large-scale Festivals.* Discussion Document. National Arts and Media Strategy Unit, Arts Council of Great Britain, London.

Hill, K.T. (1988) *Festivals, USA.* Wiley, New York.

International Energy Agency (2011) Available at: http://www.iea.org (accessed 22 December 2011).

Jago, L.K. (1998) Special events: a conceptual and differential framework. *Festival Management and Event Tourism* 5(1/2), 21–32.

Jeong, S. and Santos, C.A. (2004) Cultural politics and contested place identity. *Annals of Tourism Research* 31(3), 640–656.

Jepson, A.S. (2009) Investigating cultural relationships within the festival planning and construction process in a local community festival context. PhD thesis, University of Derby, Derby, UK.

Kearns, G. and Philo, C. (1993) *Selling Places: the City as Cultural Capital, Past and Present*. Pergamon Press, New York.

Lade, C. and Jackson, J. (2004) Key success factors in regional festivals: some Australian experiences. *Event Management* 9, 1–11.

Larson, M. (2002) A political approach to relationship marketing: case study of the Storsjoyran Festival. *International Journal of Tourism Research* 4(2), 119–143.

Larson, M. and Wikstrom, E. (2001) Organizing events: managing conflict and consensus in a political market square. *Event Management* 7(1), 51–65.

Lee, C.-K., Lee, Y.-K. and Wicks, B.E. (2004) Segmentation of festival motivation by nationality and satisfaction. *Tourism Management* 25, 61–70.

Liburd, J.J. and Derkzen, P. (2009) Emic perspectives on quality of life: the case of the Danish Wadden Sea Festival. *Tourism and Hospitality Research* 9(2), 132–146.

London 2012 Olympic Games (2011) Available at: http://www.london2012.com/press/media-releases/2008/08/olympic-park-construction-waste-will-not-be-wasted.php (accessed 25 December 2011).

Maurin, F. (2003) Festivals. *Contemporary Theatre Review* 13(4), 5.

Mayfield, T.L. and Crompton, J.L. (1995) The status of the marketing concept among festival organisers. *Journal of Travel Research* 33, 14–22.

Mehmetoglu, M. (2001) Economic scale of community-run festivals: a case study. *Event Management* 7(2), 93–102.

Mehmetoglu, M. and Ellingson, K.A. (2005) Do small-scale festivals adopt 'market orientation' as a management philosophy? *Event Management* 9, 119–132.

Mules, T. and Faulkner, B. (1996) An economic perspective on special events. *Tourism Economics* 2(2), 107–117.

Paddison, R. (1993) City marketing, image reconstruction and urban regeneration. *Urban Studies* 30, 339–350.

Pine, B.J. and Gilmore, J.H. (1999) *The Experience Economy: Work is Theatre and Every Business is a Stage*. Harvard Business School Press, Boston, Massachusetts.

Poon, A. (1993) *Tourism, Technology and Competitive Strategies*. CAB International, Wallingford, UK.

Quinn, B. (2006) Problematising 'festival tourism': arts festivals and sustainable development in Ireland. *Journal of Sustainable Tourism* 14(3), 288–306.

Richards, P. and Ryan, C. (2004) The Aotearoa Traditional Maori Performing Arts Festival 1972–2000: a case study of cultural event maturation. *Journal of Tourism and Cultural Change* 2(2), 94–117.

Robbins, D. (2000) *Bourdieu and Culture*. Sage, London.

Robinson, M., Picard, D. and Long, P. (2004) Festival tourism: producing, translating, and consuming expressions of culture. *Event Management* 8, 187–789.

Ryan, C. (1995) Finance, flowers and festivals – a case study of little economic impact. *Tourism Economics* 1(2), 183–194.

Saleh, F. and Ryan, C. (1993) Jazz and knitwear; factors that attract tourists to festivals. *Tourism Management* August, 289–297.

Sofield, T. and Li, F. (1998) Historical methodology and sustainability: an 800-year-old festival from China. *Journal of Sustainable Tourism* 6(4), 267–292.

Sofield, T. and Sivan, A. (2003) From cultural festival to international sport – the Hong Kong Dragon Boat Races. *Journal of Sport Tourism* 81, 9–20.

Walle, A. (1994) The festival life cycle and tourism strategies: the case of the Cowboy Poetry Gathering. *Festival Management and Event Tourism* 2, 85–94.

Waterman, S. (1998) Carnival for elites? The cultural politics of arts festivals. *Progress in Human Geography* 22(1), 54–74.

3 Events and Social Capital

Laura Misener*

University of Western Ontario, London, Ontario, Canada

Introduction

Event tourism has become one of the fastest-growing segments of the travel market (Getz, 2008), which can be largely attributed to the proliferation of cities vying to host large-scale events such as the Olympic Games, World Cup and World's Fair. The rationale for cities hosting sporting events is generally part of a broader agenda tied to economic initiatives designed: (i) to celebrate and promote cities (Whitson and Macintosh, 1996; Andranovich et al., 2001); (ii) to foster tourism within and around cities (Hall, 2004; Preuss, 2007); (iii) to foster development (Spilling, 1996); and (iv) more generally to garner media attention (Whitelegg, 2000; Horne, 2007). Concerns over the returns cities receive from hosting such events continue to grow, with claims that events service corporations and elites within cities (Whitson and Horne, 2006), and that economic benefits are grossly overstated (Mules and Faulkner, 1996; Baade, 2007; Porter and Fletcher, 2008). Some commentators suggest the practices surrounding the use of large-scale sporting events for civic and economic development are increasingly disconnected from local communities, neighbourhoods and local development activities (Hiller, 2000; Horne and Manzenreiter, 2006). As a result, there is a growing demand that events such as the Olympic Games also show that they positively impact other groups within the communities where Games are hosted (IOC, 1999; Eisinger, 2000; Jones, 2001; Misener and Mason, 2006, 2008; Gratton and Preuss, 2008). In fact, the International Olympic Committee (IOC) now requires all host cities to undertake an Olympic Games Impact Study to help foster an understanding that host cities and residents should be left with the best possible legacy in terms of venues, infrastructure, environment, expertise and experience (IOC, 2008).

The belief that 'sport is a universal language that can bring people together, no matter what their origin, background, religious beliefs, or economic status ... and improve the lives of whole communities' (Kofi Annan, Former United Nations Secretary-General, cited in UN, 2004) has been rarely scrutinized in the context of events. However, as cities that seek to host events are increasingly being asked to validate the events as accomplishments of social engineering above and beyond merely an entertainment and sport spectacle, emphasis on the potential for positive social impacts is growing. As an example, the bid for the London 2012 Olympic Games focused on regeneration and redevelopment of deprived areas of London with an express interest in redeveloping a sense of community in these areas through community well-being and increasing community-level social capital (DCMS, 2010).

As part of this shift to use events as feats of social engineering, scholars have recently

*laura.misener@uwo.ca

© CAB International 2013. *Research Themes for Events*
(eds R. Finkel *et al.*)

begun to focus on strategically identifying and capitalizing on the leverageable assets of events as a means to foster lasting social and economic benefits (Chalip, 2006; Kellett *et al.*, 2008). This perspective shifts focus away from evaluating event outcomes such as social and economic impact, and will allow cities to focus on what they can do to strategically position themselves within the context of more socially responsible, sustainable legacy planning for events. While there continues to be a dearth of criticism around the cost overruns, marginalization of local citizens, environmental costs and lack of sustainable legacy, this emergent focus on leveraging events to ensure communities maximize the positive outcomes is essential. With the spread to new regions of the world such as South Africa with the hosting of the 2010 World Cup and Brazil set to host the 2016 Summer Olympic Games, there is an increasing sense of urgency in these efforts to ensure that events are developed and planned appropriately to maximize positive returns and increase social well-being of local citizens (Carey *et al.*, 2011).

This chapter focuses on the potential of sporting events to help build stronger communities and influence the development of community-level social capital. The purpose is to focus on the emergence of ways to utilize sporting events to positively affect communities and showcase how events could be leveraged for greater social benefits. Through the lens of leveraging theory (Chalip, 2006), I situate the discussion on identifying and examining the positive potential of the events process as a way of: (i) building social capital; (ii) engaging communities; and (iii) improving overall social well-being of community members. From this perspective, rather than focusing on the problematic or detrimental aspects of events, I draw upon a 'strengths' or an asset-based approach (Mathie and Cunningham, 2003) to examine emerging strategies that can be used by cities and communities to maximize the positive impacts. In order to so, I begin with a discussion of the theoretical construct of leveraging, focusing on the distinction between event legacy and event leverage to highlight how events can positively influence communities' social well-being. I follow with a review of relevant literature on social capital to

help situate the discussion of leveraging events as a vehicle to acquire resources aimed at connecting communities to increase cohesiveness and overall participation in community life. A case study of the 'Playing for Keeps' strategy surrounding the 2012 Ontario Summer Games and the 2015 Pan/Para-Pan American Games in Toronto, Ontario, Canada is used to locate the discussion of key concepts related to leveraging positive social impact: (i) social leverage; (ii) community social capital; and (iii) community engagement.

Leveraging Events

Much of the literature on the outcomes of events has focused on the notion of legacy, which tends to imply automatic effects of hosting events and related projects. Mega events, in particular, usually involve substantial investment in capital projects, and can cause significant social effects in the form of new jobs, business opportunities and attracting visitors that would not otherwise have materialized. Mega events can also cause unintended and negative effects, which represent legacies of event hosting. Although the distinction is blurry, these impacts are different from effects that have been deliberately levered by attaching initiatives to events so that they deliver more optimal outcomes. The latter are referred to as 'leverage initiatives', defined by Chalip (2004) as 'those activities, which need to be undertaken around the event itself which seek to maximize the long-term benefit from events'. The event becomes the 'lever' with which wider ambitions are achieved. Other researchers call this process 'activation' (Chalip, 2006) a term that highlights that positive action needs to be taken in association with events to achieve desired outcomes.

The difference between the new approaches and those used in the past is to see it as a shift from an 'events as policy' approach to one in which the power of events and wider policy goals are synthesized (Smith, 2009). The event is effectively reduced from being the intervention to being the lever for certain effects, which are secured via parallel intermediations. To some extent, host cities have always had an eye on what they might achieve by staging events and have designed them accordingly. But there has been a lack of theoretical coherence of this approach that is brought about by Chalip's (2004) notion that events should be seen as opportunities for interventions and not merely interventions in themselves. A key distinction between leveraging and traditional approaches to event planning is that leveraging aims to produce a forward-thinking, strategic approach where both the impacts and the ways to achieve them are planned in advance of an event. This is why these authors describe leveraging as a 'more strategic *ex-ante*, analytical approach' rather than one that has an '*ex post*, impacts-driven, outcomes orientation' (O'Brien, 2007).

Leveraging of sport events has been studied from different perspectives: (i) business economics (Chalip and Leyns, 2002); (ii) destination branding (Brown *et al.*, 2002); (iii) social development (Smith, 2009); (iv) cultural benefits (Kellett *et al.*, 2008); and (v) volunteer development (Downward and Ralston, 2006). These studies demonstrate the value of a strategic leveraging approach. Kellett *et al.*'s (2008) research is perhaps the most pertinent in terms of demonstrating a strategic approach to leveraging through the celebrations of visiting teams during the 2006 Commonwealth Games in Melbourne, Australia. Port Philip, a city in close proximity to Melbourne, adopted Papua New Guinea as its 'second team', embracing the relationship as a means to build a legacy. The city planned numerous festivals, workshops and school activities, which resulted in a durable relationship with Papua New Guinea. The Port Phillip City Council was able to improve the working relationship between local government and schools and create some durable community networks of communication previously absent in the city. Geelong, another city close to Melbourne, adopted Wales as their second team; however, this was solely used as a means to represent the city's commitment to the Commonwealth Games. The city held a reception for the Welsh team and declared 'Celtic Day', but the activities did not foster cultural learning and there were no durable community relationships. This research suggests that the legacy of sporting

events can be improved by creating social or cultural activities, which can result in durable benefits for the host community.

This emerging focus on event leverage represents a paradigmatic shift away from purely impact studies to the examination of the strategies and tactics required to optimize desired outcomes from events. Leveraging recognizes that the consequences of events depend not on the mere fact that an event has taken place but rather on the ways that events are used, often in combination with other marketing and management resources, to render desired effects. The starting point (and focus throughout) is on what stakeholders want to achieve, rather than on merely what might be achieved through the mere hosting of an event. The key is to avoid being led and restricted by the requirements of the event, especially as these are often determined by outside interests that do not have a long-term stake in the host city. Thus in order to focus on social leverage of events for community benefit and building social capital, it requires an understanding of the available resources that can be drawn upon to develop specific strategic leverageable resources. This idea suggests a much more proactive attempt to positively influence the outcomes of hosting rather than merely an event 'triggering' legacies.

As Smith and Fox (2007) have suggested, one of the other innovative qualities of leveraging is that it can help host cities to move on from an approach involving top-down, physical interventions that rely on trickle-down effects, to projects that have more in common with a bottom-up approach. Large-scale top-down interventions tend to have negative implications for local communities, while leveraging allows sport events to be aligned with more enlightened development models that tend to be more focused on the 'wants' of target beneficiaries. By enhancing bottom-up initiatives (leverage), the idea is that the benefits for local community development and positive social impacts can be realized. From the perspective of leveraging theory, the event helps to inspire, frame, energize and prioritize community-based bottom-up projects that can enhance community-level social capital.

Social Capital and Sporting Events

Much of the scholarly literature on legacy for sporting events has focused on the physical, human and financial capital generated in the context of the bid process and staging of the event, with much less focus on the potential for the development of social capital (e.g. Burbank *et al.*, 2001; Walton *et al.*, 2008). Given the substantial investments in sports stadia and event-related infrastructure, it is not surprising that physical capital, which refers to equipment, real estate and physical infrastructure acquired to maximize the potential of said event, has been a central focus (Misener and Mason, 2006). While there continues to be much controversy over the building of facilities related to events, these facilities also play a vital role in either the enhancement or the prevention of building community (cf. Rosentraub, 1999, 2010; Eckstein and Delaney, 2002). Volunteers play a key role in the staging of events and as such human capital has been a significant focus in the scholarly literature. The legacy of volunteers has typically been studied from either the perspective of re-volunteering, in terms of the likeliness of volunteers to engage in a similar experience again, or in regards to enhanced employability of volunteers post-event. Recently, Nichols and Ralston's (2012) research on volunteers demonstrated the multifaceted legacy of event volunteering that has also helped increase individuals' sense of community and overall well-being. Beyond this, the connection between human capital and the development of social capital around events has received relatively little attention, despite the potential to affect community engagement strategies. A significant amount of attention has been paid to the financial capital, or lack thereof, generated by events (Mules and Faulkner, 1996). This attention typically focuses on the idea of using a multiplier analysis to determine if events bring additional visitor spending to a city and create increased flows of economic capital. The emphasis on the economic implications of event hosting is demonstrated by the Canadian Sport Tourism Alliance's Sport Tourism Economic Assessment Model (STEAM), used to generate basic knowledge of participant and spectator demographics, augmented with information contained in the event's business plan, to help determine the potential economic impact of hosting an event in Canada. Despite being a constant source of political and social tension in communities that host events, the use of economic impact analyses continues to be used to justify event-related expenditures.

Perhaps due to the tangibility of the aforementioned capitals, there are few empirical studies published that focus on the social, cultural and/or political impacts of festivals and events. In fact, despite social capital's swift rise in the policy making and community development discourses, only recently has the concept of social capital gained critical scholarly attention in the sport literature (e.g. Misener and Mason, 2006; Nicholson and Hoye, 2008). From this, very little attention has been paid to the concept in the events literature. The idea of social capital is grounded in the connectivity of human activity and, as Putnam (1993) explained, it involves 'features of social organization, such as networks, norms, and trust that facilitate co-ordination and co-operation for mutual benefit'. Thus, social capital is conceptualized in this chapter, not as a resource in itself but as a means to enhance the overall well-being of members of communities. It represents an attempt to objectify or embody the non-material social effects that are generated through the 'the structure and functioning of the social world' (Bourdieu, 1986). Social capital is characterized by relationships of mutual reciprocity embedded in social networks that enable action (Coleman, 1988, 1990; Lin, 2001). Most research on capital accumulation has often failed to recognize the importance of personal interactions and social relations that generate trust, establish expectations and create norms. Social capital's value centres upon the fact that it helps to focus attention on important aspects of community social structure and the significance of community participation. The concept is not new, but it brings together several aspects of social theory such as social structure, institutional and non-institutional relationships, trust, reciprocity, and community networking, into one theory of social action (Coleman, 1990). Thus, it can help to open up meaningful spaces of dialogue and action to advance the 'good' of society (Hutchinson and Vidal, 2004).

While there continues to be debate about the exact definition and grounding of social capital, the general premise is relatively basic: investment in social relations with expected returns in the marketplace (cf. Bourdieu, 1980, 1986; Coleman, 1988, 1990; Putman, 1993, 2001). I situate my discussion of social capital in Coleman's (1990) conceptualization that strong, healthy community networks are essential to growth and prosperity. Unlike Bourdieu (1986) who believed that only elite individuals could possess social capital, Coleman's theory of social capital is concerned with collectivity and the interpersonal connections among all community members. His idea of social capital was not limited to only the dominant class but could also beget real benefits to poor and marginalized communities (Field, 2003). The fundamental importance of this theory as it relates to events in the city lies in the collective sense of responsibility generated by broad-based participation in community initiatives. Thus it is not only elites that engage in problem solving when social capital is highly developed, rather a collective effort by members of a community. It is at this level that events can contribute to the generation of social capital in host communities.

Wilkinson and Pickett (2009) argued in their book *The Spirit Level* that societies that are more equal are generally better off in terms of infant mortality, life expectancy, violence, trust and social capital than more unequal societies. In addition, there appears to be strong theoretical support, and at least some empirical evidence to suggest that social capital 'is causally implicated in higher rates of economic growth, low crime rates, better population health, and more efficient and less corrupt government' (Halpern, 1999). This suggests a circular relationship between the notion of community-level social capital and individual well-being. While it is certainly naïve to suggest that social capital is the 'touchstone' of societal health and community well-being, social capital has been argued to benefit individuals and societies through lower rates of crime, better

health and less disadvantage. Building social capital can potentially be a powerful mechanism for planners and developers seeking to promote equity through valuing the importance of social networks and fostering social connections.

Rohe (2004) argued that social events such as street fairs and carnivals can be effective community engagement strategies if the tools exist to strategically enhance commonality and community-centred narratives that facilitate social interaction among citizens. Similarly, Briggs (2004) has suggested that leveraging civic activities to bring people together through shared celebrations and experiences will help to facilitate more social capital. Public spectacles encourage social renewal, as people feel empowered to start afresh and feel part of the transformation of their city/community (Jansson, 2005). This discussion is particularly salient in the context of leveraging events to engage communities.

Given the multidimensional nature of social capital, it is useful to differentiate between three broad types of social capital that are relevant to discussion of leveraging events for positive social impact. The first type is bonding social capital, which exists when social networks are among people who view themselves as similar. This type of social capital: (i) mobilizes solidarity; (ii) facilitates easier communication and understanding; and (iii) fosters trust. However, Sieppel (2008) also cautions that bonding social capital has the ability to reinforce narrow ideas about identity, segregation and exclusivity, which can create closed networks. The second type, bridging social capital, comprises relations of respect and mutuality between people who know that they are not alike in some socio-demographic sense (i.e. differing by age, ethnic group, class, etc.). Bridging social capital is crucial for building linkages across power differentials, especially to representatives of institutions responsible for delivering key services. Finally, linking social capital, which is perhaps the most appropriate surrounding the discussion of events (see Misener and Mason, 2006), is about the creation of opportunities for creating vertical linkages referring to alliances or associations formed to 'leverage resources, ideas, and information from formal institutions beyond the focal network' (Woolcock, 2001). These vertical bonds among less affluent individuals and those with more powerful positions (usually in formal institutions) (Middleton *et al.*, 2005) are central to beginning to break down the power relations and allow for bottom-up leveraging strategies that can positively impact community development.

Four essential elements have been discussed in the literature that help situate the discussion of the potential of civic events to facilitate social capital. The first notion centres upon encouraging behaviours including joining, participating actively in, and leading new/renewed civic institutions that help tackle tangible problems. It is perhaps pertinent at this point to note that not all forms of social capital result in positive outcomes. Encouraging citizens to join with others (i.e. bonding social capital) can result in public demonstrations, rallies and even rioting behaviour, which has the potential to further entrench the fractioning of communities. However, if social organizing is focused around a positive activity such as a sporting event, it is likely to have greater influence on the development of social capital. Second, helping people acquire new civic skills, with special attention paid to those typically disengaged citizens or those with less status in the community, is a critical element in the discussions of all forms of social capital. This can allow for a greater equity in community life, which has important results as discussed above (i.e. bridging social capital). The third element is about building more extensive, boundary-spanning and resource-rich networks to accomplish specific community building and social engagement goals (i.e. linking social capital). Finally, the essential element to make social capital 'stick' is about building supportive new norms that value and enable collectivities. This will allow for the broadening and solidifying of community participation and active citizen engagement.

While sport events are not necessarily unique in enabling and building social capital (see Arcodia and Whitford, 2006), sport is a significant socio-cultural phenomenon and a key form of associational life identified by Putnam (2001) as being important for social capital. Further, sports groups create networks that extend beyond the participants themselves, and sport plays a valuable role in building shared identities, creating a bond between different groups of people together as supporters of national, regional or local teams. Given the essential building blocks identified above, four broad strategies arise in regards to the utility of leveraging sport events to strengthen community capacity and build social capital (Chaskin *et al.*, 2001):

- enhancing the abilities of the individuals (education, leadership development);
- making community organizations stronger (capacity development);
- building links among individuals (community organizing); and
- building links among organizations (through collaborations, partnerships and so forth).

From this, I would argue that it is appropriate to examine the ways in which events can be leveraged to maximize these strategies to develop social capital in communities. Thus, the following sections will focus on a framework for leveraging event resources and related activities, using these four broad strategies as points of departure. The case study that will be presented demonstrates how events are beginning to be recognized as potential feats of social engineering, where the event-related resources present the building blocks to leverage the creation of social capital. With this in mind, the following case study examines the early planning stages of strategic leveraging tactics being employed to leverage the 2015 Pan/Para-Pan American Games in Toronto, Canada to increase social capital. The case is derived from an ongoing research project examining leveraging strategies and tactics of parasport events. Document and textual data was collected through a number of sources including: (i) community forums; (ii) online discussion forums; (iii) media outlets; (iv) bid documents; and (v) community planning documents. Two levels of textual analysis have been employed to analyse this documentation. The first was simple content analysis to determine the strategic approaches and decisions made in the delivery of legacy planning associated with the event. The second analysis involved re-analysing the texts from a discourse analysis approach (Potter, 1997) in order to formulate the 'story' of the Playing for Keeps campaign by attending to 'elements of importance that are worked up, attended to, and made relevant through interaction with external determinants' (Potter, 1997). For the purposes of representation herein, I am drawing upon primarily the textual analysis, which reveals the externalities (i.e. social forces such as youth crime, poverty reduction) driving the implementation of the strategic leveraging tactics. For example, one of the elements of developing the Playing for Keeps campaign was the use of large-scale community forums in which the outcome texts were analysed for patterns of language relating to social capital (i.e. trust, reciprocity), employed by participants, which were then reiterated in the guiding principles of the emerging strategies.

Case Study – 'Playing for Keeps': 2015 Pan/Para-Pan American Games, Toronto, Ontario, Canada

While this event has yet to come to fruition, it provides a meaningful case study given the planning processes, which have included a distinct and targeted strategy for leveraging event resources for developing social capital. I begin with a brief overview of the Games, followed by a discussion of the Playing for Keeps campaign, and conclude with a discussion of the results of the study as they relate to the four broad strategies emerging around using sporting events for strengthening community capacity.

Toronto was awarded the 2015 Pan/Para-Pan American Games in 2004. This is a large-scale multisport event. The Pan American Games involves athletes from all over the American continent participating in an international celebration of friendship and sport. The Pan American Sports Organization (PASO) governs the Pan American Games, which are held every 4 years in the year before the Summer Olympic Games, and selects the host city for each Games through a vote of its 41-member National Olympic Committees from South, Central and North America as well as the Caribbean. PASO, which is affiliated with the IOC, also has an important development mission to promote, develop and celebrate sports in the Americas and the Caribbean.

The Para-Pan American Games (specifically for athletes with a disability, similar to the Paralympic Games) were first held in 1999 in Mexico City with 1000 athletes from 18 countries competing in four sports. Rio de Janeiro (2007) was the first to host both the Pan and the Para-Pan American Games using the same venues offset in a similar fashion to the Olympic and Paralympic Games. Toronto will host the 2015 Pan/Para-Pan American Games. These Games are expected to involve 42 countries; 10,000-plus athletes and officials; and 20,000 volunteers. In addition, it is expected that the Games will create 15,000 jobs and attract more than 250,000 tourists to Toronto and the surrounding area (Toronto 2015, 2011).

Most sport event proposals and bid documents today include a legacy plan relating to infrastructure, job creation and knowledge translation; only recently have they also begun including plans for community development, social inclusion and building social capital. In the bid for the 2015 Pan/Para-Pan American Games, Toronto established its intent to service a broader legacy agenda of community inclusion and fostering social capital. 'Toronto 2015 will work to establish a consultative process that allows the region's diverse communities to engage in the decision-making process in respectful and meaningful ways' (Toronto 2015, 2011). Where traditionally major multi-sport events have focused mainly on developing the physical infrastructure and delivering the Games, often at the expense of corresponding social infrastructure, Toronto 2015 is seeking to take advantage of the opportunity to look towards enhancing social alongside human, physical and economic capital.

The Toronto Community Foundation's (TCF) report, *Toronto's Vital Signs Report*, highlighted a strongly divided city, a diminished sense of belonging, and sedentary lifestyles of Torontians (TCF, 2010). Further, the *Vital Signs Report* demonstrated the need to take action and develop a region-wide dialogue on how to improve social capital in the city. President and Chief Executive Officer of the TCF, Rahul Bhardwaj, saw the hosting of the 2015 Pan/Para-Pan American Games as a unique opportunity to open up this space for dialogue. The TCF is particularly interested in bringing community, business and government leaders together to discuss the idea of aligning common objectives (i.e. building linking social capital). TCF argued that the power of hosting the Games could provide for building stronger and healthier communities for Ontarians, and as a result became the lead social capital partner of TO2015 (Toronto 2015 Pan/Para-Pan American Games Organizing Committee).

In 2011, the TCF spearheaded the initiative called Playing for Keeps, which focuses on building upon the strengths of:

- past community consultations, summits and gatherings;
- networks of people and organizations; and
- opportunities surrounding the Games in communities.

The essence of this work is to develop social capital, which has been defined by TCF as 'networks and connections of diverse individuals and groups with shared values and assets. By investing in and leveraging social networks, social capital can be developed to help communities work, create, and play together' (TCF, 2011a). The group held three community forums during the spring and summer of 2011, in the Greater Toronto Region where the 2015 Games will be taking place. The forums were an opportunity for community organizations to gather and discuss the chance to leverage the event to: (i) build social capital; (ii) positively influence communities; and (iii) enhance opportunities for participation – in particular sport participation. Numerous partners, including the YMCA (Young Men's Christian Association), the Ontario Heart and Stroke Foundation, Toronto Parks and Recreation and the United Way, were involved in these discussions, which resulted in a report setting forth the opportunities and agenda for the Playing for Keeps campaign.

The key issues emerging from the forums relate to community regeneration, building community-level social capital, and engaging partnerships. From this, four core elements to strategically guide a campaign focused on developing community-level social capital: (i) principles; (ii) success indicators; (iii) aspirational scenarios; and (iv) challenges. To further demonstrate how these factors link to the literature on social capital, I return to the four broad strategies around using sporting events for strengthening community capacity and critically assess the current direction of the Playing for Keeps campaign.

Enhancing the abilities of the individuals (education, leadership development)

An emergent theme from the community forums was the focus on individuals typically marginalized in community life. The campaign's focus will be on youth and newcomers to Canada. This is highly representative of the geographic makeup of the region. Through the use of sports, arts and educational opportunities surrounding the Games, the intent is to engender more active, healthier and more resilient youth in the region. The implied intent is to develop far-reaching networks focused on youth engagement (i.e. bonding social capital) and the inclusion of the event in curricular and co-curricular activities. Beyond this, little is known about how the new Canadians and youth will become engaged through the hosting and leveraging processes.

Making community organizations stronger (capacity development)

The essential elements of the campaign focus on improving the capacity of community organizations and measuring these results through success stories. The Games offer the opportunity to connect otherwise disconnected groups and individuals, thus 'strengthening community bonding and belonging' (i.e. bridging social capital). In addition, leveraging Games resources to improve social inequities, improve health, well-being and happiness is described as a means to build stronger communities demonstrating success in these endeavours. The breadth of organizations involved in the community consultations is demonstrative of the intent to build capacity among the organizations involved in the project. However, from a critical perspective little is known about how the Games will be strategically positioned to enhance the capacity of community organizations. Without a concrete plan, the leveraging opportunity will potentially be missed to utilize Games-related resources for the capacity building. The next step for Playing for Keeps will ultimately be about defining the strategies to enhance the goals set forth; however, the strategic direction to develop organizational and community-level capacity remains unclear at this point. Furthermore, a key element that remains unclear is how the resources (including financial resources) will be secured to support the programmes. Many legacy programmes fail to be sustainable due to the lack of long-term financial commitment to programmes. The Playing for Keeps campaign will probably suffer the same fate if the long-term financial resources are not secured and committed to the programming early in the development processes.

Building links among individuals (community organizing)

The key element to the 'aspirational scenarios' element set forth by Playing for Keeps is the creation of a network of networks. In other words, the focus is on getting individuals in the communities involved in event-related activities and connected to one another (i.e. bonding and bridging social capital). This will be accomplished through: (i) encouraging volunteerism; (ii) creating opportunity for social events; and (iii) strengthening physical, cultural and social accessibility. In this way, the campaign aims to capitalize on the social assets of the events through celebration and community engagement opportunities. Building upon the work of Chalip (2004), who discussed the potential opportunity of the social celebration of events to bring people together, the Playing for Keeps campaign intends to utilize these social gatherings and celebratory

elements of the Games to enhance the opportunities for individual collaborations and community organizing. Again, at this point, there is no clear strategic direction in how these resources will be leveraged to ensure community organizing occurs in a positive manner to enhance social capital.

Building links among organizations (through collaborations, partnerships and so forth)

As part of the lead up to the 2015 Games, there will be efforts made to build bridges and expand networks among community organizations in the region (i.e. bridging social capital). It was clear from the community forums that there was much concern about the increasingly divided communities. Numerous organizations involved in the community forums discussed the need to enhance the opportunities for collaboration and cooperation among the diverse community organizations. This idea focuses on the collaboration and partnerships necessary to sustain connected communities. Playing for Keeps views the 2015 Games as a unique opportunity to foster these collaborations around celebratory ceremonies, cultural events and social events. The essence of this scenario is to create new pathways to connect people and provide opportunities for participation in community life. While the foundation has been laid for the development of these pathways through the community forums, there is a lack of follow-up at the current time in focusing on a strategic direction to continue to build these opportunities. For the Playing for Keeps campaign to be successful at the building these pathways, it will be necessary to examine the available resources for strategically leveraging to enhance community partnerships and opportunities for organizational engagement in the event. Without this type of strategic direction, it is unlikely that the campaign will be successful.

There is a distinct irony in the four broad strategies set forth by the TCF as the central focus of the TCF is bringing community, business and government leaders together to build common objectives and programmes (i.e.

building linking social capital). Despite this emphasis on what would typically be considered linking social capital, in which extensive, boundary-spanning and resource-rich networks are created to accomplish specific community building and social engagement goals, the Playing for Keeps campaign seems to focus on bonding and bridging social capital. Therein lies a central concern about the ability of the TCF to fulfil its objectives while meeting the goals of this particular campaign. Further, with the essentiality of financial resources to accomplish any of the goals set forth in the programmes, it is of great concern that the efforts to effect the development of social capital will go unrealized. It will take significant efforts and leadership to ensure that resources, skills and knowledge capital are invested in making this campaign a genuine leveraging strategy.

This case has demonstrated how one event is attempting to take on the task of using a large-scale event to influence the development of community-level social capital. A separate community organization has been set up with the express mission of developing strategies to capitalize on the Pan/Para-Pan American Games to: (i) encourage youth to become more involved; (ii) build inclusive and diverse collaborations that strengthen bonding social capital; (iii) improve access to active living and health lifestyle choices; and (iv) create pathways to connect people and provide opportunities (TCF, 2011b). From the perspective of social leveraging as described by Chalip (2004), the overall strategic approach is promising in that the efforts to capitalize on the social celebration of the events are a key component to engaging communities and developing social capital. However, the central concern with the strategy put forth by Playing for Keeps and the TCF in its current form is that it falls short of developing concrete, measurable actions. The plan for 'Enduring Social Capital Legacies' focuses on reiterating what has been well laid out in much of the social capital and community engagement literature related to creating networks, and actively engaging citizens. At this point in time, the organization has yet to develop a core action strategy and clearly define responsibility for enacting the lofty goals set forth in its current agenda.

Further, there are enormous challenges, such as: (i) identifying leadership; (ii) reflecting on diversity; (iii) ensuring youth and parental support; (iv) overcoming social isolation; and (v) securing the financial resources necessary to successfully meet the goals. While the efforts and direction of this organization are certainly noteworthy, it is too early to know if they will be successful at actually influencing social capital. None the less, it is highly encouraging to note that such a large-scale event is making an effort to recognize the potential to leverage the event resources to enhance the positive social impact where so many other events have failed to do so in the past.

Conclusions and Future Research

There is a growing demand that large-scale sport events show that they positively impact local communities where Games are hosted (Eisinger, 2000; Jones, 2001; Gratton and Preuss, 2008; Misener and Mason, 2008). Through the lens of leveraging theory, it is possible to move away from merely evaluating event outcomes such as social and economic impact, and to focus on what cities can do to strategically position themselves within the context of more socially responsible, sustainable legacy planning for events. Despite the lack of a clear plan to attain their objectives, it is enlightening to see Playing for Keeps piggy backing on the hosting of the 2015 Pan/Para-Pan American Games to attempt to influence community-level social capital through encouraging citizen engagement, fostering community networks, and creating pathways to support inclusivity of youth and new Canadians. These leveraging tactics demonstrate a move to a more socially sustainable approach to hosting events.

There remains much work to be done in this area. The literature on leveraging in sport events is sparse. With more events engaging in leveraging tactics to affect community development and social change, research is needed to understand the effects of these strategies. Few empirical strategies have emerged to address social capital. However, some such as Gibson *et al.* (2002) have used scales of physical income to investigate levels of social capital. Others have attempted to qualitatively investigate the development of social capital (see Kellett *et al.*, 2008). However, there remains a significant gap in the sport and social capital literature addressing the concept empirically. It is necessary to develop accurate evaluations to ensure the continued success of developing social infrastructure. It will also become all the more critical to understand how these events and leveraging tactics are affecting host communities, within and beyond the region of the Games. There is a lack of understanding about the effects of leveraging tactics on local and regional development strategies and thus future research must take an interdisciplinary approach to understanding event-related outcomes. Finally, if events are truly to make a difference in the lives of local community members, marginalized citizens and the disenfranchised, I believe researchers need to engage these individuals in the co-creation of research strategies and processes. This is truly the only way to accurately understand the effects of events on developing community-level social capital.

Questions for Students

1. What four strategies can be used to influence the development of social capital through the hosting of events? Can you give examples of how these might be implemented?
2. What does leveraging theory offer for the study of events and social impacts?

References

Andranovich, G., Burbank, M.J. and Heying, C.H. (2001) Olympic cities: lessons learned from mega-event politics. *Journal of Urban Affairs* 23, 113–131.

Arcodia, C. and Whitford, M. (2006) Festival attendance and the development of social capital. *Journal of Convention & Event Tourism* 8(2), 1–18.

Baade, R.A. (2007) The economic impact of mega-sporting events. In: Andreff, W. and Szymanski, S. (eds) *Handbook on the Economics of Sport*. Edward Elgar, Cheltenham, UK, pp. 183–196.

Bourdieu, P. (1980) Le capital social, note provisoires. *Actes de la Recherche Science Sociales* 31, 2–3.

Bourdieu, P. (1986) *Distinction*. Routledge, London.

Briggs, X. (2004) Social capital: easy beauty or meaningful resource? *Journal of the American Planning Association* 70, 142–192.

Brown, G., Chalip, L., Jago, L. and Mules, T. (2002) The Sydney Olympics and brand Australia. In: Morgan, N., Pritchard, A. and Pride, R. (eds) *Destination Branding: Creating the Unique Destination Position*. Butterworth-Heinemann, Oxford.

Burbank, M.J., Andranovich, G.D. and Heying, C.H. (2001) *Olympic Dreams: the Impact of Mega-events on Local Politics*. Reinner Publishers, Boulder, Colorado.

Carey, M., Mason, D. and Misener, L. (2011) Social responsibility and the competitive bid process for major sporting events. *Journal of Sport and Social Issues* 35, 246–263.

Chalip, L. (2004) Beyond impact: a general model for sport event leverage. In: Ritchie, B.W. and Adair, D. (eds) *Sport Tourism: Interrelationships, Impacts and Issues*. Channel View Publications, Clevedon, UK, pp. 226–252.

Chalip, L. (2006) Towards social leverage of sport events. *Journal of Sport and Tourism* 11, 109–127.

Chalip, L. and Leyns, A. (2002) Local business leveraging of a sport event: managing an event for economic benefit. *Journal of Sport Management* 16, 132–158.

Chaskin, R.J., Brown, P., Venkatesh, S. and Vidal, A. (2001) *Building Community Capacity*. Aldine de Gruyter, New York.

Coleman, J.S. (1988) Social capital in the creation of human capital. *American Journal of Sociology* 94, 95–120.

Coleman, J.S. (1990) *Foundations of Social Theory*. Cambridge University Press, Cambridge, UK.

Department of Culture, Media and Sport (DCMS) (2010) Plans For the Legacy from the 2012 Olympic and Paralympic Games. Available at: http://www.culture.gov.uk/publications/7674.aspx (accessed 1 August 2011).

Downward, P. and Ralston, R. (2006) The sports development potential of sports event volunteering: insights from the XVII Manchester Commonwealth Games. *European Sport Management Quarterly* 6, 333–351.

Eckstein, R. and Delaney, K. (2002) New sports stadiums, community self-esteem, and community collective conscience. *Journal of Sport and Social Issues* 26, 236–249.

Eisinger, P. (2000) The politics of bread and circuses: building the city for the visitor class. *Urban Affairs Review* 35, 316–333.

Field, J. (2003) *Social Capital.* Routledge, London.

Getz, D. (2008) Progress in tourism management. Event tourism: definition, evolution, and research. *Tourism Management* 29, 403–428.

Gibson, H., Willming, C. and Holdnak, A. (2002) 'We're Gators ... not just Gator fans': serious leisure and University of Florida football. *Journal of Leisure Research* 34, 297–424.

Gratton, C. and Preuss, H. (2008) Maximizing Olympic impacts by building up legacies. *International Journal of the History of Sport* 25, 1922–1938.

Hall, C.M. (2004) Sports tourism and urban regeneration. In: Ritchie, B. and Adair, D. (eds) *Sports Tourism. Interrelationships, Impacts and Issues.* Channelview Publications, Toronto, pp. 192–205.

Halpern, D. (1999) *Social Capital: the New Golden Goose?* Nexus/Institute for Public Policy Research (IPPR), Cambridge University.

Hiller, H.H. (2000) Mega-events, urban boosterism and growth strategies: an analysis of the objectives and legitimations of the Cape Town 2004 Olympic bid. *International Journal of Urban and Regional Research* 24, 439–458.

Horne, J. (2007) The four 'knowns' of sports mega-events. *Leisure Studies* 26, 81–96.

Horne, J. and Manzenreiter, W. (eds) (2006) *Sport Mega-events: Social Scientific Perspectives of a Global Phenomenon.* Blackwell Publishing, Oxford.

Hutchinson, J. and Vidal, A.C. (2004) Using social capital to help integrate planning theory, research, and practice. *Journal of the American Planning Association* 70, 142–192.

International Olympic Committee (IOC) (1999) Sustainability Through Sport – International Olympic Committee. Available at: www.olympic.org/Documents/.../Sustainability_Through_Sport.pdf (accessed 30 August 2011).

International Olympic Committee (IOC) (2008) IOC 2008 Sustainable Development Report – Rio Tinto. Available at: www.riotinto.com/documents/ReportsPublications/IOC_SD2008.pdf (accessed 30 August 2011).

Jansson, A. (2005) Re-encoding the spectacle: urban fatefulness and mediated stigmatisation in the 'City of Tomorrow'. *Urban Studies* 42(10), 1671–1691.

Jones, C. (2001) Mega-events and host-region impacts: determining the true worth of the 1999 Rugby World Cup. *International Journal of Tourism Research* 3, 241–251.

Kellett, P., Hede, A.M. and Chalip, L. (2008) Social policy for sport events: leveraging (relationships with) teams from other nations for community benefit. *European Sport Management Quarterly* 8, 101–121.

Lin, N. (2001) *Social Capital: a Theory of Social Structure and Action.* Cambridge University Press, New York.

Mathie, A. and Cunningham, G. (2003) From clients to citizens: asset-based community development as a strategy for community-driven development. *Development in Practice* 13, 474–486.

Middleton, A., Murie, A. and Groves, R. (2005) Social capital and neighbourhoods that work. *Urban Studies* 42(10), 1711–1738.

Misener, L. and Mason, D.S. (2006) Creating community networks: can sporting events offer meaningful sources of social capital? *Managing Leisure* 11, 39–56.

Misener, L. and Mason, D.S. (2008) Urban regimes and the sporting events agenda: a cross-national comparison of civic development strategies. *Journal of Sport Management* 22, 603–627.

Mules, T. and Faulkner, B. (1996) An economic perspective on special events. *Tourism Economics* 2, 314–329.

Nichols, G. and Ralston, R. (2012) Lessons from the volunteering legacy of the 2002 Commonwealth Games. *Urban Studies* 49, 169–184.

Nicholson, M. and Hoye, R. (eds) (2008) *Sport and Social Capital.* Elsevier Butterworth-Heinemann, London.

O'Brien, D. (2007) Points of leverage: maximizing host community benefit from a regional surfing festival. *European Sport Management Quarterly* 7, 141–165.

Porter, P.K. and Fletcher, D. (2008) The economic impact of the Olympic Games: *ex ante* predictions and *ex poste* reality. *Journal of Sport Management* 22, 470–486.

Potter, J. (1997) Discourse analysis as a way of analyzing naturally occurring talk. In: Silverman, D. (ed.) *Qualitative Research: Theory, Method and Practice.* Sage, London, pp. 144–160.

Preuss, H. (2007) The conceptualisation and measurement of mega sport event legacies. *Journal of Sport and Tourism* 12, 207–227.

Putnam, R.D. (1993) The prosperous community: social capital and public life. *American Prospect* 4, 13–24.

Putnam, R.D. (2001) *Bowling Alone. The Collapse and Revival of American Community.* Simon & Schuster, New York.

Rohe, W.M. (2004) Building social capital through community development. *Journal of the American Planning Association* 70, 143–144.

Rosentraub, M. (1999) *Major League Losers: the Real Cost of Sports and Who's Paying For It,* 2nd edn. Basic Books, New York.

Rosentraub, M.S. (2010) *Major League Winners: Using Sports and Cultural Centers as Tools for Economic Development.* CRC Press, New York.

Seippel, O. (2008) Public policies, social capital and voluntary sport. In: Nicholson, M. and Hoye, R. (eds) *Sport and Social Capital.* Elsevier Butterworth-Heinemann, London, pp. 233–256.

Smith, A. (2009) Theorizing the relationship between major sport events and social sustainability. *Journal of Sport and Tourism* 14, 109–120.

Smith, A. and Fox, T. (2007) From event-led to event-themed regeneration: the 2002 Commonwealth Legacy Programme. *Urban Studies* 45, 1125–1143.

Spilling, O.R. (1996) The entrepreneurial system: on entrepreneurship in the context of a mega-event. *Journal of Business Research* 36, 91–103.

Toronto 2015 (2011) About Us. Available at: http://www.toronto2015.org/lang/en/about-toronto/about-paso1. html (accessed 27 August 2011).

Toronto Community Foundation (TCF) (2010) *Toronto's Vital Signs Report.* Available at: http://www.tcf.ca/ vitalinitiatives/vitalsigns.html (accessed 30 August 2011).

Toronto Community Foundation (TCF) (2011a) Playing for Keeps. Available at: http://www.tcf.ca/ vitalinitiatives/playingforkeeps.html (accessed 30 August 2011).

Toronto Community Foundation (TCF) (2011b) About Playing for Keeps. Available at: http://playingforkeeps. ca (accessed 10 September 2011).

United Nations (UN) (2004) United Nations Sport for Development and Peace. Press release. Available at: www.un.org/sport2005/resources/statements/kofi_annan.pdf (accessed 10 June 2009).

Walton, H., Longo, A. and Dawson, P. (2008) A contingent valuation of the 2012 London Olympic Games: a regional perspective. *Journal of Sports Economics* 9, 304–317.

Whitelegg, D. (2000) Going for gold: Atlanta's bid for fame. *International Journal of Urban and Regional Research* 24, 801–817.

Whitson, D. (2004) Bringing the world to Canada: 'The periphery of the centre'. *Third World Quarterly* 25, 1215–1232.

Whitson, D. and Horne, J. (2006) Underestimated costs and overestimated benefits? Comparing the outcomes of sports mega-events in Canada and Japan. In: Horne, J. and Manzenreiter, W. (eds) *Sport Mega-events: Social Scientific Perspectives of a Global Phenomenon.* Blackwell Publishing, Oxford, pp. 73–89.

Whitson, D. and Macintosh, D. (1996) The global circus: international sport, tourism, and the marketing of cities. *Journal of Sport and Social Issues* 20, 278–295.

Wilkinson, R. and Pickett, K. (2009) *The Spirit Level.* Bloomsbury Press, New York.

Woolcock, M. (2001) Social capital in theory and practice. Where do we stand? In: Ishman, J., Kelly, T. and Ramswamy, S. (eds) *Social Capital and Economic Development: Well-Being in Developing Countries.* Edward Elgar, Cheltenham, UK.

4 Events and Volunteerism

David McGillivray,[1]* Gayle McPherson[1] and Clare Mackay[2]

[1]*University of the West of Scotland, Paisley, UK;* [2]*Glasgow Caledonian University, Glasgow, UK*

Introduction

Events and festivals are increasingly being used as the social panacea for fractured communities and neighbourhoods. The apparent crisis in the lack of civic engagement in communities and cities has seen a growth in the use of events and festivals to encourage volunteers to ameliorate this problem. This chapter examines theoretical understandings of the social and human case for events and the belief that they can work as the 'social glue' of communities by aiding capacity building and cementing a sense of place identity (whether a nation, a city or a neighbourhood). The chapter looks at how human capital, in the form of volunteering, meets social capital, through extended and sustainable networks and how this can generate useful and new knowledge for event organizers.

Structurally, the chapter first presents a review of literature that examines motivations for volunteering, volunteer management, volunteering as a public policy tool and, finally, the specifics of event volunteering. Methodological preoccupations in event volunteering research are then discussed, including the approach taken to the generation of the chapter's case study – the 2010 Delhi Commonwealth Games Handover Ceremony. The case study illustrates how 32 local councils in Scotland were asked to participate in securing volunteers to represent Scotland in the Closing Ceremony of the 2010 Commonwealth Games in India. The case study provides research insights into volunteer motivations for involvement before, during and after the event itself and explores associated issues relating to participation and identity, levels of community engagement and future volunteering intentions. The uniqueness of such a case study is that the volunteers were participating in a mass cultural performance but part of a sporting event, and this is reflected in the reasons for engagement at an individual and community level. The case study analysis is based upon the robust review of literature that is presented and thus able to offer a comprehensive analysis of the research theme and the case study, revealing how volunteer engagement can lead to successful new social networks being forged through events.

Volunteering and Public Policy

As this text is concerned with research themes for events, the literature discussed in this chapter focuses predominantly on volunteering at major sporting events. However, to embed major event volunteering in its political, economic and social context, it is necessary to open this review with a brief discussion of the role of volunteering as a public policy tool. Over

*david.mcgillivray@uws.ac.uk

the last decade, volunteering has become increasingly prevalent in public policy discourses, in the UK and further afield. This is illustrated at the global and European level by: (i) the United Nations Year of Volunteering in 2001; (ii) the Manifesto for Volunteering in Europe; and (iii) the European Year of Volunteering 2011. At the national level in the UK this is illustrated by the establishment of: (i) the Volunteer Centre (now Volunteering England); (ii) the Make a Difference initiative; (iii) Millennium Volunteers; and (iii) the Year of the Volunteer in 2001 (Rochester, 2006). The establishment of Volunteer Development Scotland in 1984 and 50 volunteer centres across the country, the Scottish Millennium Volunteers Programme and the Scottish Executive's (2004) _Volunteering Strategy_, suggests that volunteering is similarly important for the UK's devolved administrations. A growing body of evidence indicates that volunteering can benefit the economy by helping those excluded from the labour market to get back to work by providing them with skills, experience and qualifications (Scottish Executive, 2004), and allowing them to build professional networks. In addition to the economic benefits, volunteering is increasingly being seen as a means of creating 'softer', more intangible, benefits such as the opportunity to: (i) build social networks and capital (Misener and Mason, 2006); (ii) create a sense of community and citizenship (Rochester, 2006); (iii) create civic and national pride (Baum and Lockstone, 2007); (iv) aid social inclusion and cohesion; and (v) increase equality (Rochester, 2006). Volunteering strategies can, thus, be seen as cross-cutting the policy field to create positive externalities in the areas of health and well-being, education and criminal justice, as well as wider society (Scottish Executive, 2004).

While governmental and non-governmental organizations have promoted the societal benefits of volunteering in recent years, the academic community has also taken a greater (critical) interest in the professed outcomes achievable through this field. In particular, the research community has focused attention on the concept of social capital and its relationship with volunteering, which could, it is argued, reverse the decline in civic participation found in many parts of the world. Social capital has attracted a significant amount of attention in recent years as fears over the fragmentation of communities and a generalized decline in civic engagement has increased. Associated with the work of Bourdieu (1986), Coleman (1988), Putnam (1993, 2000) and Hall (1999) common definitions of the term emphasize the importance of strengthening networks, fostering community connectedness, generating feelings of trust and safety and creating a sense of belonging, reciprocity and civic participation through the development of an empowered citizenry. Theoretically, events and festivals should be able to make a contribution to the generation of social capital, given their social nature, emphasis on collectivity and, often, local setting. Moreover, because events and festivals permit dialogue and relationships to form across age, gender, social class and ethnic categories they can make a contribution to bridging long-standing social divides and encouraging citizen participation – benefits also claimed for volunteering.

The potential contribution of events and festivals in strengthening social capital is recognized in the case made for hosting a variety of large- and small-scale events, not just in the UK but also across the world. For example, Misener and Mason (2006) have tied the idea of social capital with sporting event legacy using the case of Manchester's 2002 Commonwealth Games. They argue that in studying events consideration has been given over to physical and human capital (the skills and training needs to deliver major events), but too little attention has been paid to the social capital concept. A lot is known about physical capital in terms of equipment, real estate and physical infrastructural legacies, and a growing knowledge is available on human capital relating to the recruitment of a skilled volunteer force to deliver large-scale events. However, understandings of how to secure social capital as an outcome of investments in large-scale sporting events are less well developed. It is here that human capital, in the form of volunteering, meets social capital – extended and sustainable networks – which can generate useful new knowledge for event organizers.

Taking a strategic approach to volunteering can help to combine the physical, the human and the social (and perhaps, with educational programmes, the cultural too), enhancing skills, fostering networks and widening cultural experiences. However, much of the existing research alludes to the role of events in building social and human capital but fails to adequately detail how and why these outcomes are achieved.

Volunteering at Major Sporting Events

Before focusing on the case study to illustrate a successful model for securing social capital through major event volunteering, it is important to take a step back to consider the etymology of major event volunteering strategies and policies. The importance of volunteering at major sporting events can be traced to the 1980s when 6703 volunteers were involved in the 1980 Lake Placid Winter Olympics (Green and Chalip, 2003) and the organizers of the 1984 'capitalist' Olympic Games (Burbank *et al.*, 2001) in Los Angeles built a volunteer army of an unprecedented size to help achieve their aim of maximizing profit while minimizing expenditure (Wilson, 1996; Green and Chalip, 2003). Green and Chalip (2003) note that the number of volunteers involved in major sporting events has continued to increase since the Los Angeles Olympic Games, and Auld *et al.* (2009) suggest that major sporting events have grown to the extent that they simply could not be staged without the vast numbers of volunteers that lend their support.

Baum and Lockstone (2007) build on Cnaan *et al.* (1996) and Davis-Smith's (1999) conceptual framework of volunteering to frame their critical discussion of the suitability of definitions of volunteering for major sporting event volunteers and draw a distinction between 'continuous or successive' volunteering and 'discrete or episodic' volunteering. Harrison (1995) suggests that discrete or episodic volunteers – such as major sporting event volunteers – are customized in their choice of activity. Similarly, Baum and Lockstone (2007) note the relevance of Hustinx

and Lammertyn's (2004) distinction between collective and unconditional volunteers who volunteer regularly over a period of time and have strong ties to the organization for which they volunteer, and reflexive and distant volunteers who volunteer infrequently, offer less of their time over a short-term period, yet are focused in their choice of voluntary activity and may also 'demonstrate a strong sense of loyalty to their organization and its mission' (Baum and Lockstone, 2007, p. 34). Likewise, Stebbins (2003, p. 7) suggests that sport event volunteering can be seen as participating in 'project based leisure', which he defines as 'short-term, reasonably complicated, one-off or occasional, though infrequent, creative undertaking carried out in free time'. According to Stebbins (2003, p. 7) 'project based leisure ... requires considerable planning, effort, and sometimes skill or knowledge'.

There is also evidence to suggest that major sporting event volunteers are similar to general volunteers and sports volunteers in that they are likely to be 'highly educated and come from professional occupations' (Treuren and Monga, 2002, p. 138). A number of studies suggest that major sporting event volunteers are a fairly homogenous group that reflect the gender and age profile of participants and spectators of the sports involved (Coyne and Coyne, 2001; Holmes and Smith, 2009; Pauline and Pauline, 2009). However, Holmes and Smith (2009, p. 143) and Ralston *et al.* (2005) suggest that 'the international and often intercultural appeal' of major sporting events such as the Olympics and Commonwealth Games means that they attract large numbers of volunteers with a wide range of volunteer profiles.

When considering major sport event volunteers, it is clear that there are differences between their motivations to participate, primarily because of the halo effect of the events themselves (and their international significance) and due to the expectation around temporary, yet intense, engagement. Returning to the preceding discussions, the project-based leisure and distant and reflexive nature of major sport event volunteers creates problems when trying to generate sustainable networks necessary for the achievement of social capital benefits. If wider societal benefits are to be accrued, then a more sophisticated understanding of the motivations of major event volunteers is required.

Major sport event volunteer motivations

A number of studies relating to the motivation of major sporting event volunteers have been based on scales adapted from the work of Cnaan and Goldberg-Glen (1991). Farrell *et al.* (1998), for example, developed the 28-item Special Event Volunteer Motivation Scale to explore the motivations of 300 volunteers at the Canadian Women's Curling Championship. Farrell *et al.* (1998) found that the motivations of major sporting event volunteers could be grouped into four categories:

1. Purposive (useful contribution to society).
2. Solidarity (interaction, group identification and networking).
3. External traditions (family traditions and volunteer career).
4. Commitments (external expectations and personal skills).

Farrell *et al.* (1998) found that volunteers were most likely to be motivated by the purposive dimension and least likely to be motivated by external conditions and commitments. Similarly, Wang (2006) tested five categories of motivation: (i) altruistic; (ii) community concern; (iii) personal development; (iv) ego enhancement; and (v) social approval. Yet Wang (2006) found that for major sporting event volunteers, only the latter three had positive impacts on the intention to volunteer. Ego enhancement had the largest effect on intention to volunteer, followed by personal development and social approval (Wang, 2006). Wang's (2006) findings suggest that the motivation to volunteer at major sporting events varies according to the event. This idea is supported by Coyne and Coyne (2001) who found that volunteers at the Honda Classic Professional Golfers Association (PGA) Tournament in Florida were primarily motivated by their love of golf. Similarly, Giannoulakis *et al.* (2008) developed the Olympic Volunteer Motivation Scale (VMS) and found that volunteers at the 2004 Olympic

Games in Athens were primarily motivated by Olympic-related factors. They suggest that as the greatest show on earth, the Olympic Games perhaps attracts people to volunteer for reasons that differ to other sporting events. Bang *et al.* (2009) tested a revised version of the VMS and found that expression of values was the most important motivation for the volunteers studied, followed by patriotism, love of sport, interpersonal contacts, personal growth, career orientation and extrinsic rewards. Karkatsoulis and Michalopoulos (2005, p. 588), meanwhile, reveal that findings from an opinion poll conducted 'among a sample of 2,000 individuals aged 18 through 65' who had applied to volunteer at the 2004 Olympic Games suggests that the main motivation for volunteering was to make 'a contribution to the motherland'. This was followed by the opportunity to be part of a unique experience, and 'the importance of the objective' (Karkatsoulis and Michalopoulos, 2005, p. 588).

In the UK context, Downward and Ralston (2005) conducted a qualitative study prior to the 2002 Commonwealth Games in Manchester and found that the primary motivations for volunteering were: (i) the altruistic desire to give something back to society, sport and Manchester; (ii) the desire to be involved, feel useful and be part of a team; and (iii) the desire to be part of a unique experience like the Commonwealth Games (Ralston *et al.*, 2004). These findings are supported by MacLean and Hamm (2007) who suggest that the motivation to volunteer at peripatetic events is driven by the desire to promote and advance the community. Hoye and Cuskelly (2009), however, suggest that the motivations of major sporting event volunteers change over time. Ralston *et al.* (2005) conducted research to explore the motivations of Manchester's 2002 Commonwealth Games volunteers both prior to, and post-event. Their results revealed that volunteers were primarily motivated by the excitement of the Games, the opportunity to experience 'the chance of a lifetime' and to meet 'interesting people' (Downward *et al.*, 2005, pp. 512–513). This was followed by the opportunity to support sport, do something useful for the community, and be part of a team. Over time, the chance of lifetime motivation decreased in importance, while doing something useful for the community, being part of a team, and helping Manchester and the North West became stronger motivations. Some of these changes can, of course, be put down to volunteer management interventions, but it does indicate that motivations are fluid and do not remain the same. It also suggests that, while the spectacle effect is important in the attraction and recruitment of volunteers, this wanes as volunteers become more involved in the event – and, crucially, this finding has implications for policy makers in the way they go about sustaining these positive feelings of teamwork, contributing to their city and making a difference for the community.

Managing major sporting event volunteers

The episodic and temporary nature of major event volunteering means that 'in contrast to other volunteering settings and events that take place periodically, major sporting events do not have a pool of regular volunteers' (Holmes and Smith, 2009, p. 102). In practice, the absence of this regular pool means that volunteer programmes are needed to build and manage the army of volunteers required for the event (Chanavat and Ferrand, 2010). Given the scale and complexity of major sporting events, a long leadtime is usually required. The recruitment process for the 2006 Commonwealth Games, for example, began 15 months prior to the event (Lockstone and Baum, 2009). Before recruitment, an evaluation of the roles and tasks required to stage the event is needed to determine the number of volunteers required (Chappelet, 2000) – and this cannot be divorced from the wider legacy objectives set for the event.

Although major sporting events often require vast numbers of volunteers, the supply often exceeds demand and, hence, recruitment campaigns are often targeted at universities, clubs and sponsorship communities rather than the general public, particularly for areas that require a certain type of expertise (Chappelet, 2000). While Holmes and Smith (2009) suggest that volunteer recruitment campaigns should be targeted at groups that are under-

represented in volunteering, Smith and Fox (2007, p. 10) argue that this 'has been notoriously difficult to achieve'. In addition to targeting different groups, the literature on sports event volunteering suggests targeting recruitment campaigns towards volunteer motivations (Hoye and Cuskelly, 2009), and as suggested above, the barriers faced by volunteers (Cleave and Doherty, 2005). Ralston *et al.* (2005) and Nichols (2009) thus suggest emphasizing the once-in-a-lifetime opportunity that volunteering at a major sporting event offers. Pauline and Pauline (2009) suggest that if sporting knowledge is not necessary, this should be emphasized in the recruitment materials to help attract a broader spectrum of volunteers. Given that one of the major barriers faced by potential volunteers is a lack of time, Cleave and Doherty (2005, p. 102) propose that recruitment campaigns offer volunteers flexibility and voluntary positions that require shorter commitments. Cleave and Doherty (2005) recommend that recruitment materials make the requirements and expectations of volunteers explicit to help reduce anxiety over 'the fear of the unknown, lack of skills ... and the application process'. The recruitment materials for the 'Count Yourself In' volunteer programme for the 2002 Commonwealth Games in Manchester, for example, stipulated that volunteers would be required to: (i) work 'for at least 10 days of the two week event'; (ii) attend 'an interview and training sessions'; and (iii) be 'aged 16 years or over, and be able to provide their own accommodation' (Lockstone and Baum, 2009, p. 103).

Applicants who applied to volunteer at the 2006 Commonwealth Games in Melbourne were interviewed by telephone then assessed at roadshows held in each of the Australian capitals (Lockstone and Baum, 2009). The 2006 Winter Olympics in Torino, on the other hand, benefited from the expertise of its sponsor Addecco – a recruitment company – which provided staff to aid the recruitment and selection of volunteers. A more innovative approach was adopted by the organizers of the 2000 Olympic Games in Sydney who 'trained 500 university students studying human resources to conduct many of the volunteer selection interviews' (Lockstone and Baum,

2009, p. 103). Likewise, a number of volunteers at the 2002 Commonwealth Games in Manchester were 'interviewed by other long-term volunteers' (Ralston *et al.*, 2004, p. 21). According to Chappelet (2000, p. 252) volunteer 'selection should be made on the basis of skills, candidates' preferences, and any accommo-dation and transport constraints'. Volunteers at the 2002 Commonwealth Games in Manchester, however, felt that their preferences and 'skills were rarely taken into account during the recruitment process' (Ralston *et al.*, 2004, p. 21).

Given that the psychological contract between the volunteers and the organization begins in the initial stage of correspondence, it is important that organizers nurture the relationship in the lead up to the event in order to maintain volunteer motivation and reduce attrition (Ralston *et al.*, 2004). Nichols (2009, p. 230) thus advocates making 'the psychological contract as explicit as possible'. This can be achieved by producing a written code of conduct detailing the responsibilities of both the organization and the volunteer (Nichols, 2009) or through regular communication in the form of newsletters, text messages, a dedicated radio programme, interactive websites, e-mails, greetings cards, orientation events and meetings (Chappelet, 2000; Downward *et al.*, 2005; Chanavat and Ferrand, 2010). Downward *et al.* (2005), however, suggest that volunteers at the 2002 Common-wealth Games in Manchester felt that communication prior to the event was erratic and last minute. This engendered feelings of apprehension and anxiety about the forth-coming event, particularly given that some volunteers needed to make alternative arrange-ments for childcare or reschedule work and other commitments to undertake their role. Similarly, volunteers suggested that the content of the pre-event orientation sessions was disappointing, as they did not provide training as suggested. Ralston *et al.* (2004) and Lockstone and Baum (2009) suggest that volunteers' expectations of their assignment are formed by their experience during the recruitment period and by the communication and training that they receive during the pre-event stage. Whether expectations and the expected benefits that motivated volunteers to

get involved are fulfilled during their volunteer experience impacts on their satisfaction and consequently the effectiveness of their per-formance and their retention (Kemp, 2002; Green and Chalip, 2003; Ralston *et al.*, 2004; Monga, 2006). It is also likely to affect the post-event 'benefits', because for networks, reciprocity, mutual trust and respect to be generated a satisfied volunteer pool is required.

The importance of volunteer satisfaction is reinforced in the literature, with evidence that the celebratory atmosphere, the social and altruistic elements of volunteering, and the appreciation that volunteers receive have a positive impact on their satisfaction (Elstad, 1996; Kemp, 2002; Green and Chalip, 2003; Ralston *et al.*, 2004; Reeser *et al.*, 2005). Similarly, Elstad (1996) suggests that the volunteer role, competence and welfare affect volunteer satisfaction. Likewise, Farrell *et al.* (1998) and Ralston *et al.* (2004) suggest that volunteers' satisfaction with the facilities, organization and management contributes to their overall satisfaction with the experience. Getz (1997) suggests that factors that can lead to dissatisfaction include: (i) the level of com-mitment required; (ii) over-demanding work-loads; (iii) insufficient numbers of volunteers; (iv) tensions between volunteers and others; (v) open public scrutiny; (vi) a lack of team spirit; (vii) a lack of appreciation; (viii) poor organization and leadership; (ix) a lack of tangible rewards; (x) insecurity over the appointment; and (xi) unfulfilling labour. Ralston *et al.* (2004, p. 16), however, point out that although dissatisfaction 'has implications for the effectiveness of the volunteer' – and indeed the team, if the dissatisfaction spreads (Holmes and Smith, 2009) – 'the limited duration' of major sporting events means that this may not affect retention as 'the opportunity to be involved in a unique event and the celebratory atmosphere may be more important than relinquishing the volunteer role' (Ralston *et al.*, 2004, p. 16). The problem for cities, like Glasgow, with a commitment to hosting events, is that they are likely to be looking to retain volunteers to participate on a regular basis and, therefore, high levels of volunteer satisfaction are extremely important.

To avoid dissatisfaction and resentment from arising, Holmes and Smith (2009) suggest providing volunteers with support and the opportunity to discuss any issues that they have at regular intervals. In addition to a verbal 'thank you', rewards for the efforts of major sporting event volunteers can be linked to motivation and may include souvenirs, tickets for events or the closing ceremony, parties and public recognition (Chappelet, 2000; Holmes and Smith, 2009; Chanavat and Ferrand, 2010). For example, the contribution of the volunteers at the 2006 Commonwealth Games in Melbourne was formally recognized in the official brochure, which listed each of the '14,500 volunteers by name and state of origin' (Lockstone and Baum, 2009, p. 218). The literature suggests that showing volunteers that they are appreciated is important because if volunteers are satisfied with their experience they may wish to volunteer for future events (Green and Chalip, 2003; Ralston *et al.*, 2004; Holmes and Smith, 2009; Doherty, 2010). Ralston *et al.* (2004) also suggest that volunteers can thus be considered as 'ambassadors' and 'future recruiters'. The next section turns to this idea of 'leveraging' major sporting events to create a legacy for the host city or region – crucial for the accrual of social and human capital.

Leveraging major sports event volunteering

In terms of volunteering, it has been suggested that major sporting events can be leveraged to create a legacy by: (i) increasing the human, economic and social capital of an area through developing the skill sets; (ii) expanding the professional networks and increasing the employability of volunteers; and (iii) expanding their social networks and creating a sustainable volunteer force (Ritchie, 2000; Kemp, 2002; Ralston *et al.*, 2005; Misener and Mason, 2006; Doherty, 2010). An example of success is the 1994 Winter Olympics in Lillehammer, where 70% of volunteers 'felt that they had enhanced their skills' (Kemp, 2002, p. 9). Kemp (2002) notes that these volunteers acquired language and IT skills, and work experience to improve their employability, alongside improved social skills and increased levels of confidence. Similarly, as mentioned previously, the Sydney

2000 Olympic Games were heralded as 'the Volunteer Olympics' (Downward and Ralston, 2005, p. 18) and as such it was suggested that they would create a legacy of volunteerism for the city (Auld *et al.*, 2009).

However, major sporting events can attract fairly homogenous groups of volunteers (Coyne and Coyne, 2001; Holmes and Smith, 2009; Pauline and Pauline, 2009) who are perhaps not those most in need of the benefits that can be gained from volunteering. Auld *et al.* (2009, p. 185) argue that 'unless sports event volunteering results in a broader participation base that helps establish links between dissimilar community groups, there is likely to be little long-term and systematic legacy effect … in terms of social capital'. Manchester City Council, Sport England and the organizers of the 2002 Commonwealth Games in Manchester, developed a Pre Volunteer Programme (PVP) aimed at engaging volunteers from a variety of groups under-represented in volunteering (Carlsen and Taylor, 2003; Misener and Mason, 2006). The PVP sought to engage participants from 'throughout the N[orth] W[est]' (Smith and Fox, 2007) and provide them with:

> Accredited training and … experience through volunteering at the Commonwealth Games. This training was in addition to the instruction given to conventional volunteers. Those involved were not guaranteed roles at the Games, but the aim was to encourage PVP graduates to apply for positions and, if successful, to give them extra support and guidance if they experienced difficulties fulfilling their roles.
>
> (Smith and Fox, 2007, p. 25)

The programme supplied 10% of the volunteers used in the Games (Smith and Fox, 2007) and 'the training provided as part of the PVP enabled 2,134 individuals to gain one of two qualifications offered as part of the project [and] a total of 160 individuals were recorded as having gained employment after taking part' (Smith and Fox, 2007, p. 32). Smith and Fox (2007, p. 32) suggest that the PVP thus helped to raise the aspirations of participants and gave them 'increased options and opportunities for the future'. The programme also benefited the wider community by encouraging further community and voluntary work among those individuals benefiting from participation. In addition to these benefits, 'the PVP leaves the tangible legacy of two accredited courses for event and sports volunteering' and a database of volunteers that assist at other events (Smith and Fox, 2007, p. 36). The approach taken in Manchester provides a useful example of the way in which wider social benefits and civic outcomes were integrated into the volunteer management process, something that other major sport event hosts can learn from if they are to leverage the expected planned social capital gains from their activities.

The evidence from the literature suggests that the social case for events is built on the prospect of volunteering creating the social glue of communities, bringing together people who would not otherwise meet each other and sustain communities long after the event itself has left town (Auld *et al.*, 2009). However, too little research has been conducted to assess the extent to which mass volunteer participation at large-scale events aids capacity building or specifically how and why these outcomes are achieved. The case study selected for this chapter addresses this gap in the literature.

Case Study: Delhi Flag Handover Ceremony (DFHC)

In order to illustrate the potential value of event volunteering for securing wider social benefits for host populations, a case study of a major sports event is presented. The DFHC was a project delivered by Glasgow Life (the charitable trust responsible for delivering Glasgow's sport and cultural services) on behalf of the Glasgow 2014 Local Organizing Committee. The Handover Ceremony itself took place towards the end of the 2010 Commonwealth Games Closing Ceremony in Delhi, India, reflecting the passing of the responsibility for the Games from one host to the next. Glasgow created a unique approach to the DFHC by recruiting a 'mass cast' of 348 volunteers from across Scotland to participate in an eight minute cultural performance in Delhi. There were two unique elements to the approach adopted by Glasgow. First, the Mass Cast members were citizens and not celebrities,

including a range of semi-professional and amateur performers. This is important for the theme of legacy and the (co-) creation of sustainable networks, as discussed later. Second, participation from across Scotland was secured, meeting the strategic vision of Glasgow 2014 to be Scotland's Games and extending the potential scope of social benefit in the process.

The research process that accompanied the DFHC, conducted by the authors pre-, during and post-event, sought to determine the motivations of participants to volunteer and the impact of their participation on their personal, professional, social and civic lives. Moreover, it also sought to gain greater understanding of the efficacy of the volunteer management approach and its wider implications for individuals, staff and other stakeholders. The research questions were focused on: (i) why volunteers became involved; (ii) the role that local, regional and national identity play in participation; (iii) the impacts of volunteer participation; (iv) their experience of the DFHC project; (v) the success or otherwise of the approach by the DFHC team to recruitment, selection and training of volunteers; (vi) the DFHC team's plans to maintain communication with the volunteers; and (vii) prior experience and likelihood of further participation in volunteering post-Delhi by the participants. Methodologically, research interventions took place pre-, during and post-event, employing both quantitative and qualitative techniques. In order to address the overall research objectives and specific research questions, the authors adopted a mixed methods approach, combining the measurement of volunteer motivations (quantitative, both pre- and post-Delhi) with an exploration of volunteer (and project team) narratives (qualitative), carried out over a period extending from September 2010 to April 2011, albeit some of the research data was gathered by other stakeholders prior to this timescale (i.e. the 100-word 'cases' made by each volunteer prior to their selection was analysed by us but had been gathered by the DFHC team). The research approach adopted is interesting for the events field as techniques had to be adapted to suit the scheduling of the DFHC itself. So, the major pre-event survey (with 348 Mass Cast members and with a 91% response rate) was conducted at the

'Bootcamp' where volunteers were training for 3 weeks prior to the Handover Ceremony itself. In contrast, the post-event survey had to be circulated online 3 months after the event, creating greater challenges with respect to response rate (41% response return rate). To ameliorate the weaknesses of survey design, a series of focus groups were also held with volunteer participants before and after the DFHC. These were supplemented with strategic interviews conducted with key staff involved in the management of the volunteer experience.

In terms of the key findings of the case study, evidence of potential long-term social benefits to a range of communities is present. Although the Mass Cast was unrepresentative of the traditional volunteer, being predominantly young, largely female, in further or higher education and demonstrably committed to volunteering, the findings showed that these volunteers displayed a strong desire to represent their cities, country and host organizations. Although initially motivated to participate because of the 'once-in-a-lifetime opportunity', as the DFHC project progressed, the findings suggest that representing the nation (Scotland) and being part of a major event became increasingly important motivating factors for participants. These findings were reflected in focus group conclusions with participants citing national identity, pride and the 'once-in-a-lifetime opportunity' as the key reasons for involvement. Representation was expressed as a multi-layered concept (Baum and Lockstone, 2007) as DFHC volunteers emphasized their sense of responsibility in representing Scotland (the principal focus) as well as their city, locality, workplace or educational establishment. That participants were passionate ambassadors for their localities or institutions is a positive feature of the DFHC, but there are also weaknesses in the specific approach taken to the delivery of the project that could weaken the social benefits accruable.

One potential weakness of the DFHC can also be construed as its principal strength. This event was not like other sporting events and the drive to create a mass cast from a mixture of professional and amateur groups proved more problematic than originally envisaged. The Mass Cast could be described an atypical volunteering group, comprising well-educated 'active citizens' with relatively specialist skills, previous volunteering experience and a fierce commitment to their field (dance, performance or sport). Only 3% of the Mass Cast members had never volunteered previously. This 'unique' grouping was a strength for the DFHC itself because those recruited were extremely committed, represented their nation with pride and expressed a desire to continue involvement with the Glasgow 2014 Commonwealth Games. However, the Glasgow 2014 Games have a commitment to recruit at least 15% of its volunteers from those with no volunteer experience and from the most disadvantaged communities. This is a reflection on the ambitious bid commitment to generate wider social and cultural legacies for the city of Glasgow. However the DFHC project was so unique that it recruited a very targeted population, those with the right mix of skills in the fields of performance. While these specialists will be required for the Glasgow 2014 Commonwealth Games ceremonies, the numbers are much greater and the difficulties of creating the 'team' atmosphere generated around the DFHC will be more difficult.

The findings generated for the case study (pre- and post-event surveys in particular) suggest that the Mass Cast volunteers were very satisfied with the organization of the DFHC, with the exception of some minor communication issues. Overall, the research interventions suggested a well-managed event that left positive experiences for the vast majority of participants. A 'Team Delhi' slogan empowered volunteers to make significant commitments and this ensured a positive relationship between the organizers and their Mass Cast, suggesting an understanding of the psychological contract was, in part, realized. Common to several volunteer studies, there was some evidence that skills utilization, recognition of efforts and communication could have been managed more effectively to enhance the volunteer experience. Yet, encouragingly, post-event research intervention (survey and regional focus groups) revealed that volunteering activity by members of the Mass Cast had increased by two-fifths, demonstrating the positive externalities that can be achieved, not only for the volunteers themselves but also for their host communities across the country. This is where major events can be successful at leveraging social benefits, but these will only accrue if the post-event planning is as detailed as it tends to be pre-event.

Sustaining the momentum achieved by the DFHC, which was screened around the world and received very positive media coverage, has been a real challenge for organizers. Project funding tends to elevate Games delivery to the detriment of post-event support. In the case of the DFHC, more effort (and coordination) could have been expended, post-event, to ensure that positive experiences were built upon in the lead up to Glasgow 2014 Commonwealth Games. None of the key agencies were tasked (or resourced) with the responsibility to follow-up with the Mass Cast volunteers once they had returned from Delhi – or with the 80 Handover Links that had been recruited to liaise with DFHC organizers during the event planning stage. In order to secure the much-vaunted 'legacy' benefits attributed to major events, post-event planning is crucial and this requires investment – in time and in resources – as well as being embedded in the ongoing activities of the principal delivery agents within the host city/nation.

The absence of a detailed post-event plan for engaging the 348 Mass Cast members and securing greater depth of impact in their host communities prevented the event from maximizing what can be termed its return on objectives (ROO). The DFHC project certainly gave semi-professional and amateur performers alike an appreciation of the greater good, a renewed understanding of the value of trust and thinking of others, alongside the importance of teamworking and leadership – attributes that are transferable to activities within their host communities. The event did embrace the increasingly influential idea of event *co-creation*, in that new networks of friends and volunteer communities were formed as an outcome of the DFHC. However, in a world infused with social networking and its associated practice of 'likes' and 'retweets', it is imperative to permit (and encourage) the sharing of experiences in the design of volunteer programmes to exploit the social dimension of major sport event volunteering.

Social involvement in the DFHC was overwhelmingly acknowledged as the most rewarding aspect of the event for volunteers, alongside meeting new friends and being part of a team. Opportunities were missed to engage in fundraising activity within local authority areas early on, in particular, as a means of raising awareness of the DFHC within 'local' communities and allowing the volunteers to tell 'their stories' locally, thus leading to further engagement across the country for 'Scotland's Games'. DFHC volunteers represent key ambassadorial assets for the Glasgow 2014 Games if managed effectively. In a period when social networks are created and maintained online as well as face to face, it is important for those responsible for volunteer recruitment and management to create the conditions in which self-governance and self-organization flourish. Overly stringent control of online social spaces (or their use simply as a corporate communication tool) can be counterproductive, whereas carefully managed engagement can produce significant benefits for organizers.

Conclusions

This chapter has taken as its focus the research field of event volunteering. The review of literature indicated that major sport event volunteering draws a group of people often attracted by the excitement of the once-in-a-lifetime opportunity to participate in a truly global event. However, the motivations of major sporting event volunteers appears to change over time, with contributions to the community, supporting others as part of a team and helping the host city or nation growing in importance as the event progresses. In terms of securing wider social benefits and civic outcomes attributed to major events, exploiting the more collective sentiments expressed by volunteers is of critical importance, yet this has not always been at the forefront of the volunteer management process. For example, if major events are to contribute to the generation of social capital, then organizers must be clear on what 'type' of social capital they are seeking to secure. Bonding social capital refers to a deepening of trust, respect, networks and feelings of reciprocity within relatively homogenous groups. The case study project described in this chapter, the DFHC, certainly generated bonding social capital within a relatively homogenous group of performers. While this form of social capital is valuable and could have been exploited more effectively within the DFHC project, it does not provide a means of securing bridging social capital. This form of capital requires interaction between diverse volunteer communities, opening up new networks and forms of dialogue across a heterogeneous population. For the ambitions of the Glasgow 2014 organizers to come to fruition (attracting 15% of volunteers from non-traditional volunteering routes), mechanisms for generating bridging social capital will be necessary. This will require a focus on qualifications, support and training so that the aspirations of reaching non-traditional volunteers can be met. Unless sports event volunteering results in a broader participation base that helps establish links between dissimilar community groups, there is likely to be little long-term and systematic legacy effect in terms of bridging social capital.

That said, the DFHC case study does provide an exemplar that can be drawn upon for other major event organizers. In the short term, positive impacts on the *personal* level were evident. The DFHC was a personal success for many and helped them develop valuable interpersonal and leadership skills. *Socially*, there was evidence of new networks being created face to face and online and a continuing commitment to a 'team' ethic post-event. In terms of *civic engagement* early positive change was evident with increased levels of volunteer participation post-Delhi and enhanced communication locally. However, the expressed desire of Glasgow 2014 organizers to increase participation of volunteers from those groups who have 'not previously volunteered' would need an earlier intervention strategy, using a buddy system or attracting more modern apprenticeships to the process and gaining access to people through other means, such as housing association networks, otherwise the Games will continue to attract the usual 'volunteer type' with previous experience.

This chapter has also stressed the importance of making it easier to *share* positive experiences from the outset, involving volunteers in the co-creation of the event narrative. Creating realistic expectations of roles and commitment, communicating the core values of the organization and the support volunteers can expect in return for their loyalty, engagement, ownership and passion require clear and comprehensive information management.

Further Research

Although the research conducted by the authors for the case study contributes to knowledge in the field of events and volunteering, there remains a need for further investigations into a number of discrete areas. For example, ongoing longitudinal research with cohorts of volunteers involved in major sporting events is necessary so that understandings about the longer-term legacies in communities can be strengthened. Research studies of this type will also provide a more robust evidence base to support the perceived civic benefits of major event volunteering. Furthermore, the event field needs to take cognisance of research being conducted in other disciplines and fields of study, especially around social capital (and its complexities) so that the event volunteer policies and practices developed are informed by the most robust research evidence available.

Questions for Students

1. What do you consider the advantages and disadvantages of devolving responsibility for the volunteer programme to a local organization on behalf of an organizing committee?

2. Managing volunteers and their expectations is a complex psychological relationship; do you think volunteer contracts should be considered and what would be the implications of such contracts?

References

Auld, C., Cuskelly, G. and Harrington, M. (2009) Managing volunteers to enhance the legacy potential of major events. In: Baum, T., Deery, M., Hanlon, C., Lockstone, L. and Smith, K. (eds) *People and Work in Events and Conventions: a Research Perspective*. CAB International, Wallingford, UK, pp. 181–192.

Bang, H., Alexandris, K. and Ross, S. (2009) Validation of the revised Volunteer Motivations Scale for International Sporting Events (VMS-ISE) at the Athens 2004 Olympic Games. *Event Management* 12, 119–131.

Baum, T. and Lockstone, L. (2007) Volunteers and mega sporting events: developing a research framework. *International Journal of Event Management Research* 3(1), 29–41.

Bourdieu, P. (1986) The forms of capital. In: Richardson, J.G. (ed.) *Handbook of Theory and Research for the Sociology of Education*. Greenwood, New York, pp. 214–258.

Burbank, M.J., Andranovich, G.D. and Heying, C.H. (2001) *Olympic Dreams: the Impact of Mega-Events on Local Politics*. Reinner Publishers, Boulder, Colorado.

Carlsen, J. and Taylor, A. (2003) Mega-events and urban renewal: the case of the Manchester 2002 Commonwealth Games. *Event Management* 8, 15–22.

Chanavat, N. and Ferrand, A. (2010) Volunteer programme in mega sports events: the case of the Olympic Winter Games, Torino 2006. *International Journal of Sport Management and Marketing* 7(3/4), 241–266.

Chappelet, J. (2000) Volunteer management at a major sports event such as the Winter Games. In: de Moragas, M., Merono, A.B. and Puig, N. (eds) *Symposium on Volunteers, Global Society, and the Olympic Movement*. 24–26 November 1999. International Olympic Committee, Lausanne, Switzerland, pp. 245–254.

Cleave, S. and Doherty, A. (2005) Understanding volunteer and non-volunteer constraints: a mixed-method approach. Paper presented at the Eleventh Canadian Congress on Leisure Research, Nanaimo, British Columbia, 17–20 May 2005. Available at: http://lin.ca/Uploads/cclr11/CCLR11-18.pdf (accessed 2 November 2011).

Coleman, J. (1988) Social capital in the creation of human capital. *American Journal of Sociology* 94 (Supplement), S95–S120.

Cnaan, R.A. and Goldberg-Glen, R.S. (1991) Measuring motivation to volunteer in human services. *Journal of Applied Behavioural Science* 27(3), 269–284.

Cnaan, R.A., Handy, F. and Wadsworth, M. (1996) Defining who is a volunteer: conceptual and empirical considerations. *Nonprofit and Voluntary Sector Quarterly* 25, 364–383. Available at: http://nvs.sagepub.com/content/25/3/364 (accessed 1 December 2010).

Coyne, B.S. and Coyne, E.J. (2001) Getting, keeping, and caring for unpaid volunteers at professional golf tournament events. *Human Resource Development International* 4(2), 199–216.

Davis-Smith, J. (1999) Volunteering and social development. A background paper for discussion presented at an Expert Group Meeting, New York, 29–30 November. United Nations Volunteers, Expert Group Meeting, New York.

Doherty, A. (2010) The volunteer legacy of a major sport event. *Journal of Policy Research in Tourism, Leisure, and Events* 1(3), 185–207.

Downward, P. and Ralston, R. (2005) Volunteer motivation and expectations prior to the XV Commonwealth Games in Manchester, UK. *Tourism and Hospitality Planning & Development* 2(1), 17–26.

Downward, P., Lumsdon, L. and Ralston, R. (2005) Gender differences in sports event volunteering: insights from Crew 2002 at the XVII Commonwealth Games. *Managing Leisure* 10(4), 219–236.

Elstad, B. (1996) Volunteer perception of learning and satisfaction in a mega-event: the case of the XVII Winter Olympics in Lillehammer. *Festival Management and Event Tourism* 4(3), 75–83.

Farrell, J.M., Johnston, M.E. and Twynam, G.D. (1998) Volunteer motivation, satisfaction, and management at an elite sporting competition. *Journal of Sport Management* 12, 288–300.

Getz, D. (1997) *Event Management and Event Tourism*. Cognizant, New York.

Giannoulakis, C., Wang, C.-H. and Gray, D. (2008) Measuring volunteer motivation in mega-sporting events. *Event Management* 11, 191–200.

Green, B.C. and Chalip, L. (2003) Paths to volunteer commitment: lessons from the Sydney Olympic Games. In: Stebbins, R.A. and Graham, M. (eds) *Volunteering as Leisure/Leisure as Volunteering: an International Assessment*. CAB International, Wallingford, UK, pp. 49–68.

Hall, P.A. (1999) Social capital in Britain. *British Journal of Political Science* 29, 417–461.

Harrison, D.A. (1995) Volunteer motivation and attendance decisions: competitive theory testing in multiple samples from a homeless shelter. *Journal of Applied Psychology* 80(3), 371–385.

Holmes, K. and Smith, K. (eds) (2009) *Managing Volunteers in Tourism: Attractions, Destinations and Events*. Butterworth-Heinemann, Oxford.

Hoye, R. and Cuskelly, G. (2009) The psychology of sport event volunteerism: a review of volunteer motives, involvement, and behaviour. In: Baum, T., Deery, M., Hanlon, C., Lockstone, L. and Smith, K. (eds) *People and Work in Events and Conventions: a Research Perspective*. CAB International, Wallingford, UK, pp. 171–180.

Hustinx, L. and Lammertyn, F. (2004) The cultural bases of volunteering: understanding and predicting attitudinal differences between Flemish Red Cross volunteers. *Nonprofit and Voluntary Sector Quarterly* 33(4), 548–584.

Karkatsoulis, P. and Michalopoulos, N. (2005) The national identity as a motivational factor for better performance in the public sector: the case of the volunteers of the Athens 2004 Olympic Games. *International Journal of Productivity and Performance Management* 54(7), 574–579.

Kemp, S. (2002) The hidden workforce: volunteers' learning in the Olympics. *Journal of European Industrial Training* 26, 103–116.

Lockstone, L. and Baum, T. (2009) 2006 Melbourne Commonwealth Games, Australia: recruiting, training and managing a volunteer program at a sporting mega event. In: Holmes, K. and Smith, K. (eds) *Managing Volunteers in Tourism: Attractions, Destinations and Events*. Butterworth-Heinemann, Oxford, pp. 215–223.

MacLean, J. and Hamm, S. (2007) Motivation, commitment, and intentions of volunteers at a large Canadian sporting event. *Leisure/Loisir* 31, 523–526.

Misener, L. and Mason, D.S. (2006) Creating community networks: can sporting events offer meaningful sources of social capital? *Managing Leisure* 11(1), 39–56.

Monga, M. (2006) Measuring motivation to volunteer for special events. *Event Management* 10, 47–61.

Nichols, G. (2009) Newham volunteers, United Kingdom: developing a pool of event volunteers as part of a mega event legacy. In: Holmes, K. and Smith, K. (eds) *Managing Volunteers in Tourism*. Butterworth-Heinemann, Oxford, pp. 225–235.

Pauline, J. and Pauline, G.S. (2009) Volunteer motivation and demographic influences at a professional tennis event. *Team Performance Management* 15(3/4), 172–184.

Putnam, R. (1993) The prosperous community: social capital and public life. *The American Prospect* 13, 35–42.

Putman, R. (2000) *Bowling Alone: the Collapse and Revival of American Community*. Simon & Schuster, New York.

Ralston, R., Downward, P. and Lumsdon, L. (2004) The expectations of volunteers prior to the XVII Commonwealth Games, 2002: a qualitative study. *Event Management* 9, 13–26.

Ralston, R., Lumson, L. and Downward, P. (2005) The third force in events tourism: volunteers at the XVII Commonwealth Games. *Journal of Sustainable Tourism* 13(5), 504–519.

Reeser, J.C., Berg, R.L., Rhea, D. and Willick, S. (2005) Motivation and satisfaction among polyclinic volunteers at the 2002 Winter Olympic and Paralympic Games. *British Journal of Sports Medicine* 39(20), pp. 1–5.

Ritchie, J.R.B. (2000) Turning 16 days into 16 years through Olympic legacies. *Event Management* 6, 155–165.

Rochester, C. (2006) *Making Sense of Volunteering: a Literature Review*. The Commission on the Future of Volunteering, England Volunteering Development Council, London.

Scottish Executive (2004) *Volunteering Strategy*. Scottish Executive, Edinburgh, UK.

Smith, A. and Fox, T. (2007) From 'event led' to 'event themed' regeneration: the 2002 Commonwealth Games Legacy Programme. Available at: http://westminsterresearch.wmin.ac.uk/3807/ (accessed: 28 December 2010).

Stebbins, R.A. (2003) Introduction. In: Stebbins, R.A. and Graham, M. (eds) *Volunteering as Leisure/Leisure as Volunteering: an International Assessment*. CAB International, Wallingford, UK, pp. 1–12.

Treuren, G. and Monga, M. (2002) Are Special Event Volunteers Different from Non SEV? Demographic Characteristics of Volunteers in Four South Australian Special Event Organisations. Available at: www.business.uts.edu.au/acem/pdfs/Proceedings.pdf (accessed 1 November 2011).

Wang, P. (2006) Motivations for Sports Volunteerism and Intention to Volunteer. Available at: http://epress.lib.uts.edu.au/research/bitstream/handle/10453/3129/200600548 8.pdf?sequence=1 (accessed 20 December 2010).

Wilson, W. (1996) Los Angeles 1984. In: Findling, J. and Pelle, K.D. (eds) *Historical Dictionary of the Modern Olympic Movement*. Greenwood Publishing, Westport, Connecticut, pp. 169–178.

5 Events and Motivations

Gemma Gelder* and Peter Robinson

University of Wolverhampton, Walsall, UK

Introduction

It can be argued that there are myriad of reasons to attend, spectate and participate in an event, or to be an actor within the staging of an event. Such interactions depend on multiple needs and motives: (i) the circumstances of the individual; (ii) the factors in society that influence those individuals; and (iii) the types of events that are available and accessible to those motivated to attend or participate.

This chapter explores two specific research projects on event motivation supported with broader theoretical underpinning and discusses the factors that influence decision making among audience and participants in events while attempting to explore the potential for future research in this emerging and dynamic field.

Motivations

Researching motivations in relation to event attendance addresses the key question of why people attend and participate in events. A motive is an internal factor that arouses, directs and integrates a person's behaviour. 'Motivations' refers to the process by which people are driven to act in a certain way. Motivations are usually regarded as energizing behaviour and directing it towards a goal (Wagner, 1999). According to Crompton and

McKay (1997), motivations are conceptualized as a dynamic process of internal psychological factors (needs and wants) that generate a state of tension and equilibrium through satisfying the needs.

According to Moutinho in Nicholson and Pearce (2001), a motivation 'is a state of need, a condition that exerts a "push" on the individual towards certain types of action that are seen as likely to bring satisfaction'. Events should, therefore, offer something that meets the desired need, classified as a 'pull' factor. Crompton (2003) points out that a primary goal for staging festivals and events is to create an attraction that offers visitors the potential for satisfying experiences, defined as the realization of desired intrinsic outcomes. Intrinsic motivation is defined as the doing of an activity for its inherent satisfactions, rather than for some separate consequence, and includes the personal needs of the individuals themselves, thus requiring a psychological perspective to understand event attendance motivation. Extrinsic motivation, in contrast, results from influences external to the individual and requires a sociological perspective for analysis. Extrinsic motivators are useful in explaining general motivations in event attendance; however, it is the intrinsic psychological factors that are seen as making a considerable contribution to the understanding of the motivation to attend events.

Key theories of motivation in establishing why people attend festivals and events are

* gemma.gelder@wlv.ac.uk

© CAB International 2013. *Research Themes for Events*
(eds R. Finkel *et al.*)

conceptually grounded on both the escape–seeking dichotomy and the push–pull model, originating from the discipline of tourism. Escaping is 'the desire to leave the everyday environment behind oneself' in search of change and novelty, especially new experiences, while seeking is 'the desire to obtain psychological (intrinsic) rewards through travel in a contrasting (new or old) environment'. Personal satisfaction and rewards can be obtained through relaxation, exploration, learning, aesthetic experiences and meeting challenges, to name a few (Iso-Ahola, 1982, cited in Crompton and McKay, 1997; Getz, 2008). Iso-Ahola also suggested that a consumer:

> may escape the personal world (i.e. personal troubles, problems, difficulties and failures) and/or the interpersonal world (i.e. co-workers, family members, relatives, friends and neighbours) and seek personal rewards (e.g. feelings of mastery, learning about other cultures, rest and relaxation, recharge and getting renewed, ego-enhancement and prestige) and/or interpersonal rewards.

Although it is generally accepted that push and pull factors are primarily utilized in studies relating to tourism, the general concept is applicable across the leisure sector. Push factors (e.g. escapism, curiosity) are the factors intrinsic to the individual and influence the person to make a purchase decision. They are intangible and are the psychological benefits that the person perceives they will gain from attending an event. Pull factors (those aspects of the events such as music or performance), by contrast, can be described as event-specific attributes or outer motivations that draw audiences to an event and are more tangible (Allen *et al.*, 2002). Yoon and Uysal (2005) stated that push motivations are more related to internal or emotional aspects and can be seen as the desire for escape, rest and relaxation, prestige, adventure, social interaction and excitement. Pull motives on the other hand are connected to external, situational or cognitive aspects and are inspired by the attractiveness, recreational facilities and cultural attractions of an event, entertainment and natural scenery. Kim *et al.* (2003) states that the push–pull framework provides a useful approach for examining the motivations underlying tourist and visitor behaviour.

Understanding Audience Motivations

Events are central to culture and lifestyle in today's society. Increased leisure time and discretionary spending have led to an abundance of public events, celebrations and entertainment. Most governments now support and promote events as part of their strategies for economic development, nation building and destination marketing. Festivals and events are viewed as a new form of tourism that attract thousands of visitors and encourage economic prosperity, development and regeneration. The phenomenal growth and evolution of the event industry since the early 1900s, coupled with consumer awareness and choice, requires expertise to understand and manage the sector efficiently and effectively to ensure sustained development and economic growth in the future (Shone and Parry, 2010; Bowdin *et al.*, 2011).

The contemporary world of events has not come without its recent share of problems; political uncertainties and new legislation, coupled with economic volatility and issues in the global economy, can explain the changing behaviour of consumers as they seek value for money, new experiences, and unique activities and base their judgements about the event on a wider set of previous experiences. In addition the uniqueness of an experience, its authenticity, setting and environmental impacts now influence decision making, and the industry responds with an increasing use of innovative technologies and new event concepts. Such developments address many of the motivations for attendance but at the same time drive up competition in the sector, which is arguably still led by the content and experience of the event as opposed to the peripheral activities and use of technology.

It is imperative, therefore, for event managers to better understand the motives of event attendance and the factors that enhance participation in order to design better products and services because motives are a precursor of satisfaction and a factor in decision making, which in turn can lead to better attendance figures (Crompton and McKay, 1997). Oakes (2003) contends that information regarding audience motivations can also be used to lure sponsors, who are becoming an increasingly important part of event funding. Schofield and Thompson (2007) agree that it is critically important to identify visitor motivations and to measure the performance of events from a consumer perspective. He also suggests that from an event planning and management perspective it is vital to determine visitor satisfaction and behavioural intent in considering repeat visits, as well as helping to identify the factors that affect visitor motivation and their experiential outcomes. Understanding the factors that influence people to go to events can help planners align their marketing efforts to emphasize the attributes that best reflect the mission and goals of each event. After all, different events appeal to different people, who have different perceptions, attitudes and interests. These factors will become ever more important as the growing diversity of events, and especially festivals (as it is such a saturated sector of the market), lead to heightened competition. This is especially relevant where events are initiated or expanded to encourage tourism and thus to boost local economies (Nicholson and Pearce, 2001; Daniels, 2004).

Allen *et al.* (2011) discuss the fact that it is the participants and spectators for whom the event is intended who need to have both their physical needs and their psychological needs met. These groups of stakeholders ultimately vote with their feet for the success or failure of the event. Heitmann and Roberts (2010) also discuss the importance of volunteering within the events sector and suggest that the impact of social factors, the desire for affiliation and accumulation of friendship are factors that can increase motivation for getting involved in an event.

Participation and Belonging

There has been a dramatic shift towards interactive events in order to involve audiences as participants, not just as spectators, which is closely aligned with the increased desire among consumers for active rather than passive leisure. Interactivity is thought to promote a higher level of involvement and engagement, adding to the event experience and thus making it a crucial element in event experience design. Getz (2008) suggests, 'interactive/participant events embody person–location or person–person interactivity unlike "spectator" events which are inherently passive'. He further believes that these types of events provide 'targeted benefits' due to the customized nature of the experiences that may be viewed as subcultural manifestations. Participants are, therefore, considered much more than customers or guests in that they are necessary for the event to exist.

Many cultural and historical festivals rely on the inclusion of living history and re-enactments to draw in crowds and participants, and even those seeking less engagement may be drawn into exhibitions and talks from actors creating a staged authenticity through which to narrate historical events. A relatively broad definition of 'living history' includes all instances where live 'actors' participate in the telling of a story of the past (Tivers, 2002). Living history is intended to help visitors into an authentic past ... knowing directly through sight, sound, smell, touch, taste. In contemporary society, people are generally seeking an 'immersive' re-enacting experience, trying to live, as much as possible, as someone of the period might have. The desire for an immersive experience often leads serious re-enactors to set up smaller events as well as setting up separate camps at larger events, which other re-enactors often perceive as elitism. Maybe they are seeking an alternate reality in which to set themselves, something closer to a truly authentic experience, away from gazing onlookers, wearing modern dress and peering through a contemporary lens (Tivers, 2002).

The Peter and Paul Festival in Bretton, Germany is a further example of this. This annual heritage festival, during which the local community celebrates the history of its city, features re-enactments and live recreations of the past, which both visitors and other participants are encouraged to watch and take part in. The festival features three highlight shows (re-enactment of the battle, firework and parade) and other performances including theatre, comedic performances and music. Over the years the event has attracted up to 125,000 visitors (Heitmann and David, 2010). Reasons given for participating in these kinds of events vary. Some participants are interested in getting a historical perspective on a particular period or war, especially if they can trace their ancestry back to an individual or individuals who were involved, while others participate for the escapism that such events offer and the opportunities to spend time among like-minded peers.

Motivations, Experiences and Emotions

The events industry is growing rapidly, and, as such, it is imperative that event managers strive to better understand the motives of event attendance in order to design better product offerings and services and also to ensure sustained development for future growth. As suggested by Getz (2008), it is a complex and ever-changing dynamic, but none the less there are theoretical prerequisites that help better understand and determine the processes involved in the way that individuals make decisions, and how these are understood from a research perspective. The existing body of research, albeit relatively limited, reveals some interesting and arguably unexpected results, which suggest that it may be the events traditions and ethos that determine very different motivations for audience attendance.

Motivation theorists believe that motivations are linked to intrinsic and extrinsic factors and these stimulate specific buying behaviour, meaning motivations play a key role in the decision-making process that helps determine which events consumers will attend. The marketers' view on consumer behaviour is making a product or service desirable to customers, thus making sure that consumers are motivated to purchase. The idea of experience plays a central role in the purchase of goods and services and is a key feature of modern society's choice. Experiential marketing has arisen as a response to today's 'prosumers', a combination of producer and consumer (Wood and Masterman, 2007). Experience involves a personal occurrence with emotional significance created by an interaction with a product, brand or related stimuli. Understanding participants' experiences requires knowledge of their motives, expectations and emotions.

According to Getz (2008), participants in the contemporary world of events are typically looking for mastery through meeting challenges, learning opportunities and subcultural identity. In order to achieve experiential marketing, the result must be something extremely significant and unforgettable for the consumer immersed in the experience. According to Wood and Masterman (2007), a key part of the decision-making process is an event that provides the right level of challenge or stimulation to match the skill set of the target audience. As every experience has to be extraordinary to have an effect on the consumer in today's society, event marketing, therefore, must strive to create a 'flow state experience' for the majority, which may involve surprise, novelty or challenge. A flow state experience is an optimal state of human experience in which individuals are fully immersed and engaged in creative endeavours, experiencing fulfilment, happiness, and well-being.

Case Study: Researching Motivations

Motivational studies in the events literature includes Mohr *et al.* (1993), Uysal *et al.* (1993), Backman *et al.* (1995), Crompton and McKay (1997), Formica and Uysal (1998), Nicholson and Pearce (2001), McGehee *et al.* (2003) and Ryan and Trauer (2005), to name a few, and a review by Petrick and Li (2006). Box 5.1 highlights previous international research in this area. According to Nicholson and Pearce (2001), motivations are one of the most complex areas of events research owing to: (i) its intangible nature; (ii) issues of multiple motivations theories; and (iii) questions of measurement and interpretations. Although research and studies into motivations frequently feature in events literature, current texts tend to take established tourism, sociology and marketing theories and apply them as a blunt instrument, while there remains a lack of

Box 5.1. Previous research.

Formica and Uysal (1996) conducted their research at a jazz music festival in Italy and attendees were segmented by resident status. The groups were then compared based on their motivations for attending and on their demographic characteristics. Twenty-three motivation items were factor analysed resulting in five dimensions of motivation: excitement and thrills, socialization, entertainment, event novelty and family togetherness.

Faulkner *et al.* (1999) conducted a study of visitors to a rock concert in Sweden. They investigated the relationships between motivation patterns, satisfaction levels and repeat visits, while taking into account implications of culture and festival type. Twenty-five motivational items resulted in eight motivational categories: (i) local culture/identity; (ii) excitement/novelty seeking; (iii) party; (iv) local attractions; (v) socialization; (vi) known group socialization; (vii) ancillary activities; and (viii) desire to see artists perform. In the same study through cluster analysis, Faulkner *et al.* (1999) identified three market segments: (i) local repeaters; (ii) young party set; and (iii) local families. These clusters only differed slightly and across all three clusters, known group socialization and enjoying the artists' performance were the main motivators. The younger audiences were also highly motivated by partying, while the other groups were motivated by excitement and novelty seeking.

Bowen and Daniels (2005) investigated whether music was the primary motivator for attending a music festival in Virginia (USA). The study also aimed to explore patterns of music festival attendance to determine whether definable groups of visitors emerged and to determine if the groups differed significantly in relation to demographics. The results of the study suggested that music festival organizers need to use different marketing tactics to broaden festival appeal. It also suggested that to an extent, 'festival managers who rely on a specific artist to draw large crowds or the music itself may be sorely disappointed as it is equally important to create a fun and festive atmosphere that offers ample opportunity to socialize and have non-musical experiences' (Bowen and Daniels, 2005).

(Gelder and Robinson, 2009)

applied research, with no distinct geographical patterns to develop any geo-spatial understanding of the issues. Research is often focused very heavily on the festival sector, an increasingly common theme among many student research projects.

As Oakes (2003) observes, while music-based events are a popular form of entertainment, research exploring the motivations of music festival audiences is sparse, especially from a UK perspective. Petrick and Li (2006) suggests that most studies conducted up to 2006 had been descriptive case studies developed on an ad hoc basis, which provided a gap between research findings and systematic theory building with little evidence of scientific research or the opportunity to longitudinally link any of these studies together. Petrick and Li (2006) also argues, 'festivals should be appropriately considered as recreation rather than tourism offerings'; thus, further consideration should be given to greater theorizing of the nature of event motivation as a phenomenon in its own right. This is also a view already put forward by Nicholson and Pearce

(2001). Gelder and Robinson (2009) build on the work of Petrick and Li (2006) and Nicholson and Pearce (2001) by evaluating the relationship between motivation and attendance at UK music festivals, confirming the significance of exploring motivation as a phenomenon and that socialization at events was the number one motivator in event attendance. Foster and Robinson (2010), in a related study, then evaluated the role of different members of family groups in influencing and choice and altering motivational priorities.

Petrick and Li's (2006) review indicated that a fairly consistent and practical research framework had been established, although a universal motivation scale was still yet to emerge. He drew a number of important conclusions:

- Most studies were grounded in the 'escape–seeking' motivation theory and the similar push–pull model.
- There was no agreement on whether motivations were common across all types of events.

- It was also suggested that as knowledge about event and festival motivation has accumulated over time, research is starting to progress beyond simple case studies of motivation theories.

Petrick and Li (2006) believes that individual characteristics of event motivation have started to emerge partly because of the hybrid nature of festivals as both recreation for local residents and tourism offerings for visitors. Box 5.2 defines music festivals in order to understand the motivational factors for audiences more holistically.

However, and as already noted, it is suggested that more efforts in theoretical conceptualization are needed for understanding festival and event attendees' motivations, and related psychology, sociology and marketing literature may provide useful insights on this issue, as they have done for other studies in the leisure sectors. On a final note, Petrick and Li (2006) argue, 'from a meta-theoretical perspective, it can be seen that existing festival and event motivation research has been heavily dominated by a naturalistic tradition, with a strong emphasis on formal logic analysis and quantitative methods', rather than the qualitative methods that may offer greater insight into socio-cultural and socio-psychological factors such as motivation.

Following the work of Petrick and Li (2006), a comparative study of motivation at two of the largest UK music festivals by Gelder and Robinson (2009) found a more complex and diverse range of motives based upon a mixed-method approach to data collection, as explained in Box 5.3.

By adopting Nicholson and Pearce's (2001) research approach, the study has enabled more thorough details to be captured than would have been possible from the list of motivational statements alone. This qualitative technique offers greater insight into why people attend events. In addition, the results highlight the importance of multiple means of analysis and the value of a comparative approach in the study of motivations.

The results provide evidence that watching an artist or hearing their music was an important motivational factor at V Festival (49%) as was the location of the festival (close to home) and the availability of free tickets. Box 5.4 illustrates further comments regarding motivations to attend these festivals. These were interesting findings that support the assertion that the festival could be a recreational rather than a tourism product.

The research revealed that the main motives for attending the Glastonbury Festival were the atmosphere and opportunities for socialization. Again, these motives would not have been established without an open-ended question or by following previous festival motivational studies by using only predetermined categories through a Likert-scale approach. These motives not only support the view of including ancillary activities not specifically related to the main purpose or theme of the event (Daniels and Norman, 2003) but also confirm that festivals should be treated as a service, focusing on their intangible nature. The opinions from respondents also identified many aspects of socialization across both festivals and explored the variance between Glastonbury and V Festival, which can be attributed to the

---

Box 5.2. Defining the music festival.

Waterman (1998) states that 'music is often presented as a universal and universalizing art form, transcending social and cultural fault lines, appreciated if not understood by all'. Allen *et al.* (2002) point out that festivals are an important expression of human activity that contribute much to our social and cultural life and they are also increasingly linked to generating business activity and providing income for their host communities. Yeoman *et al.* (2004) adds that festivals are attractive to communities looking to address issues of civic design, local pride and identity, heritage, conservation, urban renewal, employment generation, investment and economic development. Bowen and Daniels (2005) state that music festivals can also have a broad appeal because they typically include activities beyond the music and may include workshops and sideshows. Mintel (2006) defines music festivals as musical events held on consecutive days in which various musical artists perform a live set.

Box 5.3. The methodology.

First, a research framework for surveying festival and event motivation was developed; second, the relationship between motivation and other variables was investigated. This was owing to similar research designs and methods being employed in all of the research projects relating to festival motivation. A list of motivational items was developed and respondents were asked to indicate the importance of each item in their festival-attending decision based on previous research drawing on examples they provided (Formica and Uysal, 1996; Faulkner *et al.*, 1999; Nicholson and Pearce, 2001; Thrane, 2002; Bowen and Daniels, 2005). For the study in hand to have points of comparison with other studies, the data was collected on a similar basis. Questionnaires from previous studies were part of the input into the questionnaire design. A self-completion questionnaire was designed to survey visitor motivations for attending Glastonbury, V Festival or for both.

Previous studies identify six principal motives to explain why attendees visited music festivals: (i) socializing with friends/family; (ii) the music or artists playing; (iii) novelty or excitement; (iv) general entertainment; (v) to escape everyday life; and (vi) for cultural exploration. These items were listed and measured in this study on a five-point Likert scale to indicate the extent to which respondents agreed or disagreed on the importance of each item. Following Nicholson and Pearce's (2001) approach, the list of statements was succeeded by the questions: (i) 'What was your main motive for attending Glastonbury, V Festival or both?'; and (ii) 'Would you attend the festival(s) again?'. For the latter question there was a yes/no tick box and underneath 'Please give reasons for your answer'.

As Nicholson and Pearce (2001) suggest, these open-ended questions were included to ensure other possibilities were recorded that may have been overlooked in previous studies. Furthermore, they provide qualitative information, which, as Dann and Phillips (2000) cited in Petrick and Li (2006) point out, generates more complete, unbiased motivational information. Ryan (2002) also argues that this qualitative approach potentially allows researchers to gain new insights on actual experiences and attitudes.

The final section of the questionnaire collected the socio-demographic information. Finn *et al.* (2000) state that most questionnaires include demographic questions in order to classify the respondents. In this study, gender, age, ethnic background and town of residence classified the respondents. This survey was conducted using a random sampling approach.

The qualitative data was then coded and the classified responses to the open-ended questions were ranked and examined. The quantitative data was analysed by using frequency counts, proportions and percentage calculations. Cross tabulation was then used to explore the relationships between categorical variables. Once the mean scores of the motivational statements had been compared between the two festivals, they were subject to two-way ANOVA tests to investigate if there were any significant differences between the motivation statements and the demographics of respondents.

(Abridged from Gelder and Robinson, 2009)

Box 5.4. Comments from qualitative data.

Self-expressed motives for attending V Festival:

    'The V Festival offers a new look into live music and discovering new bands.'

    'To enjoy a new experience and listen to lots of my favourite bands playing live.'

    'The bands, the best acts of any festival.'

Self-expressed motives for attending Glastonbury Festival:

    'Wanted to see what the hype was and experience the atmosphere.'

    'The atmosphere was portrayed as amazing and it was.'

    'A great atmosphere, really good vibe.'

    'Being part of Glastonbury's famous festival.'

    'To experience festival life.'

    'Nothing really juicy or exciting happened, it was just us enjoying ourselves, nice to be there, just to get away, escaping. The total atmosphere of it all. Your mindset changes completely.'

heritage of Glastonbury and its socio-cultural traditions, where socialization is a part of the festival experience. Not only has socialization been a primary motive for attendance in this study, but it has also emerged as a salient dimension in a number of other motivation studies.

The quantitative data in the study revealed that the music or artists were the most important factor for visiting the V Festival. This was less important at Glastonbury, and escaping everyday life and cultural exploration appear as less significant motives in both studies, especially in relation to the V Festival where they were considered the least important factors; however, both of these are considered the most important factors in relation to tourism motivation in terms of the escape–seeking and push–pull theories.

The seeking dimension was deemed much more important to festival participants and was the more dominant factor; however, the escape component was still present and was considered as less central in this study. This further supports Petrick and Li (2006) in that these results have led the authors to the argument that festivals should, therefore, be considered as recreation rather than tourism offerings. Further consideration should be given to greater theorizing of the nature of event motivations as a phenomenon in its own right, rather than simply as a component of tourism in general (Nicholson and Pearce, 2001).

The study revealed that a wide range of motivational factors need to be considered, suggesting that multiple motivations are important and that, as a result, festival managers who rely specifically on the music or artists to draw in large crowds may be disappointed by the result, as considerable emphasis is placed on broader social factors at festivals. The research revealed that it is equally important to create a festival atmosphere that offers ample opportunities to socialize and to provide new and non-musical experiences. Furthermore, it highlights that event organizers should focus on service strategies that create an atmosphere which promotes a sense of escape from daily routine, and second on infusing an ambient environment that focuses on family togetherness

and excitement (Kyungmi *et al.*, 2002). An extrapolation of the data would probably show this to be true in the case of all the hallmark musical festivals, but with the more recently established commercial festivals the line-up of music and artists is still a key factor.

Music festival organizers need to use different marketing tactics to broaden the appeal of festivals, and evidence in recent years suggests that this is a saturated marketplace with many festivals being cancelled or running into financial difficulties at the early stages of planning (Benn, 2007). No single theory of motivation could be expected to fully explain attendees' behaviour. Indeed, most studies conducted have seen a combination of theories used in relation to event motivation. The research highlights that there is a clear need for event motivation theory to be developed in the future as event management is emerging into its own distinct and dynamic industry. Likewise, in understanding why people attend or participate in events, a marketing approach that seeks only to satisfy one single need or pertain to the main theme of the event will not be enough to get people to an event without there being some ancillary package of benefits that greatly encourages socialization.

However, this research project only considers individual responses within the methodology. A parallel study into group motivations was used to validate these findings, using a sample of family groups to consider the dynamics of different group members and their influences in defining decision making and their role in group motivation and peer choices. Previous studies on event motivation concentrate on the factors that influence an individual to attend an event, but within family groups different group members have different ideas, opinions and motivations.

Research by Foster and Robinson (2010) recognizes that it is essential to identify the motivational factors that influence event attendance in family groups because the nature of the family leisure relationship remains poorly understood in the events industry (Couchman, 1988, cited in Zabriskie and McCormick, 2001). Zabriskie and McCormick (2001) also suggest:

Examinations of family leisure have consistently demonstrated a positive relationship between family recreation and aspects of family functioning such as satisfaction and bonding. It has also been suggested that in modern society, leisure is the single most important force developing cohesiveness between parents and their children.

This indicates that when a family attends an event or indulges in a leisure activity, it is creating a bond between members. Uysal *et al.* (1993) believe that events encourage family togetherness. This is also supported by Crompton and McKay (1997), who add that a need to interact with the family is often inhibited by the independent actions of individuals in the home environment. Attending events as a family provides an opportunity for family bonding and cohesiveness.

Bowdin *et al.* (2006) states:

The need for family cohesion and building familial ties is a strong leisure motivator for many people. It explains the large numbers of children and exhausted parents who congregate at agricultural shows around the UK, like the Great Yorkshire Show. Many festivals focus on children's entertainment for this reason.

Robinson (2008) also suggests, 'a happy child should result in satisfied parents and carers. For this reason alone those with children will make their travel decisions with the child's entertainment in mind.' The research recognizes that it is important to gain a clear understanding of the term 'family' in order to assess the motivational factors that influence event attendance in family groups, especially because, as Giddens (2005) notes, the domination of the traditional nuclear family was steadily eroded over the second half of the

20th century. Newman and Grauerholz (2002) state that in the UK, where the research was carried out, less than a quarter of all families conform to the model of the so-called 'traditional' British family. The functionalism of family is changing with step parents, single parents and same-sex parents all becoming part of the equation of 'family life'.

The study here evaluated families' responses to a survey based around the same six factors selected by Gelder and Robinson (2009), with the results highlighting some interesting differences between the results found here and those of previous studies, including Backman *et al.* (1995), Formica and Uysal (1996, 1998), Crompton and McKay (1997) and Schofield and Thompson (2007). Box 5.5 explains the methodology for this aspect of the research.

The research showed that the most important motivational factor – family togetherness – was consistent across the research sample, regardless of the age of the children and the composition of the family groups. In other datasets in this research, age was a specific factor and the data collection classified families based upon three age categories for their children. Socialization was ranked as the second most important priority for respondents with older children, but for families with younger children, the second most important motivational factor of event attendance was the chance to escape from everyday life. Bowdin *et al.* (2006) define 'escape' in this context as the chance to get away from the usual demands of life, having a change from daily routine and recovering from life's stresses, which could be because, as Morss (1995) notes, young children are often hard work for parents. Where families have older children, 'escape from everyday life' appears lower down on the list of motivational

Box 5.5. The methodology.

The research gathered from other reports on surveying festival and events motivation has been linked into the questionnaire of this project, in order to see if the same motivational influences apply to families. A self-complete questionnaire was designed to survey the motivational factors influencing event attendance in family groups and was based upon the same questions used in the earlier study discussed here (Gelder and Robinson, 2009). However, during the design process additional questions were added to take into account the evaluation of different family group members. Socio-demographic information was collected, for example, to understand the differences in motives to attend events in family groups depending upon certain socio-demographic factors.

factors. It also worth noting that while individuals are motivated by socialization (Gelder and Robinson, 2009), this factor is secondary when the needs of others in a family have to be considered, and arguably socialization with one's family group is encompassed within the heading of family togetherness, suggesting that socializing within a family group is a priority over socializing outside the family group.

Respondents with children of all ages agree that 'excitement' is the third most popular reported motivational factor, which is unsurprising, as Bowdin *et al.* (2006) note that excitement is a common motivational factor found in event motivation studies since the event gives the attendee/s the opportunity to do something new, stimulating and exciting. From analysing the results, the least important motivational factors that encourage families to attend events are learning about other cultures and the novelty or uniqueness of the event. This differs from Nicholson and Pearce's (2001) theory, which states that the dominant reasons for attending events/festivals are directly related to the theme of the event and are specific to the activities and attractions on offer.

The results also identify that families want to visit events that will entertain the whole family. However, while events will always encourage visitors who share common interests to attend, families are not necessarily made up of members who share the same interests, as friendship groups can be. While an event may not be of interest to all family members, it will still achieve the more important benefits of family togetherness, socialization and excitement.

Future Research

Event and festival research continues to develop around the subject of consumer behaviour and event motivation. For future research, a combination of quantitative and qualitative data is needed in order to generate more complete and unbiased information and to better understand event motivation. Further-more, Gelder and Robinson (2009) highlight that festivals and events should be considered as recreational offerings and that multiple motivations are important in creating a desire to attend an event. As the event industry is becoming more distinct, the need to develop and underpin research with grounded theories will become increasingly important, especially as events can lead to, support or develop tourism and therefore may occur before tourism develops.

It can also be argued that 'intrinsic' motivation is at the heart of leisure theory and can be applied to many events; hence, Getz (2008) believes there is a need for more research and theory on 'extrinsic' motivation in the event sector as it is the extrinsic motivators that are useful in explaining general motivations to attend events. To date many researchers have looked at festival motivation, confirming the 'escape–seeking' theory of leisure and travel motivation. Also sport motives have been examined and researched frequently, but the motives for attending other types of events have been studied much less. For example, limited research has been reported on motivations to attend art exhibitions.

It is also evident that research into event motivations predominantly focuses on mega events (usually sports events) or festivals, and when it comes to other types of events, research is rather limited or non-existent. For example, Lee and Back (2005) conclude that more attention should be given to the decision processes regarding attendance at conventions, along with meeting participation behaviour, as it is largely overlooked because researchers are more concerned about economic impacts and locational decisions for meetings. Furthermore, Getz (2008) argues that the probable assumption of why people attend conferences and meetings is for extrinsic reasons, or because it is part of the business or job description and, thus, very little pertinent research has been conducted to date. While it could be expected that motivations to attend meetings and business-related events would be quite different from leisure motivations, and specifically that extrinsic motives will dominate, it is certainly wise to point out that event marketers need to understand how to attract and satisfy their clientele.

Conclusions

This chapter has considered the broad and complex area of event motivation and has also introduced contemporary research into the factors that influence families to attend and participate in events. The chapter has provided an overview of emerging consumer behaviours, and it has highlighted the need for a shift towards marketing benefits of the event experience through a focus on key motivational research and theories that influence decision making.

Understanding consumer behaviour and motivations is of vital importance to the marketing and promotion of event products and services, and understanding the event consumer is essential for event managers and organizations to survive and succeed in such a competitive, challenging and ever-changing environment. However, identifying motivations to attend events is not straightforward, and, as the chapter has highlighted, a range of factors and determinants that influence consumer behaviour and event motivation require further research to establish and strengthen the development of theory. Central to the idea of event motivations is the idea that motivations are about satisfying needs, be it intrinsic, extrinsic or both, and the shift towards the 'immersive experience' is clearly a key motivator in the decision-making process.

Questions for Students

1. Critically assess the differences and similarities in tourism motivations and event motivations suggested in the research outlined in this chapter.
2. Provide an evaluation of the importance of understanding event consumer motivations in making decisions to attend events.

References

Allen, J., O'Toole, W., McDonnell, I. and Harris, R. (2002) *Festival and Special Event Management*, 3rd edn. Wiley, Milton, Queensland, Australia.

Allen, J., O'Toole, W., McDonnell, I. and Harris, R. (2011) *Festival and Special Event Management*, 5th edn. Wiley, Milton, Queensland, Australia.

Backman, K.F., Backman, S.J., Uysal, M. and Sunshine, K.M. (1995) Event tourism: an examination of motivations and activities. *Festival Management & Event Tourism* 3(7), 15–24.

Benn, M. (2007) UK Festival Market Has Hit Saturation Point. Available at: http://www.virtualfestivals.com/latest/news/3996 (accessed 12 September 2011).

Bowdin, G., Allen, J., O'Toole, W., Harris, R. and McDonnell, I. (2006) *Events Management*, 2nd edn. Elsevier, London.

Bowdin, G., Allen, J., O'Toole, W., Harris, R. and McDonnell, I. (2011) *Events Management*, 3rd edn. Elsevier, London.

Bowen, H.E. and Daniels, M.J. (2005) Does the music matter? Motivations for attending a music festival. *Event Management* 9, 155–164.

Crompton, J. (1979) Motivations for pleasure vacation. *Annals of Tourism Research* 6(4), 408–424.

Crompton, J.L. (2003) Adapting Herzberg: a conceptualization of the effects of hygiene and motivator attributes on perceptions of event quality. *Journal of Travel Research* 41, 305–310.

Crompton, J. and McKay, S. (1997) Motives of visitors attending festival events. *Annals of Tourism Research* 24(2), 425–439.

Daniels, M.J. (2004) Beyond input-output analysis: using occupation-based modelling to estimate wages generated by a sport tourism event. *Journal of Travel Research* 24(2), 425–439.

Daniels, M.J. and Norman, W.C. (2003) Estimating the economic impacts of seven regular sport tourism events. *Journal of Sport Tourism* 8(4), 214–222.

Faulkner, B., Fredline, E., Larson, M. and Tomljenovic, R. (1999) A marketing analysis of Sweden's Storsjoyran music festival. *Tourism Analysis* 4, 157–171.

Finn, M., Elliott-White, M. and Walton, M. (2000) *Tourism and Leisure Research, Methods, Data Collection, Analysis and Interpretation*. Pearson Education Limited, Harlow, Essex.

Formica, S. and Uysal, M. (1996) A market segmentation of festival visitors: Umbria Jazz Festival in Italy. *Festival Management & Event Tourism* 3, 175–182.

Formica, S. and Uysal, M. (1998) Market segmentation of an international cultural-historical event in Italy. *Journal of Travel Research* 36(4), 16–24.

Foster, K. and Robinson, P. (2010) A critical analysis of the motivational factors that influence event attendance in family groups. *Event Management* 14(2), 107–125.

Gelder, G. and Robinson, P. (2009) A critical comparative study of visitor motivations for attending music events: a case study of Glastonbury and V Festival. *Event Management* 13, 181–196.

Getz, D. (2008) *Event Studies: Theory, Research and Policy for Planned Events*. Butterworth-Heinemann, Oxford.

Giddens, A. (2005) *Sociology*, 4th edn. Polity Press, Cambridge.

Heitmann, S. and David, L. (2010) Sustainability and event management. In: Robinson, P., Wale, D. and Dickson, G. (eds) *Event Management*. CAB International, Wallingford, UK, pp. 181–200.

Heitmann, S. and Roberts, C. (2010) Successful staffing of events. In: Robinson, P., Wale, D. and Dickson, G. (eds) *Event Management*. CAB International, Wallingford, UK, pp. 113–136.

Kim, S.S., Lee, C. and Klenosky, D.B. (2003) The influence of push and pull factors at Korean national parks. *Tourism Management* 24, 16.

Kyungmi, K., Uysal, M. and Chen, J.S. (2002) Festival visitor motivation from the organisers' point of view. *Event Management* 7, 127–134.

Lee, J. and Back, K. (2005) A review of convention and meeting management research. *Journal of Convention and Event Tourism* 7(2), 1–19.

McGehee, N., Yoon, Y. and Cardenas, D. (2003) Involvement and travel for recreational runners in North Carolina. *Journal of Sport Management* 17(3), 305–324.

Mintel (2006) *Music Concerts and Festivals*. Mintel International Group Ltd, London.

Mohr, K., Backman, K., Gahan, L. and Backman, S. (1993) An investigation of festival motivations and event satisfaction by visitor type. *Festival Management & Event Tourism* 1(3), 89–97.

Morss, J.R. (1995) *Growing Critical: Alternatives to Developmental Psychology*. Routledge, Oxford.

Newman, D.M. and Grauerholz, L. (2002) *Sociology of Families*, 2nd edn. Sage Publications, Thousand Oaks, California.

Nicholson, R. and Pearce, D.G. (2001) Why do people attend events? A comparative analysis of visitor motivations and four South Island events. *Journal of Travel Research* 39, 449–460.

Oakes, S. (2003) Demographic and sponsorship considerations for jazz and classical music festivals. *Services Industry Journal* 23(3), 165–178.

Petrick, J.F. and Li, X. (2006) A review of festival and event motivation studies. *Event Management* 9, 239–245.

Robinson, P. (2008) Holiday decision-making: the family perspective. In: *Tourism Insights*. Visit Britain, London. Available at: http://www.insights.org.uk/articleitem.aspx?title=Holiday+Decision+Making%3A +The+Family+Perspective (accessed 2 May 2013).

Ryan, C. (2002) *The Tourist Experience*, 2nd edn. Continuum, London.

Ryan, C. and Trauer, B. (2005) Sport tourist behaviour: the example of the Masters games. In: Higham, J. (ed.) *Sport Tourism Destinations: Issues, Opportunities and Analysis*. Elsevier, Oxford.

Schofield, P. and Thompson, K. (2007) Visitor motivation, satisfaction and behavioural intention: the 2005 Naadam Festival, Ulaanbaatar. *International Journal of Tourism Research* 9(1), 329–344.

Shone, A. and Parry, B. (2010) *Successful Event Management*, 3rd edn. Cengage Learning, Andover, Hampshire.

Thrane, C. (2002) Jazz festival visitors and their expenditure: linking spending patterns to musical interest. *Journal of Travel Research* 40, 281–286.

Tivers, J. (2002) Performing heritage: the use of live actors in heritage presentations. *Leisure Studies* 21, 187–200.

Uysal, M., Gahan, L. and Martin, B. (1993) An examination of event motivations: a case study. *Festival Management & Event Tourism* 28(1), 5–10.

Wagner, H. (1999) *The Psychobiology of Human Motivation*. Routledge, London.

Waterman, S. (1998) Place, culture and identity: summer music in Upper Galilee. *Transactions of the Institute of British Geographers* 23(2), 253–267.

Wood, E.H. and Masterman, G. (2007) Event marketing: experience and exploitation. Paper presented at Extraordinary Experiences Conference: Managing the Consumer Experience in Hospitality, Leisure, Sport, Tourism, Retail and Events. Bournemouth University, Bournemouth, UK, 3–4 September 2007.

Yeoman, I., Robertson, M., Ali-Knight, J., Drummond, S. and McMahon-Beattie, U. (2004) *Festival and Events Management – an International Arts and Culture Perspective.* Elsevier Butterworth-Heinemann, Oxford.

Yoon, Y. and Uysal, M. (2005) An examination of the effects of motivation and satisfaction on destination loyalty: a structural model. *Tourism Management* 26, 45–56.

Zabriskie, R.B. and McCormick, B. (2001) The influences of family leisure patterns on perceptions of family functioning. *Family Relations* 50(3), 281–289.

6 Events and Sexualities

Kevin Markwell[1]* and Gordon Waitt[2]

[1]*Southern Cross University, East Lismore, Australia;* [2]*University of Wollongong, Wollongong, Australia*

Introduction

In 2000, the inaugural WorldPride event was held in Rome to coincide with the Great Jubilee of the Catholic Church. WorldPride is an event to celebrate sexualities but particularly those discriminated against by heterosexual norms. Organized by InterPride, an internationally based organization first established as the National Association of Lesbian and Gay Pride Coordinators in 1982, WorldPride is held irregularly, with the first event held in Rome and the second in Jerusalem in 2006. The object of InterPride is: (i) to promote the notion of gay and lesbian pride at an international scale; (ii) to facilitate and enhance networking across its membership; and (iii) to encourage and support a diverse range of events from a broad constituency of communities (InterPride, 2011a). WorldPride Roma was a provocative event, outraging the Vatican. The event, which included a parade estimated to comprise more than 250,000 participants, attracted people from around the globe seeking to celebrate diverse sexualities within a programme of entertainment, workshops and speakers. At the same time, the event challenged the manner in which a particular type of heterosexuality is naturalized by the Catholic Church. Pope John Paul II was allegedly reported as saying:

In the name of the Church of Rome, I cannot fail to express bitterness for the affront to the Great Jubilee of the year 2000 and for the offence to Christian values in a city that is so dear to the hearts of Catholics around the world.

(Ferrisi, 2000)

Pope John Paul's statement reproduced the prevailing moral standards that demonize sexualities that do not conform to heterosexual norms of married (heterosexual) couples. This event, then, opened up not just a celebratory space but simultaneously a political space that brought attention to the persecution and discrimination that many would argue has been inflicted on gays, lesbians and transgendered people by the Catholic Church. 'World Pride Roma, with its volatile mix of politics, celebrations, art and activism, is emblematic of how leisure spaces opened up by festivals help to subvert heteronormativity and sustain counter hegemonic identities...' (Waitt and Markwell, 2006, p. 203).

In 2012, WorldPride was hosted in London, coinciding with the Olympic Games. Organizers hoped to attract one million visitors to the 2 week event (InterPride, 2011b). Staging this event in London at around the same time as the Olympic Games meant that WorldPride was able to garner maximum exposure and attention from a global media

*kevin.markwell@scu.edu.au

© CAB International 2013. *Research Themes for Events*
(eds R. Finkel *et al.*)

gaze. Unlike the situation in Rome, where there was not state-sanctioned support, both VisitLondon (the city of London's marketing body) and the Lord Mayor, Boris Johnson, supported the event very publicly. InterPride reported the Lord Mayor saying that he was:

> absolutely thrilled that London has won the right to host WorldPride in 2012. London has one of the largest and most diverse LGBT [lesbian, gay, bisexual and transgender] communities on the planet and it is a fantastic opportunity to inspire cities across the globe. In an Olympic year, the eyes of the world will already be on London and the city will give an enormous welcome to LGBT people, their friends and families, for what we want to be the most colourful and exciting WorldPride festival yet.
>
> (InterPride, 2011b)

While not doubting the Lord Mayor's sincerity in his delight that WorldPride would be staged in London, his public support of the event and of the interests of his gay and lesbian constituents helps to consolidate the place-image or brand of London as a sophisticated, world-class, gay- and lesbian-friendly city. In turn this reputation may have substantial economic benefits to London following the logic of both neo-liberal economic discourses of the so-called 'creative cities' as advocated for by Florida (2005) and the place-marketing of the gay tourism industry (Waitt and Markwell, 2006).

These two WorldPride events make visible how sexuality is constantly being produced, reproduced and challenged and they illustrate how events, sexualities, space, morals and politics are inextricably linked. Understanding the relationships between events and sexualities is important, whether it is 2000 or 2012, whether you identify as straight or gay, whether you are a Catholic or atheist, or if it is Rome or London.

WorldPride is just one example of an increasingly diverse range of events that are organized to explicitly celebrate sexualities that have a history in Western culture of being persecuted and discriminated against. Events celebrating sexuality range in size and scale from the International Gay Games, OutGames and the Sydney Gay and Lesbian Mardi Gras (SGLMG), which attract hundreds of thousands

of participants, through to smaller-scale events, such as: (i) the ChillOut Festival in regional Victoria, Australia; (ii) Hamilton Pride in provincial New Zealand; (iii) Peoria Pride, Illinois; and (iv) the Gainesville Pride Picnic, Florida. Pride events also vary in relation to the constituency to which they appeal. The larger, mega events such as WorldPride and International Gay Games appeal to a very broad base of people, including, of course, those who identify as heterosexual; whereas others such as the Folsom Street Fair in San Francisco or Los Angeles Leather Week appeal to those who seek a more overt opportunity to publicly celebrate sexual acts, in the case of the Folsom Street Fair, or those who identify with the leather subculture, in the case of Leather Week. There is today a constellation of events celebrating sexualities ranging from film festivals, street fairs, community picnics, sporting events and music festivals. This diversity of events is also reflected in the literature that has focused on sexualities and events such as: (i) the International Gay Games (Krane *et al.*, 2002; Markwell and Rowe, 2003; Waitt 2003, 2004; Stevenson *et al.*, 2005; Rowe *et al.*, 2006); (ii) pride events (Brickell, 2000; Kates and Belk, 2001; Luongo, 2002; Markwell, 2002; Kates, 2003; Johnston, 2005; Browne, 2007; Junge, 2008; Waitt and Gorman-Murray, 2008; Markwell and Waitt, 2009; Tomsen and Markwell, 2009a,b); (iii) gay circuit parties, particularly in relation to sexual health and recreational drug use (Mansergh *et al.*, 2001; Mattison *et al.*, 2001); and (iv) gay and lesbian film festivals (Gamson, 1996; Kim, 2007).

To explore the relationships between special events and sexualities the chapter begins by sketching out in a literature review the ways in which scholars have made theoretical and methodological advances. Particular attention is given to introducing five key terms in the literature: (i) 'impact'; (ii) 'the body'; (iii) 'sexuality'; (iv) 'pride'; and (v) 'the closet'. The focus then turns to our case study, the SGLMG, with which to illustrate conceptual and empirical advances identified in the literature review. Finally, the chapter concludes by drawing out the ramifications of the discussion for festival and event management.

Understanding Events and Sexualities

Contemporary studies of events and sexualities are heavily influenced by a set of philosophical ideas developed in the 1980s and termed postmodernism. At the core of postmodernism is the rejection of single truths and grand theories. Instead, a postmodern approach acknowledges that all knowledge is situated and partial (see Jennings, 2001). Several important implications arise for understanding the relationships between events and sexualities from the recognition of multiple truths, social difference and that knowledge is often contradictory. In the remainder of this section we define and discuss terms and concepts used frequently in analysis of the relationships between events and sexualities from a post-modern approach – terms including impact, the body, sexuality, pride and the closet.

The meaning of the term 'impact' in event management research may seem obvious. And yet there is a multiplicity of ways of thinking about the impacts of events. Drawing on positivist approaches, these impacts conventionally refer to something that is measurable such as the revenue that a festival or event generates, the number of people in attendance, or the levels of participant satisfaction. However, the impacts of an event are not always as clearly demarcated as might be assumed by scientific rationalization. Furthermore, the ways in which impacts have been conceptualized have varied greatly. In the 1960s the Russian scholar, Mikhail Bakhtin (1965), drawing on a Marxist theoretical perspective, argued that through mediaeval carnival, the everyday world and its power relations were turned upside down, however temporarily. In Bakhtin's view, carnival provided an opportunity for the socially, economically or politically marginal to be liberated from the prevailing social order. In other words, the carnival, as represented through contemporary forms of special events and festivals, provides a kind of authorized transgression, enabling participants access to opportunities for the expression of ideas, beliefs and practices that might normally not be tolerated. The 'tolerance' afforded by the state and its apparatus is made available because it is only temporary. Following Bakhtin, all festivals and events are characterized by spatial and temporal boundaries, they take place within spaces and times that have been sanctioned by authority.

In the early 1990s the priority given to social class and to the spatial and temporal limits of Marxist analysis of carnivals began to be questioned by work framed by postmodern theorists. The work in Picard and Robinson's edited book, *Festivals, Tourism and Social Change* (2006) illustrates how it is not possible to say where and when the impacts of a festival actually stop. Nor is it possible to extract the individual and collective identities forged through events from their social context. Identities, whether they are based on class, gender, sexuality or race, cannot be assumed to be either stable or pre-given. Impacts, events and the social are always inextricably linked. Extending Picard and Robinson's (2006) argument about festival, the impacts of special events are also interconnected with bodies, societies, cultures, economies, places and time. Following a postmodern approach, the impact of festivals and events may be explored *through* bodies and how events provide opportunities for individual, collective identities to be made, remade, performed and transformed, fashioned and refashioned. Following a postmodern approach, bodies are at once material (the physical body), social (the interpersonal body), cultural (the discursive body) and psychical (the emotional, perceptive body). Understanding the impact of these events can therefore be explored by 'unpacking' the body as a site of pleasure and pain, social and cultural inscription and the ongoing performance of subjectivities. In other words, a postmodern approach understands participation in a festival or event as transcending Urry's (1990) 'tourist gaze' with its emphasis on the visual, to an embodied experience in which the participant's body is the product not just of biology but also of society and culture. The way the body looks, how it is presented, how it acts and how it is used to make sense of experience are expressions of social and cultural forces and practices as much as of biological processes.

Postmodern approaches conceptualize events as platforms for the construction of individual and collective identities. Much of the literature on the psycho-socio-cultural dimensions of festivals and special events has tended to address issues around national identities, often overlooking how the events are often unintended celebrations of state-sanctioned expressions of sexuality. There has been, however, a shift in more recent times to examining how events produce, reproduce and challenge gendered and ethnic identities, and, to a lesser extent, sexuality. The term sexuality refers to the expression of an individual's sexual desires and behaviours. Sexuality, from a postmodern perspective, is conceptualized as something that is performative. Therefore, postmodern approaches challenge thinking of sexuality that assumes stable sexual desires that underpin the categorization of individuals as either heterosexual (straight), bisexual or homosexual (gay men and lesbians). Postmodern approaches acknowledge that the lived experiences of sexual desires may rarely be this stable or clear-cut. There is an array of difference surrounding the categories of heterosexual, bisexual and homosexual, which has, in part, led to the emergence of the term queer, which rejects traditional understandings of sexual categorizations (Jagose, 1996). The term has also come to mean all non-heterosexual forms of sexuality – lesbian, gay, bisexual, transgender and queer (LGBTQ).

Events play a central role in Western politics of sexuality. Many events celebrating queer sexualities take their starting points from what has become known as the New York Stonewall Rebellion or Stonewall Riots, which took place in Greenwich Village, New York City, in June 1969 (Duberman, 1986, 1993). Police raids on gay bars were a regular occurrence at a time when male homosexuality was illegal in the USA, with patrons being regularly subjected to hostility, aggressive behaviour and often arrest. The 3 days and 2 nights of rioting were the first time that lesbians and gays in the USA publically and stridently resisted police harassment. A year after the Stonewall Riots, the Gay Liberation Day March was organized in New York as a mass action to commemorate the bravery of those resisting discrimination. Mass action marches were also organized shortly afterwards in Los Angeles and San Francisco

on what was termed Gay Freedom Day (Duberman, 1986). However, by the mid-1980s, a gradual shift in philosophy occurred from an oppositional politics of resistance, to a celebratory politics that included humour and frivolity. A carnival atmosphere helped to avoid the hardening of social divisions along identity lines of heterosexual/homosexual. Furthermore, as Shepherd (2005) suggests, the carnival atmosphere of the mass actions demonstrates the possibilities of a joyous existence.

Reflecting the change in politics, the marches became known as pride parades (Duberman, 1993). What is striking is the way in which the embodied act of marching as a form of highly visible civic or social protest transformed relatively quickly into a somewhat different embodied act of a celebratory parade. While a march has connotations of protest and struggle, a parade is generally a more overtly performative, carnivalesque, celebratory and often humorous act. Event organizers wish joy to become the organizing feeling between bodies. Over time, many of these carnival-style parades have become integrated festivals with the parade being the 'spine' around which various other events such as art exhibitions, dances and fair days have been attached. Initially an American metropolitan concept, the carnival atmosphere of the pride parade and its variants have been adopted through the processes of globalization in a large number of European cities (which, ironically have their own narratives about the liberation of sexual minorities that well precede the Stonewall Riots), Australia, Aotearoa/New Zealand and a number of South-east Asian nations (Waitt and Markwell, 2006).

As will have become clear, a term that appears frequently in research on the relationship between events and sexuality is 'pride', a term that is central to Western sexual politics. The antecedents of pride can be traced back to the Stonewall Riots in the USA and the brave resistance to the taken-for-granted culture of shame surrounding individuals who refused to conform to the norms of heterosexuality. While a number of scholars and commentators have argued that it is not accurate to view the Stonewall Rebellion as the marker of the beginning of a gay and lesbian liberation movement (see for example Jagose, 1996; Reynolds, 2002), the incident did give rise to what has become known as the modern Gay and Lesbian Pride Movement. The politics of pride are fundamental to this social movement and its trans-global network. One of the key drivers in the initial sexual politics of pride parades is to vanquish its opposite, that of shame. However, postmodern approaches encourage a rethinking of the dynamics of pride and shame that move beyond a binary understanding of pride and shame as separate entities. Indeed, postmodern theorists such as Eve Sedgwick (2003) and Elspeth Probyn (2004) argue that the politics of pride are inseparable from the politics of shame. Shame is conceptualized as both productive and corrosive of sexuality. Drawing on this conceptualization, Johnston (2007) explores how pride and shame are constantly negotiated by participants in Pride Scotland, Edinburgh. She argues that a 'pride/shame tension is created that brings subjectivities into being, at the same time it isolates. Shame is equally and simultaneously identity defining and identity erasing' (Johnston, 2007, p. 42). Waitt and Staple (2011) explore the mobilization of pride and shame to better understand the multiple and often conflicting understandings of the SGLMG within the rainbow community in the provincial centre of Townsville, Queensland. Within the Townsville community understandings of sexualities made visible through television broadcasts of the SGLMG into homes and clubs are both praised and condemned.

Equally, the term 'closet' requires special attention. Events, which are highly visible celebrations of queer cultures and identities, are often understood in Western sexual politics as a means to open the metaphorical 'closet door' and 'come out' in a very public way. This is sometimes referred to as the 'politics of visibility'. Indeed, a common rallying-cry of early pride parades in the 1970s was 'out of the closets/bars and on to the streets' (Mason, 1994; Carbery, 1995). The 'closet' calls upon particular spatial imaginaries to account for the motivations of attending an event celebrating queer sexualities. Emphasizing the roles of oppression and marginalization produced

through heterosexism and homophobia, such spatial imaginary necessitates the logic that attendance at an event celebrating queer sexualities is essential to consolidate an individual or collective identity. Indeed, offering the promise of finding one's 'true self', queer events now play important drivers in gay and lesbian tourism (see Markwell, 2002; Johnston, 2005; Hughes, 2006; Waitt and Markwell, 2006; Markwell and Waitt, 2009).

However, postmodern approaches question the spatial imaginary of the closet. At one level this spatial imaginary may strengthen Western dichotomous categorizations of homosexuality and heterosexuality as distinct, separate and hierarchical subjectivities. The closet is at the forefront of binary notions that pre-configure the space of events along the lines of the heterosexual and the homosexual. Postmodern approaches acknowledge that sexuality is embedded in space, but the relationship between sexuality and spatiality is co-constituted or reciprocal. These ideas moved thinking about the relationship between spatiality, sexuality and events beyond applying a dualism within a pre-existing sexual order that 'fixes' sexuality at events within heterosexual/homosexual identities. Instead, sexuality, along with other subjectivities, is negotiated in, and through, the social, discursive material and emotional relationships that comprise the spaces of events. At another level, it would be naïve to claim that an event that facilitates the politics of visibility can, or will, alleviate systemic oppression or discrimination by opening the 'closet', becoming visible and challenging normative ideas of sexuality. Nevertheless powerful, if limited, political and social gains can be achieved. Kim (2007, p. 618) notes how the First Seoul Queer Films and Video Festival, in 1998, caused a scandal as queers had, up until then, little to no opportunity to 'claim their cultural rights and make them public'. This festival created a space in which queer Koreans could consume a queer cultural form, debate ideas around identity and community and facilitate the leaking of those discussions and debates into wider Korean society that began to challenge state-sanctioned discourses of sexuality. While the film festival was 'bounded' physically, being conducted within a cinema, the debates, discussions and ideas generated from it, leaked out into spaces beyond just the physical space of the cinema.

Methodological Considerations

Postmodern approaches have important methodological implications for researching the relationships between events and sexuality. Methods must provide a critical, yet nuanced understanding of pyscho-socio-cultural and spatial practices that help shape and reshape meanings of these events. According to the aims and objectives of the particular research project a number of different qualitative methods may be appropriate. Research exploring the production and circulation of sets of ideas, or discourses, that structure knowledge surrounding events have made use of a variety of texts from various media reports, websites and blogs of events, and the publications and reports of LGBTQ organizations (Markwell, 2002; Markwell and Waitt, 2009; Tomsen and Markwell, 2009a,b).

Other projects utilize successfully ethnographic approaches that involve the researcher participating in the event under study, either as part of the audience, in the parade itself or in some kind of organizational role. Ethnographic approaches enable the researchers to use their own bodies as instruments of research. For example, Johnston (2007) explored how she felt both dismayed and encouraged with the effects of her participation as a drummer in a gay pride parade in Edinburgh, Scotland. Ethnographic approaches also mean research activities are less intrusive to the participants, who won't necessarily appreciate more conventional methods such as questionnaire surveys or highly structured interviews that might interfere with their enjoyment (see Browne, 2007). Such approaches are more readily achieved if the researcher and the participants of the event or festival share socio-cultural characteristics or similar worldviews, but even then, it can be difficult for the researcher to be accepted by particular communities hosting an event with a relatively narrow constituency. For example, Saldanha (2005, p. 709), in her examination of the Goa Rave parties in southern India, noted

that in carrying out her field research, she came up against a party-culture core that was:

> violently hostile to any investigation, whether from the media, police, government, industry or academia. Most of my material, therefore, came from covert participant observation – I had to be doing stuff among the research populace to develop a perspective adequately sensitive to the messy processes I was trying to map.

As illustrated by the work of Johnston (2007) and Saldanha (2005), research diaries and critical reflexivity both become integral methods. As researchers, they found themselves constantly in a process of negotiation involving the ethics and internal contradictions apparent in the events under study.

Equally, researchers often use a 'mixed-methods' approach, referring to the mixing of methods appropriate for different conceptualizations of research questions. Researchers have used multiple methods within qualitative approaches such as ethnography and participant observation (Waitt, 2005; Rowe et al., 2006; Johnston, 2007; Waitt and Gorman-Murray, 2008) and interviews along a continuum from informal conversations through to structured interviews and focus groups (Tomsen and Markwell, 2009a,b). On the one hand, these projects illustrate how mixed methods can enhance the trustworthiness of findings. Credibility of results is enhanced through a combination of methods that facilitate different spaces of knowledge production. On the other hand, these projects illustrate how the application of mixed methods is often negotiated throughout the project. Research using mixed-methods approaches is understood as iterative rather than linear.

Mixed methods can also involve the mixing of qualitative and quantitative methods. For example, Tomsen and Markwell's (2009a,b) work on the SGLMG incorporated an online questionnaire survey, with ethnography, and short, almost 'vox pop'-style interviews. Pragmatic considerations influenced the use of the web-based survey. The survey was relatively inexpensive to construct and maintain, and it was easily promoted throughout Australia to its target population. The survey was also straightforward for participants to enter their answers and the data set could then be easily transferred into SPSS, a statistics software package, for quantitative analysis. However, such a method assumed that the target population had access to the Internet and had sufficient skills to be confident answering the questionnaire online.

Case Study: Sydney Gay and Lesbian Mardi Gras (SGLMG)

The SGLMG held annually in Sydney, Australia, serves as an interesting case study to gain a better understanding of the relationships between events and sexuality. The first Mardi Gras was held on 24 June 1978, and was the finale to a day of protest as part of the International Day of Gay Solidarity, which in turn commemorated the Stonewall Riots (Carbery, 1995; Markwell, 2002). The event consisted of a parade along a number of streets and roads in Darlinghurst, an inner-city suburb of Sydney that was becoming known as a recognizable gay and lesbian precinct. Participants were encouraged to wear costumes in the hope of creating a more celebratory event that served to distinguish the parade from the protest march that had occurred earlier in the day (and which was attended by many of the same people). The parade attracted between 500 and 1000 participants and a similar number of onlookers (Carbery, 1995). However, what was considered as unnecessary interventions by the police, who wanted to end the parade prematurely, created a situation of civil disorder. Fifty-three people were arrested for taking part in what the police referred to as an illegal procession. A parade that began as a joyful celebration of gay and lesbian pride ended in a riot. The public visibility afforded by this first parade is often invoked as a politically significant act, because at this time not only was male homosexuality a crime punishable with a gaol sentence in New South Wales (NSW) but when the prevailing contemporary attitudes were hostile to any sex acts other than those between married heterosexual couples.

Within the space of 1 year, a number of other events were organized to create a week-long event including what was called a 'Gay Alternative Fair' in addition to the street parade

(Carbery, 1995). However, even at this stage, tensions began to emerge among those who identified as part of the lesbian and gay community between those who wanted the march to remain as a protest and those who wanted the march to embrace elements of the carnival and become more celebratory. Had the event become a party without politics? Some of these tensions also ran along gender lines, with disagreements being played out between gay men and lesbians about the attributes of the event (Markwell, 2002). In 1983, the Sydney Gay Mardi Gras (as it was known then, the word 'Lesbian' was not incorporated into the event's name until 1988) was rescheduled from its late summer June date – as a commemorative event of the Stonewall Riots – to February, at the height of Sydney's summer. This decision caused considerable debate. However, the February timing was fundamental to the emergence of a festival that enabled bodies to become sexualized and eroticized. The generally warm temperatures and humidity of a Sydney Gay summer facilitates many in the parade to present their bodies in near-nakedness. In Western culture, nudity is often read as a display of sexuality. In other words, the summer climate provided the perfect context for a level of hedonism, and slippage of the codes that contextually attempt to keep nakedness separate from the sexual in public spaces.

Mardi Gras' momentum was maintained throughout the 1980s and through the 1990s, with the number of participants in the parade increasing significantly along with the number of onlookers. Unlike the pride parades of North America, however, the Mardi Gras parade takes place at night time and is a much more theatrical and playful event. Considerable resources (time, money, creativity) are invested in the creation of floats that incorporate sophisticated sound systems, lighting rigs and elaborate costumes. Whereas many pride parades comprise lots of individuals marching together, the Mardi Gras tends to be made up of groups of people ranging in size from a few to several hundred in the case of groups such as the Asian Marching Boys or Dykes on Bikes.

During the 1980s, the Mardi Gras parade was, in part, an act of defiance against the catastrophic effects that acquired immuno-deficiency syndrome (AIDS) was having on the gay community in Sydney and elsewhere. Pressure to cancel the 1985 event was brought to bear by some religious commentators and elements of the media, and there was also some debate within the gay and lesbian community as to whether or not it was appropriate to stage the event (Carbery, 1995). Nevertheless, the parade took place, although with noticeably fewer floats and onlookers. While the increasingly devastating effects of human immunodeficiency virus (HIV)/AIDS would continue to be felt by the Mardi Gras for the next two decades, the parade and associated festival would come to be seen as an important means of extending the reach of safe sex education through the promotion of safe sex practices and information. Later, the parade would become, in part, an act of commemoration of those people who had died from AIDS.

The relationship between the SGLMG, sexuality and capitalist market forces of the tourism industry is also an important focus in understanding more broadly the impacts of such an event. During the 1980s, SGLMG was marketed largely through the rapidly growing gay and lesbian tourism industry. Influential gay travel guides such as *Spartacus* and Damron's *Gay Guide* provided information about the event to North American and Western European markets eager to travel to other nations to collectively celebrate gay and lesbian identities through festivals and events (Waitt and Markwell, 2006). It was not until the 1990s, however, that the NSW State Government, through its Tourism Commission, began promoting the SGLMG as a major event in the Sydney tourism events calendar. Indeed, in 1989, the Minister for Tourism, Gary West, instructed the Tourism Commission to stop supplying information about Mardi Gras through its information centres (Carbery, 1995). As pointed out by Markwell (2002), however, the incorporation of sexuality into the marketing strategies of the neo-liberal imperatives of the NSW Government demands careful questioning. Bell and Binnie (2002) and Stychin (2003) argue that the incorporation of sexuality into the neo-liberal marketing strategies of cities is a politically limiting

process. They argue that lesbian and gay visitors who are welcomed into the neo-liberal market place are sanitized and respectable versions; queer visitors who pose no challenge to the norms of heterosexuality. The relationships between events and sexuality in a neo-liberal market place works towards a particular sanitized expression. Events that embrace neo-liberal marketing are critiqued as stabilizing, normalizing and assimilating particular expressions of 'respectable' homo-sexuality into the mainstream life of a city rather than celebrating sexual diversity in all its diverse forms and expressions.

The bodies attending the SGLMG are an equally important focus of research. Rather than assuming bodies arrive with an entirely pre-formed or pre-existing sexuality and gender at an event, research attention is now being given to how bodies become gendered, sexed and sexualized through the social relationships comprising events such as the SGLMG parade. Johnston (2001) demonstrated that rather than conceptualizing 'straight' and 'gay' as distinct and separate entities, these bodies became (re) sexualized through attending the SGLMG parade. Indeed, for some bodies, Johnston illustrated how attending the SGLMG parade was a mechanism to normalize and assert heterosexuality by constructing homosexuals as deviant. For others, the parade offered possibilities to celebrate diverse sexualities through encounters that allow bodies to become sexualized as lesbian, gay, trans or bisexual. Her focus on gendered/sexed and sexualized embodiment at gay pride parades foregrounds sexual subjectivity as always spatial, fractured and multiple. In other words, each individual negotiates their sexuality, in and through the material, social and emotional relationships of the event. Furthermore, paying attention to how gender and sexuality are performative has demonstrated the instability of how bodies become sexualized as gay. Historical analyses of images taken of pride parades reveal shifts in the ways in which gay men and lesbians construct and present their bodies. In the case of gay men, dominant tropes have been the moustached and leather-pants-wearing 'clone' in the 1970s, through to the 'muscle marys' of hypermasculine, buffed, muscular and often shaven bodies, which began to emerge in the 1990s. The Bear subculture presents a different form and style of body, which celebrates hairy faces, chests, bellies and backs and a much more relaxed approach to the presentation of self.

Orthodox notions of gender performance are destabilized through the involvement of drag queens and drag kings as participants and spectators. Arguably, it is the people who dress in drag who create the most 'gender' and 'sexuality' trouble. The bodies of drag kings and queens deliberately bring into question naturalized assumptions about masculinity and femininity, respectively. Yet, parade bodies are interpreted in a multiple of ways. Parade bodies celebrating gender and sexual diversity are always a source of considerable debate within the gay and lesbian communities. The questions repeatedly debated are:

- Does the SGLMG challenge the everyday assumptions about sexuality?
- Do the SGLMG celebrations serve to reinforce certain stereotypes around 'butch lesbians' and 'sissy men'?
- Does the SGLMG encourage transformation of how participants know themselves and others?

Postmodern approaches warn against responding with a resounding 'yes' or 'no'. Instead, postmodern approaches suggest that SGLMG is read in multiple ways, with no guarantee with respect to the political influence of the event. Furthermore, when Mardi Gras is interpreted through a postmodern lens, what it means to become transgender, male or female, or gay, bisexual or lesbian is in a continuous state of becoming contested, and will always be, from people who both identify and do not identify with the gay and lesbian community.

Thus, the growing body of research on this one particular LGBTQ event, the SGLMG, demonstrates the complex and often contradictory ways of understanding and performing gender and sexuality. On the one hand, there may be a common, uniting thread to such events that celebrates LGBTQ pride and fosters a greater awareness within the broader community of a range of pertinent social and political issues such as marriage equality, HIV/

AIDS and anti-gay and lesbian violence. On the other hand, these events are the outcome of ongoing contestations and debates about what it means to be gay, lesbian, bisexual, transgendered or queer in the 21st century. Mardi Gras, like many other pride events, both reinforces and ruptures normative sexuality.

Conclusions: Implications for Event and Festival Management

Postmodern approaches to understanding social phenomena such as special events and festivals are challenging. They raise questions that deliberately provoke different ways of thinking about events, sexuality and the ways by which they are connected.

First and central to this approach was the aim of disrupting ideas that work against the casting of sexuality along neat dualist categories of straight or gay. Instead, sexuality is conceptualized as performative that intersects with nationality, age, class, race and gender. Event managers must remain mindful of the diversity of genders and sexualities within and between participants and think beyond fixed categories of male/female and heterosexual/homosexual. This line of thinking also suggests that participants do not arrive at an event with their sexuality already entirely predetermined. Instead, events may be conceived as creating spaces through which the social relationships facilitate bodies to become sexualized. Bodies become sexualized through the spaces of an event, at the same time as the space of the event becomes sexualized through the bodies of participants. When event managers become alert to the spatial imperative of sexuality they must become advocates for space and bodies, simultaneously considering the material, emotional, personal and interpersonal aspects. The spatial imperative of sexuality is not only a set of ideas about events that have implications for 'impacts' but also: (i) how bodies are allowed to move and dress; (ii) the connection and disconnection between bodies; and (iii) how sounds, light and temperature 'press on to' bodies.

A second implication relates to the sexual politics of events. Many events celebrating sexuality have the politics of visibility at their core. Event managers must remain alert to the proposition that pleasure and politics, while sometimes problematic, are not mutually exclusive. Previous research suggests that tensions can arise when events start to collude with transnational corporations or neo-liberal governments for funding. Concerns are raised that through the workings of capitalism in particular, and very narrow, expressions of sexuality are privileged – in the case of the SGLMG, relatively wealthy, young, male, white and gym-toned bodies.

A final, methodological, implication arising from examining the relationship between events and sexuality is the necessity to embrace methods beyond those advocated by scientific rationalization. Ethnography, semi-structured interviews, focus groups, research diaries, videos, photographs and critical reflexivity all become essential to the event manager's research and evaluation tool box.

Questions for Students

1. Why might it be a mistake to consider pleasure and politics to be mutually exclusive in the context of an event such as the Sydney Gay and Lesbian Mardi Gras? Can an event be a success and engender an atmosphere of fun and celebration while at the same time remaining political?

2. To what extent do you see an event such as Mardi Gras bounded in space and time? Is this event entirely contained or do the impacts of the event 'leak out' across space and through time?

References

Bakhtin, M. (1965) *Rabelais and His World.* Indiana University Press, Bloomington, Indiana.

Bell, D. and Binnie, J. (2002) Sexual citizenship: marriage, the market and the military. In: Seidman, S. and Richardson, D. (eds) *The Handbook of Lesbian and Gay Studies.* Routledge, London, pp. 443–458.

Brickell, C. (2000) Heroes and invaders: gay and lesbian pride parades and the public/private distinction in New Zealand media accounts. *Gender, Place and Culture* 7(2), 163–178.

Browne, K. (2007) A party with politics? (Re)making LGBTQ Pride spaces in Dublin and Brighton. *Social and Cultural Geography* 8(1), 63–87.

Carbery, G. (1995) *A History of the Sydney Gay and Lesbian Mardi Gras.* Australian Lesbian and Gay Archives, Melbourne, Australia.

Duberman, M. (1986) *About Time: Exploring the Gay Past.* Presses of New York, New York.

Duberman, M. (1993) *Stonewall.* Dutton, New York.

Ferrisi, S.A. (2000) World Gay Pride 2000 Seen as Targeting Church. Available at: http:www.osvpublishing.com/peropdicals/show-article.asp?pid=326 (accessed 3 March 2004).

Florida, R. (2005) *Cities and the Creative Class.* Routledge, New York.

Gamson, J. (1996) The organisational shaping of collective identity: the case of lesbian and gay film festivals in New York. *Sociological Forum* 11(2), 231–261.

Hughes, H.L. (2006) *Pink Tourism, Holidays of Gay and Lesbians.* CAB International, Wallingford, UK.

InterPride (2011a) Mission and History. Available at: http://www.interpride.org/mission-history (accessed 2 September 2011).

InterPride (2011b) WorldPride 2012. Available at: http://www.interpride.org/world-pride (accessed 26 August 2011).

Jagose, A. (1996) *Queer Theory.* Melbourne University Press, Melbourne, Australia.

Jennings, G. (2001) *Tourism Research.* Wiley, Milton, Queensland, Australia.

Johnston, L. (2001) (Other) bodies and tourism studies. *Annals of Tourism Research* 28(1), 180–201.

Johnston, L. (2005) *Queering Tourism: Paradoxical Performances at Gay Pride Parades.* Routledge, London.

Johnston, L. (2007) Mobilizing pride/shame: lesbians, tourism and parades. *Social and Cultural Geography* 8(1), 29–45.

Junge, B. (2008) Heterosexual attendance at gay events: the 2002 Parada Livre Festival in Porto Alegre, Brazil. *Sexuality and Culture* 12, 116–132.

Kates, S.M. (2003) Producing and consuming gendered representations: an interpretation of the Sydney Gay and Lesbian Mardi Gras. *Consumption, Markets and Culture* 6(1), 5–22.

Kates, S.M. and Belk, R.W. (2001) The meaning of lesbian and gay pride day. *Journal of Contemporary Ethnography* 30(4), 392–429.

Kim, J. (2007) Queer cultural movements and local counterpoints of sexuality: a case of Seoul Queer Films and Videos Festival. *Inter-Asia Cultural Studies* 8(4), 617–633.

Krane, V., Barber, H. and McClung, L.R. (2002) Social psychological benefits of Gay Games participation: a social identity theory explanation. *Journal of Applied Sports Psychology* 14, 27–41.

Luongo, M. (2002) Rome's World Pride: making the eternal city an international gay tourism destination. *GLQ* 8(1–2), 167–181.

Mansergh, G., Colfax, G.N., Marks, G., Rader, M., Guzman, R. and Buchbinder, S. (2001) The circuit party men's health survey: findings and implications for gay and bisexual men. *American Journal of Public Health* 91(6), 953–958.

Markwell, K. (2002) Mardi Gras tourism and the construction of Sydney as an international gay and lesbian city. *GLQ* 8(1–2), 81–99.

Markwell, K. and Rowe, D. (2003) The International Gay Games: subverting homophobia or selling out? *International Sports Studies* 25(1), 5–20.

Markwell, K. and Waitt, G. (2009) Festivals, space and sexuality – gay pride in Australia. *Tourism Geographies* 11(2), 143–168.

Mason, A. (1994) Introduction. In: Healey, E. and Mason, A. (eds) *Stonewall 25, the Making of the Lesbian and Gay Community in Great Britain*. Virago Press, London.

Mattison, A.M., Ross, M.W., Wolfson, T. and Franklin, D. (2001) Circuit party attendance, club drug use and unsafe sex in men. *Journal of Substance Abuse* 13, 119–126.

Picard, D. and Robinson, M. (eds) (2006) *Festivals, Tourism and Social Change: Remaking Worlds*. Channel View, Clevedon, UK.

Probyn, E. (2004) Everyday shame. *Cultural Studies* 18, 328–349.

Reynolds, R. (2002) *From Camp to Queer: Remaking the Australian Homosexual*. Melbourne University Press, Melbourne, Australia.

Rowe, D., Markwell, K. and Stevenson, D. (2006) Exploring participants' experiences of the Gay Games: intersections of sport, gender and sexuality. *International Journal of Media and Cultural Politics* 2(2), 149–165.

Saldanha, A. (2005) Trance and visibility at dawn: racial dynamics in Goa's rave scene. *Social and Cultural Geography* 6(5), 707–721.

Sedgwick, E.K. (2003) *Touching Feeling: Affect, Pedagogy, Performativity*. Duke University Press, Durham, North Carolina.

Shepherd, B. (2005) The use of pleasure as a community organizing strategy. *Peace & Change* 30(4), 435–468.

Stevenson, D., Rowe, D. and Markwell, K. (2005) Explorations in 'event ecology': the case of the International Gay Games. *Social Identities* 11(5), 447–465.

Stychin, C. (2003) *Governing Sexuality: the Changing Politics of Citizenship and Law Reform*. Hart Publishing, Oxford.

Tomsen, S. and Markwell, K. (2009a) *When the Glitter Settles: Safety and Hostility at and around Gay and Lesbian Public Events*. Australian Institute of Criminology Research and Public Policy Series 100, Australian Institute of Criminology, Canberra.

Tomsen, S. and Markwell, K. (2009b) Violence, culture display and the suspension of sexual prejudice. *Sexuality and Culture* 13(4), 201–212.

Urry, J. (1990) *The Tourist Gaze*. Sage, London.

Waitt, G. (2003) Gay Games: performing community out from the closet of the 'locker room'. *Social and Cultural Geography* 4(2), 167–184.

Waitt, G.R. (2004) Boundaries of desire: becoming sexual through the spaces of Sydney's 2002 Gay Games. *Annals of the Association of American Geographers* 96(4), 773–787.

Waitt, G. (2005) Sydney 2002 Gay Games and querying Australian national space. *Environment and Planning D, Society and Space* 23, 435–452.

Waitt, G. and Gorman-Murray, A. (2008) Camp in the country: renegotiating sexuality and gender through a rural lesbian and gay festival. *Journal of Tourism and Cultural Change* 6(3), 185–207.

Waitt, G. and Markwell, K. (2006) *Gay Tourism: Culture and Context*. The Haworth Press, New York.

Waitt, G. and Staple, C. (2011) Fornicating on floats: the Sydney Mardi Gras Parade beyond the metropolis. *Leisure Studies* 30(2), 197–216.

7 Events and Economics

Leo Jago[1]* and Larry Dwyer[2]

[1]*University of Nottingham, Nottingham, UK;* [2]*University of New South Wales, Sydney, Australia*

_____

Introduction

While it is widely recognized that there are many reasons for a host destination to stage an event, one of the most important is the economic impact that events are seen to generate. The attraction of economic benefits for the host destination has underpinned the fierce competition that often takes place for the right to stage an event and helps explain the fact that governments are prepared to invest substantial sums providing the infrastructure needed to host the event and to subsidize its operation.

There is an expectation that the economic performance of events be evaluated after they are staged in order to confirm that they have generated the return that was expected. Unfortunately, the manner in which many economic evaluations of events have been undertaken has resulted in grossly overstated outcomes. As a consequence, the credibility of the figures that are generated has fallen to such an extent that some government agencies no longer accept the findings and, indeed, has led to some auditor reviews of the way these evaluations have been conducted.

This chapter provides an historical overview of the way that the economic performance of events has been evaluated with commentary as to the theoretical and practical advantages and disadvantages of the different approaches. A case study based on the Auditor General's evaluation of the Melbourne Formula One Grand Prix is then presented to highlight issues in relation to some of the more advanced techniques to assessing the performance of a major event. Recommendations are then made as to the manner in which the performance of events should be evaluated in the future.

Although many regard the staging of events and the supportive role that events play for tourism as relatively recent phenomena, history shows this not to be the reality, with people throughout the ages coming together to attend sporting, religious and cultural events. Indeed, some of the earliest examples of tourism were based on trips to attend events, with the first Olympic Games in 776 BC being commonly regarded as the first major sporting event that underpinned substantial tourism activity. While the staging of events per se has a long tradition, the 'explosion' in the number of events being staged, and the range of destinations that see events as important, if not core, to the profile of the destination, has occurred largely since the 1980s.

Australia in general, and Melbourne in particular, are destinations that were early to recognize the important role that events could play as generators of tourism activity that had substantial economic impacts. In both cases,

* leo.jago@nottingham.ac.uk

© CAB International 2013. *Research Themes for Events*
(eds R. Finkel *et al.*)

this strong interest in events was no doubt born out of necessity with Australia being such a remote destination that it needed events or activities that could create an international profile and be an incentive to attract tourists to travel to Australia. Melbourne had been the host of international sporting events dating back to its hosting of the Olympic Games in 1956, but it was not until the early 1990s that events were identified as the core strength of Melbourne's tourism industry. Events were seen as a way for Melbourne to compete with other key destinations in Australia that had stronger natural attractions. Events became a key economic driver for Melbourne and were fundamental in repositioning the city image.

As the staging of events is an expensive exercise, especially for large-scale events that often require substantial investments in new infrastructure, it is critical that funds be obtained from the public sector. In the early days of the modern event era (from the 1980s) it was really only the economic impacts of events that were seen as the benefit for the host destination. Thus, public sector agencies needed to see strong projected economic returns prior to funds being provided in support of staging events. This led to the development and rapid growth in the number of agencies that provided economic evaluations of events, most of which were undertaken prior to the event itself in order to justify the support of the public sector.

There is now wide recognition of the diverse range of benefits that events can generate for a host destination and the fact that many of these benefits have lasting effects for the host community. However, in the early days of the modern event era, there was an almost total focus on the economic impact of events with barely any mention given to other benefits. As the old adage 'bigger is better' was prevalent in the event industry, there was substantial pressure on those conducting evaluations to produce the largest possible economic impact results. Although economic evaluations were conducted prior to most major events in order to obtain public sector funding, relatively few post-event evaluations were conducted in the early days and it was very rare for comparisons to be done between pre- and post-evaluation studies.

An economic evaluation of an event should be undertaken in order to objectively assess the impact that the event generates. This evaluation can then be used to determine whether this event or event type should be supported in the future and if so, what modifications should be made in order to enhance its impact. To be able to effectively manage an event, one must be able to accurately measure its performance. However, in the 1980s and 1990s, it would appear that many of the economic impact evaluations of events were conducted with the main intention to simply claim that they had a substantial economic impact on the community rather than assessing the size of this impact. The models that were used in these early studies and the assumptions that were made were all geared towards maximizing the economic impacts generated; they were 'boosteristic' in nature and ultimately, they were not seen as credible.

Economic Impacts of an Event

The economic impact of an event is the net sum of the economic consequences of the new money that is attracted to the host region by the event as it flows through the local economy. It is important to recognize that impact studies do not take into account the opportunity cost of resources used in staging the event and thus produce a larger result than would be obtained via a cost–benefit study. While economic impact studies have been used to determine the desirability of an event, it is not possible to actually make such a decision without an understanding of the resources required to generate the impact, that is, an assessment of the net benefit should be considered (Dwyer and Forsyth, 2009).

The new money that is attracted to the local economy by the event is the direct impact of the event. As these funds flow through the local economy they produce indirect (production induced) and induced (consumption induced) impacts. The indirect impacts occur when organizations that make sales to visitors purchase goods and services from other organizations in the region, which in turn make purchases from other suppliers in the region.

Once all of the direct funds have leaked outside the host community, the rounds of the indirect impact cease. The total of these subsequent purchasing rounds adds to the indirect impact. The induced impact results from employees in the host region who receive wages from the direct spending of the visitors to the event, purchasing goods and services themselves within the region. The induced impact also includes the consumption made within the host region when business owners who have made sales to visitors subsequently spend some of their profits on goods and services within the region. The total economic impact of the event is the sum of the direct, indirect and induced impacts. The economic impacts of an event include such variables as income, value added and employment generated.

The ratio of the total impact to the direct impact is called the multiplier and the larger the multiplier, the greater the impact that the direct spending has on the local economy. A larger multiplier indicates that the direct funds circulate more frequently in the economy before they 'leak' away, which suggests that an economy is more diverse and better able to provide more supplies within the economy itself.

The two most common types of multipliers are: (i) 'output'; and (ii) 'value added'. As output multipliers involve multiple counting of economic activity at each stage in the process, they are much larger in size. Value-added multipliers consider only the increase in economic activity at each stage in the process and thus produce more conservative results. It is not surprising, therefore, that many of the early event economic impact studies used output multipliers in order to maximize the results achieved. Although the economic impact studies of events using output multipliers produced very large results that were 'music to the ears' of event supporters including local politicians, government treasury officials became increasingly vocal in their condemnation of the use of such multipliers. Indeed, economic impact results achieved using output multipliers are now regarded as unacceptable by many government treasury officials, prompting a move to the more widespread use of value-added multipliers.

Inscope Expenditure

It can be seen in the previous section that the type of multiplier used in an analysis can greatly affect the size of the economic impact that an event is estimated to have achieved. Another factor that can influence the result is the calculation of inscope expenditure, which is defined as the new expenditure that is generated in the host region that would not have occurred if the event did not take place. Inscope *visitor* expenditure only includes the spending of visitors to the region who were specifically attracted to the region by the event. It does not include the spending of visitors who simply changed the timing of their visit to coincide with the event or visitors who were in the region anyway and attended the event while they were there. Inscope *sponsorship* expenditure includes only sponsor funding that is specifically generated by the event and which would not otherwise have been spent in the destination.

In many of the early event economic impact studies, the direct expenditure included expenditure well beyond inscope expenditure, which meant that the final economic impact figure was grossly inflated after the multiplier had been applied. Some of these studies included the expenditure of local residents based on the argument that the spending generated by the event was different to what would have been spent otherwise (Li and Jago, 2013). While the timing and categories of expenditure made by local residents may be different as a result of the hosting of the event, it can be assumed that the equivalent expenditure would have been made within the local economy by these residents in the absence of the event. Thus, event-related expenditure by residents is regarded simply as 'transferred' expenditure and not as new money. The questionnaires used to capture the inscope expenditure have become more sophisticated in relation to their ability to identify residents and visitors who would have come to the region at another time in the absence of the event (time switchers) and visitors who were in the region for another purpose besides the event (casuals).

Attendee Numbers

Another way in which early event economic studies inflated the results was via the over-estimation of attendees, especially for non-ticketed events. While there can be no debate about the number of attendances at an event derived from the total ticket sales at ticketed events, this does not always indicate the number of attendees, as for some events, individuals may purchase tickets to multiple performances or sessions. For example, an event may run over 2 days and have separate tickets for each day. The fact that 5000 tickets are sold could mean that there are 5000 different attendees or it could mean that there were 2500 attendees who each bought tickets for both days. When one ramps up the expenditure obtained from a sample of attendees to the total population, knowing whether the total population is 2500 or 5000 will make a substantial difference to the final economic impact.

While there are some challenges in determining the total number of attendees from ticketed events, these problems are magnified many times over for non-ticketed events. Crowd estimation is a difficult task, especially if multiple venues are used over a number of days and some components of the event are indoors as well as outdoors. In many of the early event economic impact assessments that were undertaken, concerns were raised that the most optimistic crowd estimates were used to underpin the analysis resulting in overstated economic impact estimates. In order to produce credible economic impact assessments, it is critical that the crowd estimates are as accurate as possible. While this is far from an exact science, there are techniques that can be used to enhance the reliability of the estimates. Such techniques include: (i) aerial photography; (ii) tag and re-capture; (iii) hotel occupancy; and (iv) proportional occupancy in venues. Jago and Dwyer (2006) provide an overview of some of these techniques and highlight the importance to the final economic impact figure of having accurate attendee estimates.

Economic Models to Estimate Economic Impacts

In most of the early studies undertaken to assess the economic impact of an event, Input–Output (I–O) models were used. An I–O model lists the relationships between inputs per unit of output for each sector of a particular economy. Each of these supplying sectors will in turn require inputs from other sectors, ultimately involving the whole production system in the economy. These models show the flow on effects throughout the local economy caused by the initial spending of an event attendee. As indicated earlier, the money injected into the economy by the event attendee continues to work through the economy in multiple rounds until all of it leaks out of the economy when the process stops. The main forms of leakages are: (i) retained earnings; (ii) taxes; and (iii) imports (Fletcher, 1994).

I–O models have been the most commonly used method for assessing the economic impact of events due largely to the following:

- The model is easy to use.
- The model is relatively cheap to operate.
- The results are easily interpreted and communicated (Mules, 1999).

I–O models are based on some key assumptions that include:

- There are no resource constraints.
- Prices and costs remain fixed as economic activity expands.
- There are constant proportions between inputs and outputs (Briassoulis, 1991; Fletcher, 1994).

While these assumptions facilitate the operation of I–O models, they also limit the ability of I–O models to truly represent the economic impact of a change in demand for goods and services. As there are resource constraints in most economies, an injection into one sector of the economy may attract resources from another, thus leading to a reduction in the output of a sector that may have more benefit for the economy than the sector into which the initial injection was made. I–O models are not able to show this effect and always produce a positive result, which may not always reflect the reality of the situation.

The key alternative to I–O models is Computable General Equilibrium (CGE) models. These are comprehensive models of the economy that incorporate the relationships between all of the key stakeholders, which facilitate a more accurate assessment of the impact of shocks to the economy. The comprehensive set of relationships included in CGE models enables them to be calibrated to the actual conditions within an economy in a manner that I–O models can't match. CGE models can be used to explore scenarios in the economy involving: (i) flexible or fixed prices; (ii) various exchange rate regimes; (iii) differences in the degree of mobility of factors of production; and (iv) different types of competition.

One of the key advantages of CGE modelling over I–O modelling is that CGE models permit the estimation of the negative effects on non-tourism sectors of an initial injection into the economy, as well as the positive effects on tourism-related industry sectors. As the negative effects on industry value added and employment can sometimes actually exceed the positive effects, the ability to assess both sides of the ledger is very important (Adams and Parmenter, 1999; Dwyer *et al.*, 2005). CGE modelling has replaced I–O modelling in most areas of economic evaluation. 'Indeed, event evaluation by tourism researchers and consultants is one of the few areas left in which I–O based multiplier models are still used for evaluation and policy advice purposes' (Jago and Dwyer, 2006).

The main criticisms that are levelled at the use of CGE models for evaluating the economic impact of events as described by Jago and Dwyer (2006) are:

- CGE models are not needed for other than very large events.
- CGE models are not necessary for events held in regional areas.
- CGE models require too many assumptions, which make them too complex to use.
- CGE models are costly and are often not available in various regions.

Proponents of CGE models have examined all of these criticisms and provide arguments for their rejection (for example see Dwyer *et al.*, 2005).

Trends in the Economic Evaluation of Events

While the authors of this chapter have some knowledge as to how the economic evaluation of events has been handled in different parts of the world, they are more familiar with the Australian scene having been closely associated with the event sector over many years. Thus, much of the discussion of trends in this section relates to the Australian experience and it is likely that this will accord with many of the trends in other jurisdictions. Since Australia was a very early adopter of events as drivers of economic development and Australia's public sector is a major provider of funds and the infrastructure that events require, the economic evaluation of events in Australia occurred from an early stage and has influenced the development of event evaluation elsewhere.

As indicated previously, many of the early economic evaluations of events have had a 'boosteristic' feel to them. More often than not they were undertaken prior to the event in order to provide some justification for financial support from the public sector and as such, the most optimistic assumptions were used in their preparation. Projections of attendee numbers tended to be at the very high end of possibility and very generous output multipliers were often used to predict the likely economic impact of the event. As these studies generally produced the very high numbers that politicians like, public sector funding was not often a problem. Within a few years, state government budgets allocated to providing the infrastructure and marketing needed by events increased quite substantially, which led to the appropriate call by government treasuries to verify that these events were, indeed, generating the economic impacts that had been projected.

Although the move to *ex post* event evaluations was an important step forward, there were still concerns that the focus of many of these evaluations was to justify the support that the event had received, rather than to objectively assess its performance. As before, optimistic assumptions were used in many of these evaluations leading to higher economic impacts than necessarily reflected what actually took place. It soon became recognized that some of the assumptions and methods being used to evaluate the economic impact of events lacked credibility and by the mid-1990s output multipliers were no longer used in these evaluations. Although this move to value-added multipliers produced more conservative economic impacts than had been the case using output multipliers, the size of the value-added multipliers that were used in some of the studies were too high and still produced inflated outcomes.

Australian Capital Territory (ACT) Auditor General's Performance Audit Report of V8 Car Races in Canberra

While there was growing disquiet among treasury officials about the manner in which some of the economic evaluations of events had been conducted, this issue became 'front-page news' around the country with the release in 2002 of the ACT Auditor General's Performance Audit Report of V8 Car Races in Canberra (Auditor General for the ACT, 2002). This audit report examined the manner in which the projected economic impact of the event had been forecast and communicated to government as well as the method by which an *ex post* event evaluation had taken place. The audit was highly critical on both issues.

In relation to the forecast, the audit made the following observations:

- It did not discount future revenue and cost flows to account for the cost of capital, which resulted in exaggerating the estimated net benefit.
- Its use of visitor expenditure figures from another event exaggerated the estimated visitor impact on spending by over 50%.
- It included optimistic forecasts as well as arbitrary and unjustified assumptions that favoured the project.
- It assumed an unrealistically high level of job creation.

- It included optimistic ticket-sale forecasts that were inconsistent with experience with other car races.
- It did not follow standard practice and provide information on the financial risk associated with the project.

As a consequence, the audit found that the economic and financial forecasts contained in the submission to ACT Cabinet in relation to a request for funding for the event were not reliable as a basis for sound decision making. The audit found that 'if better information had been available, Cabinet may not have decided to conduct the races' (Auditor General for the ACT, 2002).

One of the key recommendations of the audit was that a cost–benefit analysis (CBA) should have been undertaken in addition to the economic impact assessment, as without knowing the cost to the host community of producing the event, government is not in a position to make a decision about the true merit of its investment. That aside, however, the audit also identified a range of flaws in the approach adopted in the conduct of the economic impact assessment of the V8 Car Race in Canberra. These flaws included:

- The evaluation did not take into account the direct financial flows from the project, such as the public funds spent to establish and run the event.
- Expenditure by interstate tourists and locals on race tickets and merchandise was included even though such expenditure was also included in the direct operating revenue for the race, which is double counting.
- It included as a benefit the expenditure by tourists who would have come to Canberra whether or not the race was held (i.e. time switchers).
- It included expenditure by local residents at the race, which is simply expenditure switched from other activities.
- It included expenditure on local contracts as a benefit, which is actually a cost.
- Surveys of spectators at the event overstated the increase in tourist expenditure from the race.

A key recommendation in the audit report was that the value of events should be assessed using a CBA rather than simply an economic impact analysis. The primary reason for this is that an economic impact analysis considers only the gross benefits whereas a CBA takes into account the cost to deliver the benefit, thus producing a net benefit for the region. A CBA also takes account of the benefits (consumer surpluses) received by residents due to the hosting of an event, whereas in economic impact analysis all resident expenditure is classified as 'transferred expenditure' and thus not counted as 'new money' associated with the event.

The findings from this audit report provide a useful summary of many of the issues that led to the economic evaluations of events being overstated, grossly so in some cases. The fallout from this audit report was substantial both for ACT, where it led to the complete restructuring of the agency responsible for managing and assessing the impact of events, and for event agencies around Australia. As none of the other state governments wanted the very public humiliation that occurs when a state Auditor General produces such a damning report into the evaluation of events as occurred in the ACT, the government bureaucracies in each state recommended the adoption of a more conservative approach to the economic evaluation of events, taking into account the recommendations made in the ACT Audit Report. While this did help to produce more accurate evaluations, some of the State Government Ministers responsible for events worked against such a change as they were keen to be seen publicizing huge economic impacts for the events for which they had provided government financial support in their state.

Comparability of Economic Evaluation Studies

There are a number of reasons for undertaking an economic evaluation of an event. The driving force should be to determine whether the event produced the economic impact that was expected and to identify what changes could be made to the event and the way that it is promoted in order to enhance this impact in the future. There is also substantial merit in being able to compare the economic impact of an event to other similar events, which provides guidance as to how the event is performing; considering it in isolation does not provide this important comparative element.

With the support of all state government tourism agencies, a study was undertaken (Jago and Sherwood, 2005) to identify the key indicators of the economic performance of events and then to develop measures for these indicators that would facilitate comparison between events. This study entailed the collection and analysis of a large set of economic evaluation reports from events conducted around Australia in the previous few years. As relatively few of these reports are released publicly, the various state government agencies agreed to provide copies from their internal research libraries and a total of 105 event evaluation reports was supplied for analysis. This analysis showed that there were some general trends in relation to patronage and visitor expenditure profiles, but there was minimal consistency between reports in terms of the type of data collected and the manner in which they were analysed. This meant that it was virtually impossible to benchmark the economic performance of different events because the bases used and approaches adopted varied so much from study to study. Indeed, there were examples of specific events for which different approaches had been adopted in their economic evaluation from one year to another. This highlights a serious flaw in the way in which the economic evaluation of events has been undertaken.

Victorian Auditor General's Report on State Investment in Major Events (2007)

Even though there was pressure to adopt more conservative approaches to the economic evaluation of events after the release of the ACT Audit Report in 2002, there was a tendency to slip back towards being more 'boosteristic' in estimating economic impacts within a few years. This prompted some 'anti-event' lobby groups to start questioning the value of the financial support that governments were providing event agencies. Nowhere was this more obvious than in the State of Victoria where events form the centre piece of the state's tourism agenda and the government provides more funds in support of events than any other state (Tourism Victoria, 2009).

In response to these concerns, the Victorian Auditor General commenced an investigation into the means by which events were managed and evaluated in the state and its report was released in 2007. The manner in which the Formula One Grand Prix had been evaluated in 2005 was the prime focus of this audit, largely because this event receives substantial funding from the state government and like so many motorcar races around the globe, tends to polarize the community. The audit confirmed that the state had a sound framework for managing major events but recommended that 'the economic assessment models currently used now warrant concerted re-evaluation and further development' (Victorian Auditor General, 2007).

The audit used the primary data that had been collected for the 2005 Formula One Grand Prix and then commissioned a consultant to undertake a CGE analysis of the data and another consultant to undertake a CBA in order to compare the findings with the results produced from the original economic impact assessment. The consultants were also asked to comment on the bases used in the original assessment.

Key recommendations from this audit were as follows:

- Reconciliations should be undertaken between pre- and post-event evaluations in order to improve accountability and to better inform future decisions.
- Post-event evaluations should be broadened to include the social and environmental impacts.
- CBA and CGE modelling represented the most methodologically sound approaches to economic assessment of events, but economic impact analysis, including CGE modelling, cannot address the issue of whether an event should be supported.
- CBA should be used at the pre-event stage to assess the degree to which anticipated net benefits match the funding sought.

- CGE modelling should be used in post-event evaluations for larger events to assess their impact on the economy.
- Key performance indicators such as the level of direct inscope expenditure should be used in post-event evaluations for smaller events.

Conclusions

As a result of the 'boosteristic' approach that was adopted in preparing the early economic evaluations of events (whereby overly optimistic assumptions were used, some costs were ignored and additional revenues were claimed) the evaluation reports had low credibility. Indeed, many treasury officials had such low regard for some of these evaluations that the reports were simply ignored. Given that the methods needed to collect the data to assess the economic impact of an event have been well documented for many years, it has been deliberate decisions rather than a lack of knowledge that has led to the overstatement of event benefits.

The two government audit reports that have been conducted into the evaluation of events over the last decade have highlighted many of the pitfalls in these evaluations making similar recommendations about what is needed to enhance the accuracy of these evaluation reports. It is clear that CGE modelling is the most appropriate method to assess the economic impact of an event on the host economy. For smaller events, where the economic impact is smaller and it may not be possible to justify the expense of undertaking a CGE analysis, an approximation is to use the size of the direct inscope expenditure that the event generates (Jago and Dwyer, 2006).

As event evaluations have been so obsessed with the economic dimension, this has meant that the very important social and environmental costs and benefits have been largely ignored, which has been a major gap. The reports demonstrate that there are many potential effects of events that are often not accounted for in a standard economic impact analysis. In order for a government funding agency to be more comprehensively apprised, event assessments need to be broadened to take, where practicable, a more comprehensive approach embracing not only economic but social and environmental factors. Once these wider effects of events are acknowledged, we can appreciate why estimation of the economic impacts of events is only part of the evaluation story. To determine the extent (if any) of government assistance to be provided, it is necessary that the cost of these funds be compared to the wider costs and benefits from the event (Abelson, 2011).

Some events are staged largely for a local audience and as such have a very low economic impact yet may produce very substantial social benefits for the host community. Assessing such events on purely an economic basis will suggest that they are total failures, which may not be the case at all. A strong recommendation in the Victorian Auditor General's (2007) report was that the social and environmental impacts of staging an event should also be considered as equal partners with the economic dimension. This is vital for truly understanding the impact of an event on a local community and offers strong support for the use of CBA in event assessment. Although some are seeing this as a new development in the event evaluation field, it is far from new. Some 25 years ago, Burns *et al.* (1986) presented a comprehensive CBA assessment of the first Formula One Grand Prix in Adelaide. Assessments of this kind are essential to understand the full impact of an event on the local community.

Questions for Students

1. What are the benefits and challenges of the economic evaluation of events?
2. How do the perceived economic advantages of hosting an event have an impact on the host destination and its communities?

References

Abelson, P. (2011) Evaluating major events and avoiding the mercantilist fallacy. *Economic Papers* 30(1), 48–59.

Auditor General for the Australian Capital Territory (ACT) (2002) ACT Auditor General's Performance Audit Report of V8 Car Races in Canberra, 2002. Available at: http://www.audit.act.gov.au/auditreports/reports2002/Report_5_02.pdf (accessed 12 November 2012).

Adams, B. and Parmenter, B. (1999) General equilibrium models. In: *Valuing Tourism: Methods and Techniques*. Occasional Paper No. 28. Bureau of Tourism Research, Canberra, pp. 985–994.

Briassoulis, H. (1991) Methodological issues: tourism input–output analysis. *Annals of Tourism Research* 18, 435–449.

Burns, J., Hatch, J. and Mules, T. (eds) (1986) *The Adelaide Grand Prix: the Impact of a Special Event*. The Centre for South Australian Economic Studies, Adelaide, Australia.

Dwyer, L. and Forsyth, P. (2009) Public sector support for special events. *Eastern Economic Journal* 35(4), 481–499.

Dwyer, L., Forsyth, P. and Spurr, R. (2005) Estimating the impacts of special events on the economy. *Journal of Travel Research* 43, 351–359.

Fletcher, J. (1994) Input–output analysis. In: Witt, S. and Moutinho, L. (eds) *Tourism Marketing and Management Handbook*, 2nd edn. Prentice Hall, Upper Saddle River, New Jersey, pp. 480–484.

Jago, L. and Dwyer, L. (2006) *Economic Evaluation of Special Events: a Practitioner's Guide*. Common Ground, Altona, Victoria, Australia.

Jago, L. and Sherwood, P. (2005) The economic performance of special events: a framework for comparison. Proceedings of the Third International Event Conference: *The Impacts of Events: Triple Bottom Line Evaluation and Event Legacies*. University of Technology Sydney, Sydney, Australia, July, pp. 63–75.

Li, S. and Jago, L. (2013) Evaluating economic impacts of international sports events. In: Shipway, R. and Fyall, A. (eds) *International Sports Events: Impacts, Experiences and Identities*. Routledge, London, pp. 13–26.

Mules, T. (1999) Estimating the economic impact of an event on a local government area, region, state or territory. In: *Valuing Tourism: Methods and Techniques*. Occasional Paper No. 28. Bureau of Tourism Research, Canberra, pp. 123–134.

Tourism Victoria (2009) *Tourism Victoria Business Plan 2008–2011*. State Government Printer, Melbourne, Australia. Available at: http://www.tourism.vic.gov.au/images/stories/Documents/StrategiesandPlans/Tourism-Victoria-Three-Year-Business-Plan.pdf (accessed 16 August 2012).

Victorian Auditor General (2007) State Investment in Major Events. Available at: http://download.audit.vic.gov.au/files/20070523-Investment-in-Major-Events.pdf (accessed 13 September 2012).

8 Events and Management

Joe Goldblatt*

Queen Margaret University, Edinburgh, UK

Introduction

According to Bowdin *et al.* (2010), since the dawn of time, human beings have found ways to mark important events in their lives: (i) the changing of the seasons; (ii) the phases of the moon; and (iii) the eternal cycle of birth, death and the miraculous renewal of life each spring. Whether these celebrations are tied to agricultural cycles or human life cycles, they provide, as Bowdin *et al.* (2010) and Goldblatt (2010) both note, benchmarks and milestones by which human beings record their lives. Getz (2007) identified a typology of planned events that includes three distinct streams. First, cultural celebrations, political and state, and arts and entertainment are clustered, as are business and trade, with educational and scientific events separately categorized. Second, sport competition and recreation are bundled together, and, third, private events, such as weddings, bar and bat mitzvahs and anniversaries, are given their own category. Some may disagree with Getz's (2007) typology, but it does provide a helpful categorization for examining a field of study that is both broad and deep.

Between 2000 and 2010, the planned events industry has grown in both professionalism and scale (Getz, 2007). This growth can be evidenced by the Scottish Government's decision to encourage the development of over 400 events during a year-long celebration of Robert Burns' birthday in 2009. The signature event for this celebration was a 2-day festival and Highland Games programme called 'The Gathering'. This diasporic event attracted individuals from throughout the world who wished to connect with fellow Scots and particularly their clan organization. Over 120 clan organizations exhibited in individual marquees during The Gathering, and it is estimated that over 40,000 people attended the overall event. Nearly 40% of the people attending came from the USA and Canada, and others came to Scotland from as far away as Australia and New Zealand (EKOS, 2010).

First, this chapter will analyse the growth and development of research in planned events, especially as it pertains to the concepts of management processes and practices within planned events. Second, the chapter will provide a comprehensive case study analysis of The Gathering 2009 as related to management research in the field of planned events. Third and finally, as a result of this analysis, recommendations will be provided for further research and recommendations for additional reading in the area of events management.

* jgoldblatt@qmu.ac.uk

© CAB International 2013. *Research Themes for Events*
(eds R. Finkel *et al.*)

Planned Event Eras of the 20th and 21st Centuries

Goldblatt (2010) identified seven major eras of event development throughout the world. These are as follows.

1950s, the Age of Discovery

In the post-World War II economic boom, the private sector discovered the potential of planned events to generate new revenue. One example of this is the opening of Disneyland in 1954 when Walt Disney asked his director of public relations, Bob Jani, to create an event to extend the visitor stay. Jani discovered that by creating a daily parade that was illuminated with electric lights, guests would extend their stay and the per capita spending would significantly increase. The Main Street Electric Light Parade became a major feature at the Disney theme parks for many years and generated significant new revenues for the corporation.

1960s, the Age of Exploration

As a result of increased economic prosperity throughout the developed Western world, individuals and organizations began to explore the creation of events of greater scale than previously experienced in earlier eras. Further, advances in transportation, including the commercial use of the jet aeroplane, enabled events to market to international audiences. Events such as the US Woodstock Festival (music festival) and the New York World's Fair of 1964 experimented with new event locations, architecture and technology to reach and engage new audiences.

1970s, the Age of Invention

The rapid development and expanded use of computers enabled event planners and their suppliers to automate many of the tasks that were previously performed through manual operations. These new technologies enabled the development of automated database systems and online communications systems, such as computer-assisted design, and resulted in the improved functionality of lighting, sound and other key event elements.

1980s, the Age of Expansion

The rapid increase in the use of events by corporations and not-for-profit organizations to promote education, training, sales, brand building and other outcomes, greatly raised the profile for events as an accepted modern profession. Corporate leaders, such as the founder and chairman of *Forbes Magazine*, Malcolm Forbes, organized lavish events to promote his brand. In addition, the 1984 Summer Olympic Games, held in Los Angeles, California, was the first Olympic Games in modern history to generate a net surplus as a result of corporate sponsorship contributions.

1990s, the Age of Education and Research

As a direct result of the age of expansion, a new professional standard was required by which employers could hire appropriate individuals to plan and manage their events. In the final decade of the 20th century, universities and colleges throughout the world developed modules, courses and continuing professional development programmes to provide appropriate training for workers in the growing events industry. According to Getz, in 1989 Goldblatt wrote the first textbook in this field and with others developed the first comprehensive programme for training event managers within higher education (Getz, 1997). During this same period, event research greatly expanded and conferences were conducted by organizations such as the Australian Centre for Event Management at the University of Sydney and resulted in publications of the first scholarly proceedings such as *Events Beyond 2000: Setting the Agenda* (Australian Centre for Event Management, 2001). Finally, the development of a professional as well as academic qualification rapidly increased towards the end of the 20th century with the creation of the Certified Special Events Professional (CSEP) (ISES, 2010) and the Certified Festival and Event Executive (CFEE) (IFEA, 2010).

2000–2001, the Age of Global Celebrations

The events held by nation states and destinations throughout the world on 31 December 1999 to mark the beginning of the 21st century received global attention through internationally televised broadcasts. Nation states and city destinations competed to attract the greatest attention through their festivities. These events were also conducted to promote civic pride and to engage thousands of participants in developing and delivering these programmes. One example of events held during this period occurred when Joe Goldblatt was summoned to Bethlehem, Palestine, to assist the Mayor of this city with training for volunteers who were producing events in Manger Square. Goldblatt provided training on behalf of the World Bank to help ensure their multi-million dollar investment in these events was secure as a result of a comprehensive training and evaluation programme.

2001–2010, the Age of Reinvention and Meaning

Throughout the 1980s and 1990s events as phenomena of business and public life grew exponentially. However, as a result of the terrorist attacks on 11 September 2001 in the USA, the field of events required reinvention and sought ways to produce events that brought appropriate and deeper meanings. Further changing the landscape of planned events both in the USA and throughout many other regions was the financial recession that commenced with the collapse of Lehman Brothers in 2008. As a result of government financial injection into the US banking and automobile sector, these corporations were more cautious about the use of events for ostentatious display of their power and benefits (Goldblatt, 2010). These two paradigm shifts, the increased security that resulted from the

events of 11 September 2001 and the hesitation of corporations to spend funds for events after 2008 for fear of attracting ill will from the public, significantly changed the landscape for events. Event planners, who were surveyed by a leading publication in the field, noted that although corporate spending was reduced, spending for social life-cycle events such as weddings actually increased (Special Events Magazine, 2010).

As planned events have grown in professionalism and scale so has the need to promote greater accountability and understanding of these events increased as well. According to Getz (2007), in 2000 a study of the research articles submitted to the leading journal in the event management field indicated that the majority of research being conducted was in the area of economic impact studies, with a secondary focus upon corporate sponsorship. In the past decade, especially since the global economic crisis of 2008, the research in international planned events has begun to expand its focus and methodological approach.

Review of Literature

It is unclear when management as a profession was first developed. Some believe that its origins may be found as early as 6th century (BC) through the writings of the Chinese general, Sun Szu. He recommended being aware of and acting on strengths and weaknesses of both a manager's organization and a foe's. Fayol (1966) defined management as having six basic functions: (i) forecasting; (ii) planning; (iii) organizing; (iv) commanding; (v) coordinating; and (vi) controlling. The profession of management rapidly developed during the 17th and 18th centuries.

The term 'manage' is derived from the Latin term *manus* that means *hand*. The 19th-century American social worker and management pioneer Mary Parker Follett defined management as 'getting things done through people' (Follett and Graham, 1995). However, Drucker (2007), often credited as the guru of modern management, stated in the mid-20th century that the basic task of management is the combination of marketing and innovation. Therefore, there is no single, clear and unequivocal definition for the term management, as it has evolved over numerous centuries of development. This evolution appears to be the result of exogenous variables such as the greater emphasis upon marketing in the mid-20th century as contrasted with the greater focus on industrial approaches in the early 20th century (Fayol, cited in Dunod, 1966).

The term 'management' appears 755 times in Getz's (2007) book, *Event Studies*, compared with the terms 'studies' (501) and 'planned' (367). The only term that appears more frequently than 'management' is the title itself, 'event', with over 1200 appearances. Getz (2007) and others (Bowdin *et al.*, 2010; Goldblatt, 2010) have recognized that planned events are observable management phenomena that are largely dependent upon getting work done through people.

In 2000, Getz conducted an analysis of refereed journal articles that had appeared in *Festival Management & Event Tourism* (now *Event Management, an International Journal*) to identify historic trends in research as reported by this journal. After reviewing the first six volumes of this journal, Getz (2000) determined that economic impact studies were the most frequently published studies (26 articles) while studies examining consumer benefits of attending events were among the least frequently published (one article). This analysis clearly identified that as the events management field was moving from a period of adolescence into maturity, measurement of economic impacts had been seen as most important to event organizers and researchers to use empirical knowledge to provide clear evidence of performance. However, this evidence only provided one type of evidence.

The field of events management has been linked to a wide ranging number of classical foundation disciplines. Getz (2007) identified these foundation disciplines to include anthropology, sociology, psychology, environmental psychology, social psychology, philosophy, religious studies, economics, management, political science, lay history, human geography and even future studies. Both sociology and anthropology developed as disciplines at the

same time and share common interests in the concept of social organization (Schultz and Lavenda, 2005). Within both foundation disciplines, the core concept is culture. According to Schultz and Lavenda (2005), culture is both learned and transmitted to others. Events management may also be learned through exposure to others and transmitted through the act of developing, delivering and evaluating the event (Goldblatt, 2010).

Within social and cultural research, a key research methodology used by both anthropologists and sociologists is ethnography. Ethnography is one method in qualitative research. Qualitative research is a naturalistic, interpretative approach concerned with understanding the meanings that people attach to actions, decisions, beliefs, values and the like within their social world, and understanding the mental mapping process that respondents use to make sense of and interpret the world around them (Ritchie and Lewis, 2003). According to the UK Office of National Statistics, qualitative methods may play an important part in developing, maintaining and improving survey quality by assessing vital issues that field pre-tests and pilot surveys alone cannot address. They are better able to identify the problems experienced by respondents in answering questions because they place a more systematic and in-depth spotlight on each question and its administration as well as routing and instructions (National Bureau of Statistics, 2008).

According to Krugman and Wright (2007), all events, local or international, begin with an analysis of the rationale or purpose and the type of event that will serve the purpose best. In the case of The Gathering, these questions were explored without the advantage of a formal market research study and this may have contributed to the later challenges faced by this event. The motion picture entitled *Field of Dreams* (1989) used the mantra, 'If you build it, he will come,' to suggest that the mere idea itself is strong enough to achieve the marketing aims of the organizers. According to Hoyle (2002), the concept of an event as a place where dreams come true was achieved by this film as evidence that over two decades later thousands of tourists continue to annually visit the maize field where the filming took place. Although The Gathering did not benefit from systematic market research, the organizers were acutely aware that if they created their own Scottish field of dreams, thousands of tourists would potentially visit.

The Gathering 2009 Case Analysis

The Scottish Government, led by First Minister Jack McConnell, decided to utilize the historic milestone of the 250th birthday of Scotland's national poet, Robert Burns, to develop a major event entitled 'Homecoming Scotland' in 2009. This event, at the time of its delivery, was the only homecoming programme in the world focused upon drawing individuals of Scottish ancestry or those who have an affinity for Scottish culture to visit Scotland. The Scottish diaspora includes over 40 million people (Scottish Government, 2009). Therefore, by targeting those of Scottish ancestry living outside Scotland in North America, Australia, Europe and other continents, The Gathering 2009 was a globally focused programme of events.

The Homecoming Scotland 2009 programme adopted the following four key objectives:

1. To deliver additional tourism visits and revenue for Scotland.
2. To engage and mobilize the Scottish diaspora.
3. To promote pride in Scots at home and abroad.
4. To celebrate Scotland's outstanding contributions to the world.

Beginning in 2007, individuals and organizations throughout Scotland were invited to submit ideas and proposals for events and programmes that would accomplish these objectives. Hundreds of ideas and recommendations were received and eventually over 400 events were funded by EventScotland as part of the final official programme of events. While most of the events were small community-based programmes, one event that received significant public financial support

would ultimately be described by the Scottish Parliament as a 'signature' event of the Homecoming Scotland 2009 programme (Scottish Parliament, 2011).

Supovitz and Goldblatt (1999) discuss whether success in the business of events is measured in profits, lifestyle or the acquisition of wealth. They conclude through the examination of dozens of event entrepreneurs' success factors that the event organizer's overall reputation must be guarded as something of great value. Regrettably, as a result of the financial losses resulting from The Gathering, the organizers as well as public officials from the Edinburgh City Council experienced severe negative publicity over an extended period that damaged individual as well as civic reputations.

One of the early seminal books in the field of event management is entitled *ISES Gold* and was published by the International Special Events Society (ISES) in 1994. This anthology of examples, best practices and anecdotes by international leaders in the field of events management includes a chapter entitled, 'The Chemistry of Leadership: a Table of Elements' by Marc Rose, a past president of ISES. Rose (1994) states that, according to Max De Pree, leaders are obligated to provide and maintain momentum, tangibly as well as intangibly. It is the feeling that among a group of people their lives are intertwined and moving towards a recognizable and legitimate goal. Within The Gathering organization, this leadership was both tangible and intangible and despite the financial failures of this event, the key stakeholders of this organization and Homecoming Scotland 2009 did indeed have a sense of moving toward their goals.

The Gathering 2009 was a private venture that would eventually record final debts of £726,000. Although The Gathering 2009 was organized by a private concern, it received £490,500 in public funding support (EKOS, 2010). The research conducted by the authors found that 40% of the visitors to The Gathering 2009 were attracted from outside of Scotland. Thirty per cent of the people who attended The Gathering would not have attended Homecoming Scotland 2009 had The Gathering 2009 not been held. Forty-one per cent of those people who attended The Gathering 2009 stayed in hotels. Over 98% of the people who attended The Gathering 2009 rated their experience as good or very good. Seventy-three per cent of visitors further stated that they would most likely visit The Gathering again in the next 4 years. The Gathering 2009 contributed, according to the economic impact study conducted by EKOS, an additional £10,000,000 to Scotland. This presented a return of £21 for each £1 invested.

The EKOS study primarily focused upon economic impact and the collection of demographic data for future marketing usage. The organizers of The Gathering 2009 then contracted with the International Centre for the Study of Planned Events (ICSPE) to conduct a complementary study of the outcomes of their programme of events (ICSPE, 2009). The principal investigators for this project were Professor Joe Goldblatt, CSEP and Claire Seaman, DBA (Diploma in Business Administration). Goldblatt and Seaman met with The Gathering 2009 officials and were informed that as this was a first-time-ever event the organizers were seeking evidence of the human impacts this event would generate in order that they could promote future versions of the event to sponsors in Scotland as well as other destinations where there are large numbers of people of Scottish descent.

The Gathering used carefully selected mixed-method evaluation tools to examine their event management practices. However, this was not a systematically planned process; rather, it was an ad hoc solution to provide further evidence for their financial and other contributions to Homecoming Scotland 2009. As a result of the review of literature, it may be determined that there is a need to join up this evaluation process in the future to provide an Olympic Games Knowledge Services (OGKS)-type evaluation and transfer-of-knowledge system that will benefit future hallmark events, such as the second edition of Homecoming Scotland in 2014. The following examines in depth the case of the evaluation system used for The Gathering 2009.

Goldblatt and Seaman determined that the most effective methodology for the delivery of this research would be through using qualitative methodologies. The Gathering 2009 approved this approach to their research study and the principal investigators then developed a comprehensive research plan to accomplish the objectives identified by the organizers. The research plan consisted of the use of triangulation methodology. This called for 15 researchers to conduct 152 semi-structured interviews with visitors to the event using a convenience-sampling approach during The Gathering 2009. These interviews focused upon their perception and future memories of the event. In addition, the researchers conducted 150 h of direct observation of the guests attending The Gathering 2009 and then recorded field notes regarding their behaviours (demeanour, engagement, audience participation and other key factors). The researchers also documented the event using ethno-photography and recorded 500 images that would later be analysed to determine if there was congruence between the responses from the semi-structured interviews, the ethnographic observations and the final photographic documentation. Finally, the researchers used counting clickers to record the number of people at each activity within The Gathering 2009 at the start as well as at the end to determine slippage (audience attrition) during the programme. The combination of these three methods created a robust picture of the perceptions, behaviours and attendance at the event.

Figure 8.1 depicts the results of one observation activity performed by the researchers. Using a five-point Likert scale, the researchers were able to identify various levels of engagement among the guests attending The Gathering 2009 during an individual activity.

Figure 8.2 depicts the average involvement of the spectators versus the actors. A spectator is defined as one who is primarily cognitively involved in the event activity whereas an actor is one who is physically involved.

Individual activities such as those recorded in Figs 8.1 and 8.2 were then compared with all the activities observed during The Gathering 2009. Figure 8.3 compares the overall audience response by individual activity. The Scotland Lives Exhibition, Clan Parade and Clan Village achieved the highest scores. This was also reflected in the final report prepared by EKOS.

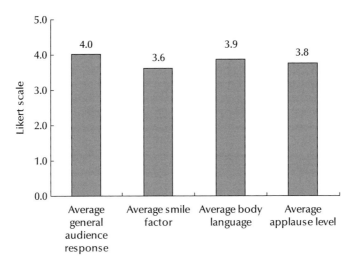

Fig. 8.1. Ethnographic observation scoring.

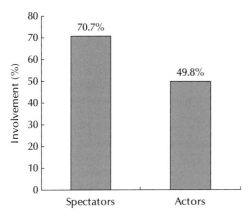

Fig. 8.2. Ethnographic scoring of average involvement of spectators and actors.

Recent research examining the happiness factor at events has focused upon the number and type of 'smiles' that are observed among the participants during the event activity. Happiness is defined as a state of well-being and contentment and a pleasurable or satisfying experience. Furthermore, recent happiness research has been shown to have a direct economic correlation, as evidenced by its research potential for determining: (i) future economic policy; (ii) the effect of institutional conditions; and (iii) the formation of subjective well-being (Frey and Stutzer, 2001). Therefore, 'smile factor research' may

provide additional insights into the perception guests have of their event experience. Figure 8.4 depicts the various smile factor observations by individual activity. The highest smile factor was recorded during the Clan Parade along the Royal Mile. This may be attributed to the historic first-time-ever parade of over 125 different Scottish clans and the responses being generated through broad smiles by their clan members in the audience of nearly 20,000 people.

The semi-structured interviews further confirmed the results of the ethnographic observations. Figure 8.5 depicts the a priori and post hoc attitudes regarding the guests' perception of The Gathering 2009. The majority of the people interviewed were satisfied or very satisfied after attending The Gathering 2009. One of the assumptions that the researchers made about this high level of satisfaction was that this was a first-time event and the overall programme had not been clearly described by the organizers. Therefore, the expectation level of the guests may have been somewhat low and this resulted in a final impression that was highly positive. These research results also further confirm the survey research conducted by EKOS.

The researchers also observed the tone of voice used by the people who were interviewed to further identify their pre-event expectation

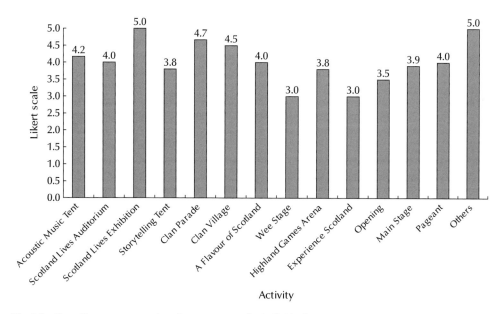

Fig. 8.3. Overall average general audience response by individual activity.

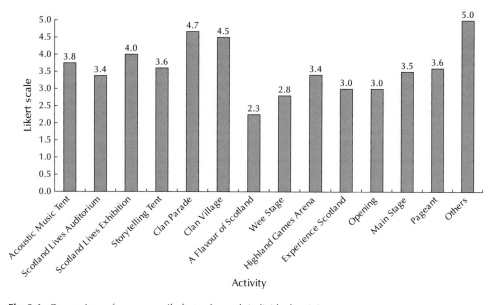

Fig. 8.4. Comparison of average smile factor for each individual activity.

levels as evidenced by their tone and rate of speech. These expectation levels are shown in Fig. 8.6. The aggregate score of 3.1 demonstrates that the guests showed very high expectations when they responded to the ethnographers' questions.

Discussion

The Gathering 2009 research project served as an opportunity to pilot test new methodologies for exploring events management practices. As a result of this exploration, the researchers

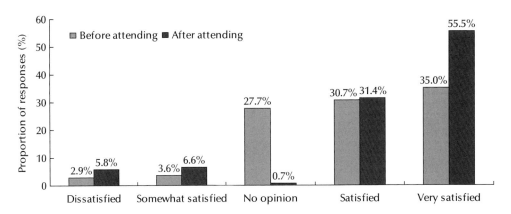

Fig. 8.5. Pre- and post-attitudes about The Gathering 2009.

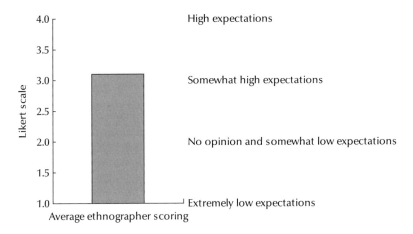

Fig. 8.6. Average score for guest pre-event expectation levels as observed by ethnographers.

were able to identify several key factors that may provide future event organizers with evidence that events such as The Gathering 2009 may achieve their goals and objectives through proper management practices. The original research goals of organizers of The Gathering 2009 were to measure the human impacts and to provide evidence that would make the event attractive to future sponsors. As a result of this study, the evidence is clear that the human impacts were very positive, especially as related to Scottish culture as shown through high responses to the Clan Village and Clan Parade. However, what may be equally important is what was not mentioned

by the guests but was captured in the research conducted by EKOS. The EKOS study described high levels of dissatisfaction with the operational aspects of the event as evidenced by the long queues for the loos and food and beverage stalls. This type of criticism did not appear in the semi-structured interviews conducted by the researchers, and they even observed people smiling while waiting in inordinately long queues. This may be attributed again to the low pre-event expectations of the guests or the myriad of distractions that could be experienced while standing in a queue. Regardless, one of the important outcomes of this research is that due to the low-profile marketing provided by The Gathering 2009 prior to the event, the guest expectations may have been better managed and this resulted in a better experience outcome as reported by the guests during and after the event. This new research methodology is a direct paradigm shift from the earlier research in planned events conducted at the turn of the 21st century that was primarily related to solely economic or sponsor impacts.

Furthermore, through the use of triangulation, the researchers were able to compare and contrast the spoken responses by the guests with their actual behaviour as observed in speech (tone and rate) and physical behaviour (cognitive engagement, physical audience participation and 'smile factors'). This opportunity to provide an alternative assessment, measurement and evaluation of the overall guest experience may be helpful to future event organizers as they seek to better manage the guest experience. This was particularly useful and applicable to The Gathering 2009, as over 40% of the visitors were from outside Scotland and this allowed for a determination of how, in anthropological terms, 'the other' would experience the indigenous culture of Scotland as defined through the clans.

The literature reviewed for this study clearly confirms the linkage between events management and anthropology, sociology and other scientific fields of study. However, prior to this study, the majority of research conducted regarding events management concentrated upon quantitative approaches to measuring outcomes. Therefore, through the use of a wide range of qualitative methods, the results obtained as shown in the figures above demonstrate it is possible to draw general conclusions from observation, participation and the use of semi-structured interviews.

Getz (2007) and others have described several foundation disciplines, including anthropology and sociology, that have important influences upon the field of planned events. These foundation disciplines were evidenced through the research for The Gathering 2009 as guests: (i) returned to their anthropological roots through high levels of cultural symbolism; (ii) connected as a clan through the sociological experience of establishing stronger social networks; and (iii) reported positive psychological experiences through their high levels of overall satisfaction during the event. These foundation disciplines may be further incorporated by events managers to address the potential for increasing best practices, which may be experienced before, during and following the event.

A well-designed event evaluation process enables the client and the organization to determine if the event met the goals and objectives as well as the needs and opportunities for future events (O'Toole and Mikolaitis, 2002). In the case of The Gathering, the comprehensive evaluation conducted by Goldblatt and Seaman (2009) and EKOS (2010) demonstrate that despite the significant financial losses and resulting tarnished reputation of the organizers and government funders, the participants generally rated the event very highly. Furthermore, the overall economic impact resulting from The Gathering was significant and reflected nearly 10% of the total impact of the entire Homecoming Scotland 2009 programme of 400 events. Finally, as evidenced by the literature, the careful evaluation and documentation of management practices is critically important to ensure continuous improvement.

Future Research Opportunities

This study has since been replicated at three other planned events in Scotland. These events include: (i) the Saltire Celebration (the celebration of the birth of the Scottish flag); (ii) the papal visit to Edinburgh by Pope Benedict XVI; and (iii) the programme of events entitled 'Celebrating Fife 2010', which was conducted in Scotland's Kingdom of Fife. Each of these studies further refined and advanced the early research conducted on behalf of The Gathering 2009. Now, there is a need to conduct longitudinal studies of these and other events to determine if this methodology will provide valid and reliable results over an extended period of time in a wide range of geographic locations. One opportunity for this will be the return of The Gathering in 2014, which will be held in

Stirling near historic Stirling Castle. Only through the incorporation of longitudinal studies will researchers of planned events be able to determine if this type of robust research practice will be useful in the mid- and long-term future as we seek to better understand the management processes of events through a wide variety of different cultures.

Conclusions

From the early study by Getz (2000) regarding a future research agenda for research in planned events, there has been a need to broaden and deepen the way events are examined by using new and complementary methodological approaches. In the case of The Gathering 2009, many of these new approaches were piloted and their results have been utilized by the organizers of similar events in an effort to improve their final outcomes. Looking to the future of research in events management, the work achieved during The Gathering 2009 will be replicated and expanded during the repeat of this programme in 2014. As a result of the baseline data collected in 2009, the researchers will be able to expand their research through: (i) a larger sample size; (ii) the incorporation of new technological methodologies such as perhaps radio-frequency identification (RFID) to determine crowd behaviours; and (iii) improved interpretation systems drawn from standardized psychological and sociological instruments. Through this longitudinal approach the researchers plan to further extend the role and scope for using qualitative research to bring greater meaning and understanding to the study of events management processes and practices.

Although The Gathering 2009 was unsuccessful financially owing to lack of proper internal financial controls, EKOS reported a significant economic impact directly attributed to this event for Scotland. In addition, the media reports and impressions generated a significantly higher than normal return on marketing investment for this type of event. Finally, as evidenced by the study conducted by the ICSPE, The Gathering 2009 was very well received by its guests and, as a result of its cultural and social successes, is scheduled to be repeated in 2014. Therefore, in terms of management practices, it may be argued that while the marketing and expectation management was extremely well managed for this event, the internal financial operations, as recommended by the Scottish Government parliamentary committee, should be improved in the future to provide greater and closer oversight. When international financial inspection is addressed in the future, this event should be able to grow from strength to strength through the evidence provided from more in-depth research studies such as the one described here. The combination of well-planned internal and external management practices for all events is one that must be given greater scrutiny by event organizers and their sponsors in the future.

Questions for Students

1. How would you select the appropriate methodology to evaluate the management aspects of an event with global participants who do not share a common written or spoken language?
2. How does the management of an event have an impact on how the event is perceived and evaluated?

References

Australian Centre for Event Management (2001) *Events Beyond 2000: Setting the Agenda*. University of Technology, Sydney.
Bowdin, G., Allen, J., O'Toole, W., Harris, R. and Mcdonnell, I. (2010) *Event Management*, 3rd edn. Butterworth-Heinemann, Oxford.
Drucker, P.F. (2007) *The Practice of Management*. Butterworth-Heinemann, Oxford.

EKOS (2010) Homecoming Scotland 2009 Economic Impact Report. Available at: http://www. homecomingscotland2009.com/Repository/review/Homecoming_Scotland_2009_-_Economic_Impact. pdf (accessed 1 August 2011).

Fayol, H. (1966) *Administration Industrielle et Générale: Prévoyance, Organisation, Commandement, Coordination, Contrôle.* Dunod, Paris.

Follett, M.P. and Graham, P. (1995) *Mary Parker Follett: Prophet of Management.* Harvard Business School Press, Cambridge, Massachusetts.

Frey, B.S. and Stutzer, A. (2001) *Modern Developments in Behavioral Economics: Social Science.* Princeton University Press, Princeton, New Jersey.

Getz, D. (1997) *Events Management and Event Tourism.* Cognizant Publications, Elmsford, New York.

Getz, D. (2000) Developing a research agenda for the events management field. In: *Proceedings: Events Beyond 2000.* Australian Centre for Events Management, Sydney, July 2000. Australian Centre for Events Management, Sydney, Australia, pp. 9–20.

Getz, D. (2007) *Event Studies.* Elsevier, Oxford.

Goldblatt, J. (2010) *Special Events,* 6th edn. Wiley, New York.

Goldblatt, J. and Seaman, C. (2009) *The Gathering Research Report.* Queen Margaret University, Edinburgh, UK.

Hoyle, L. (2002) *Event Marketing.* Wiley, New York.

International Centre for the Study of Planned Events (ICSPE) (2009) Agreement of work. Internal documentation. ICSPE, Edinburgh, UK.

International Festivals and Events Association (IFEA) (2010) Certified Festival and Event Executive (CFEE) Certification Programme. Available at: www.ifea.com (accessed 1 August 2011).

International Special Events Society (ISES) (2010) Certified Special Events Professional (CSEP) Certification Programme. Available at: www.ises.com (accessed 1 August 2011).

Krugman, C. and Wright, R. (2007) *Global Meetings and Exhibitions.* Wiley, New York.

National Bureau of Statistics (2008) What Is Qualitative Research? Available at: http://www.ons.gov.uk/about/ who-we-are/our-services/data-collection-methodology/what-is-qualitative-research- (accessed 2 August 2011).

O'Toole, W. and Mikolaitis, P. (2002) *Corporate Event Project Management.* Wiley, New York.

Ritchie, J. and Lewis, J. (eds) (2003) *Qualitative Research Practice: a Guide for Social Science Students and Researchers.* Sage Publications, London.

Rose, M. (1994) The chemistry of leadership: a table of elements. In: Goldblatt, J., Surbeck, L. and Weirsma, B. (eds) *ISES Gold: an Anthology of Expertise from Members of the International Special Events Society.* International Special Events Society (ISES), Chicago, Illinois.

Schultz, E. and Lavenda, R. (2005) *Cultural Anthropology: a Perspective on the Human Condition.* Oxford University Press, Oxford.

Scottish Government (2009) The Characteristics of Each Diaspora. Available at: www.eventscotland.org (accessed 23 November 2011).

Scottish Parliament (2011) Lessons Must Be Learned from The Gathering 2009 Event. Presented to Scottish Parliament 24 February 2011. Available at: http://www.scottish.parliament.uk/nmCentre/news/news-comm-11/cpac11-s3-004.htm (accessed 1 August 2011).

Special Events Magazine (2010) *Social Event Spending Rises.* Pentland Communications, Malibu, California.

Supovitz, F. and Goldblatt, J. (1999) *Dollars and Events, How to Succeed in the Special Events Business.* Wiley, New York.

9 Events and Sport Tourism

John Nauright,[1]* Andrea Giampiccoli[2] and Seungwon 'Shawn' Lee[3]

[1]University of Brighton, Eastbourne, UK and George Mason University, Fairfax, Virginia, USA; [2]Durban University of Technology, Durban, South Africa; [3]George Mason University, Manassas, Virginia, USA

Introduction

In this increasingly unified yet divided world, sports mega events (SMEs), particularly the Olympic Games and the Fédération Internationale de Football Association (FIFA) World Cup, have become high-demand focal points that have symbolic value well beyond the results on the fields of sporting competition. Major sporting competitions and tournaments are regarded as 'events' to be 'marketed' and 'managed', and terms such as 'hallmark' and 'mega' suggest that size really does matter. The lure of large and spectacular events is thought to be an expedient way to attract media interest in a host city and nation, which, it is hoped, will translate into an influx of capital through tourism and new investment. In this chapter we discuss the role of sports events in economic development with particular focus on tourism.

By the 1990s it was clear that recurring sports events (RSEs), such as Super Bowls in American football, FA (Football Association) Cup finals in association football, the Tour de France, and numerous smaller-scale events and professional sports matches, generated income for local and regional economies through increase in spending at and near event sites and as a result of an increasing number of tourists coming to view an event who also used the occasion to participate in an array of tourist

activities. Several textbooks appeared in the late 1990s and early 2000s attempting to establish sport tourism as a distinct sub-field of both sports studies and tourism studies (cf. Standeven and de Knop, 1998; Turco et al., 2002; Weed and Bull, 2003; Adair and Ritchie, 2004). Over the past few years, however, sports events have been conceptualized within literature on mega events or considered in events management frameworks. A critical literature has also emerged that examines the claims for economic return proposed by event promoters and the actual costs as well as associated economic and social benefits. A framework of event legacy has now emerged as the focal lens for assessing the relative long-lasting impact of hosting a sports event.

The branding of destinations as desirable sites for new investment and tourist consumption has included sport and sporting events as key elements of new economic development strategies. We now live in an age of special events and a major part of national, regional and local politics is tied up with 'boosterism' and branding through the hosting of special events. The two most common of such events are sports events and festivals. Among sports events, there are two main types: (i) one-off mega events such as the Olympic Games or FIFA World Cup, for which special-purpose facilities are constructed; and (ii) recurring, usually smaller-scale, sports events

*jnaurigh@gmu.edu

© CAB International 2013. *Research Themes for Events*
(eds R. Finkel *et al.*)

(RSEs) for which the same facilities are used each year or which use primarily existing facilities. Examples of these include a local 5k road race, the US Masters Golf Tournament, and the Tour de France.

The relevance of both the mega event and the small sport events industries is their growing connection with other relevant spheres of local and regional political economies. SMEs have been the object of numerous studies in recent years in relation to the political economy of globalization, and focusing on developing countries and real or imagined attempts at poverty reduction (cf. Black and van der Westhuizen, 2004; Matheson and Baade, 2004; Nauright, 2004; Lee and Taylor, 2005; Saayman *et al.*, 2005; Bohlmann, 2006; Cornelissen and Swart, 2006; Cornelissen, 2007; Pomfret Pillay and Bass, 2008; Giampiccoli and Nauright, 2010). Mega events are large-scale economic phenomena and have increased in global relevance to become important factors in local and national economic development strategies. In this process local community interests and democratic practices are often ignored, and business and governments align in support of events-driven economies as part of growth strategies. In substance, business and political leaders view SMEs as significant channels for local and regional economic development and as a way to facilitate urban redevelopment using the event as a catalyst to leverage additional resources that might not otherwise be forthcoming. This strategy is justified through projecting increases in tourism, resulting infrastructural improvements, and the increase in short-term employment opportunities. Tourism and planned new investment in the specific locality or nation are key aspects of the heightened interest in hosting SMEs as they are thought to be the most expedient way to attract global media interest in a host city or nation, which, it is hoped, will translate into an influx of outside capital through tourism and new investment (Nauright, 2004). It is appropriate, therefore, as Nauright (2004) outlines, to analyse mega events in terms of a sport–media–tourism complex that is at the centre of many local, regional and national development strategies not only in developed countries but also in a number of developing globally focused economies such as Brazil, Russia or South Africa, or as Perelman (2012) suggests in terms of an entire mode of production that has emerged around globalized sport.

SMEs also need to be understood from political and social viewpoints, because mega events involve the political leadership of a host country and often shape legacies that governments and leaders envision for themselves. Governments are often keen advocates for promoting the positive impact that these events have, not only on a country's economy but also on its developmental legacy (Schulz Herzenberg, 2010). While political factors form the power behind the willingness to host SMEs, the hosting itself, beside the usually advertised economic and 'image' impacts, can have a variety of social consequences. Thus, SMEs should examine social impacts on residents and account for their concerns in planning for the event and in designing potential legacies. Examples of social costs that impact local day-to-day life include: (i) traffic congestion and overcrowding of roads; (ii) increased potential for criminal activity; (iii) disruption to daily schedules; and (iv) increased pollution (Turco *et al.*, 2003). The political willingness to host SMEs can, therefore, involuntarily (or not), ignore negative consequences faced by the local community such as: (i) residential displacement; (ii) breakdown of historic communities; and (iii) cost overruns that impact negatively upon citizens' quality of life (Nauright, 2004; Ritchie, 2004).

In general, SMEs have gained greater significance since the 1980s due in large part to: (i) an expansion of global media markets; (ii) new technologies enabling great exposure to be achieved; and (iii) the profits generated by the 1984 Olympic Games in Los Angeles. As a result, many countries began to link their economic development strategies to the attraction of major international sporting events that they hoped would leverage exposure into an increase in tourism income and outside business investment while encouraging the rapid development of supporting infrastructure that could be used more widely post-event (cf. Cornelissen, 2004; Nauright, 2004). Therefore, even though mega-sporting events are vulnerable to imprecise impact studies (Barclay, 2009) and much ambiguity exists with the meaning of the concept of SME 'legacy', it is a reality that a continually growing number of cities compete to host large-scale events. As Preuss (2007) has outlined, cities, usually with the support of national governments, base many aspects of their developmental strategies on events, with only vague ideas about the complexity of 'legacy' and long-term social and economic consequences.

The Olympics provide a prime example of complexities in utilizing SMEs as economic development strategies that promote the common good. The concept associated with the creation of the Olympic Games in the latter half of the 19th century was associated with the perpetuation of class distinction while shrouding the games with an aura of universalism (Wamsley, 2002; Nauright, 2012). Alternative international sporting movements were marginalized as the governing body for the Games, supported by business and governmental elites, established control of the governance and operation of global sport (Nauright, 2012). The rise of neo-liberal economic strategies in the West in the 1980s enabled the Olympic 'Movement' as a single institution with the capital to organize events, to define, delineate and sustain particular meanings about sport and human society to tie human aspirations with economic development issues (Wamsley, 2002; Nauright, 2012). In addition, the hegemonic ideology of Olympism has been coupled with a financial capitalist ideology through association with trans-national corporations. Thus, SMEs exist to legitimate political, economic, diplomatic and militaristic institutions supporting and gaining benefit from them (Perleman, 2012). At the same time, competition in sport event production has led corporate interests to demand that event organizers demonstrate value or return on investment (ROI) resulting from sponsorship and public exposure.

The Olympic Games, ultimately, are as much about selling endemic consumer processes and dominant political ideologies as they are about promoting peace. The Olympics are intensely political; they always have been.

Unfortunately, the disturbing testimony to their success is that most people do not complain, and in fact actively support the Games (Wamsley, 2002; Nauright, 2012; Perleman, 2012). The Olympics are, therefore, historically linked to the process of modern capitalist development, and since the 1980s have been rejuvenated by neo-liberalism and its connected globalization processes in a context of total monopoly of the ownership of the concepts and values that have defined and sustained dominant interpretations of 'sport' (Wamsley, 2002). The International Olympic Committe (IOC) controls the bargaining power of potential bidders. The situation of monopoly is not exclusive to the Olympics but is evident in all SMEs.

RSEs also have been objects of study; however, the overwhelming majority of work on the operation and wider impact of sporting events have focused on SMEs (Ritchie, 2004). Following Marsh (1984), it is argued that RSEs receive little attention because of the perceived small economic significance. RSEs can allow many smaller communities to organize sporting events and the operation of numerous RSEs on a recurring basis can collectively create significant impact. As a result, following Daniels and Norman (2003), we argue greater recognition should be given to RSEs by businesses, politicians and tourism planners.

RSEs can include a great variety of sporting categories such as regular team or individual sporting competitions in a local, regional or national league or tournament circuit, plus outdoor/adventure, distance running, cycling, boating, automobile races, etc. (Yusuf et al., 2009). As with SMEs, RSEs are closely connected with the tourism sector. Increased tourism is in fact the primary reason to promote RSEs and where consequential economic impacts can be measured (cf. Kotze, 2006; Yusuf et al., 2009). RSEs are often repetitive and have close connections to local contexts and opportunities; they are not, like SMEs, a one-off event. RSEs are based on existing local infrastructure, are repetitive, locally connected and evolve in relation to local opportunities and needs. While SME strategies are originated and managed within specific neo-liberal global frameworks and discourses to assist large-scale political, economic and cultural interests, RSEs hold out the possibility of greater local control. As with SMEs, the economic impact and local benefits of RSEs are usually a paramount factor in determining their value. They also rely on sponsorships and local and regional government support (Saayamn and Saayman, 2012). Horne (2000) argues that a sustained series of smaller events, often based on amateur sport, can provide wider exposure sufficient to create a 'host' city image and thus increase tourist revenue. The positive impact of RSEs also has been noted by Daniels and Norman (2003) in affirming that recurring sport tourism events have a more sustainable potential for host locales. Following Higham (1999), they suggest that the seven events they investigated had positive outcomes including: (i) zero to low bidding expenses; (ii) use of existing infrastructure; and (iii) little or no burden on public funds or problems for local residents (Daniels and Norman, 2003).

The Measurement of Impacts of SMEs and RSEs and Related Issues

Researchers often legitimate the sport–media–tourism complex through the production of reports suggesting expenditures on mega event infrastructure should be considered investments that generate long-term growth (Barclay, 2009). As Barclay (2009) and others argue, these reports are commissioned by stakeholders with political and economic interests in legitimating the hosting of the SME in order to maximize personal or organizational benefit. As early as the 1990s, researchers began to suggest the dangers inherent in SMEs (Baade and Dye, 1990; Baade, 1996; Coates and Humphreys, 1999; Porter, 1999; Baade and Matheson, 2002). As early as 2000, Siefried and Zimbalist found no statistically significant correlation between sports facility construction and positive long-term economic development (Siegfried and Zimbalist, 2000). In 2002, Baade and Matheson applied the same statistical techniques directly to SMEs (Baade

and Matheson, 2002). Yet, numerous promotional studies continue to appear, conducted by well-compensated consulting firms, using: (i) unrealistic assumptions about added local value; (ii) spending estimates that exclude many added costs; and (iii) inflated associated multipliers used as indicators of value added by tourists and spectators before, during and after an event. Public spending and 'biased' estimates are important factors in SME legitimation. Indeed, these are really not economic indicators but political tools to legitimate public support and limit protest (cf. Chalip and Leyns, 2002). While there have been multiple reports of how successful the 2010 FIFA World Cup was as a sports event itself, as well as its overall positive impact on the South African economy and tourism industry (e.g. FIFA, 2010), some doubt the reliability of projected numbers and assessment methods for measuring the impacts of SMEs on tourism and business industries (Lee and Taylor, 2005).

A number of authors, such as Gibson *et al.* (2003), Ritchie (2004), Saayman *et al.* (2008) and Yusof *et al.* (2009), have started to produce an increasing body of research suggesting regular localized sporting events can produce substantial economic benefits for a host community (Daniels and Norman, 2003), such as the Argus Cycle Tour in the Western Cape region of South Africa. Saayman *et al.* (2008) using an input–output and multiplier analysis found the 2008 Tour cost R80.7 million yet generated R131 million in expenditures yielding a 1.40 multiplier effect. Additionally, 1403 specific jobs were present due to the event.

Another way to compare relative costs versus impact is to examine *leverage ratios* of public sector input versus private sector response. The leverage ratio is illustrative of the amount of money that is accrued by the private sector with every unit of currency spent by the public sector. The leverage ratio does not consider overall tourist spending, or other general multiplier effects such as revenue from transport, external financial transactions, product suppliers, tours, or ongoing businesses and informal traders (Turco *et al.*, 2003).

South Africa as a Destination for SMEs and RSEs

Post-apartheid South Africa provides an instructive example of how large-scale sporting events have been sought in the hope of promoting tourism and economic development. South Africa has bid for and hosted an array of different SMEs in terms of scope and global awareness/impact. Since 1995 South Africa has hosted the Rugby World Cup (1995), the Cricket World Cup (2003) and the FIFA World Cup (2010). Although the Olympic Games have yet to come to Africa, Cape Town bid unsuccessfully for the 2004 Olympics (after winning a national competition with Johannesburg and Durban which also wanted to host the Games). Plans are in place for Durban to bid for the right to host the 2024 Summer Olympic Games. In a situation where many African countries have bid for SMEs, only South Africa was successful as of 2012 with no other nation on the immediate horizon of SME hosting. As a result, South Africa has become representative of the entire continent of Africa as to whether major events can be successful or not. This pressure provides a rationale for overriding traditional participatory planning processes, and, while the corporate sport–media–business alliance has never been open, countries and cities themselves have operated in a covert manner, continuing the undemocratic process running mega events (Tomlinson *et al.*, 2009).

Studies of RSEs in the South African context have emerged alongside those examining SMEs.

- Kotze (2006) investigated the impact of the Two Oceans Marathon in Cape Town.
- Turco *et al.* (2003) analysed the impact of various sport events of different size and local/international exposure at municipality level in Durban.
- Saayman *et al.* (2008) examined the economic impact of visitor spending at the Cape Argus Pick 'n Pay Cycle Tour.
- Sookrajh (2008) researched the relationship between nature-based sports events and the physical environment using the Halfway-Telkom Midmar Mile sport event as a case study.

- Saayman and Saayman (2012) explored determinants of visitors spending in three major sport events within South Africa: the Two Oceans Marathon, the Argus Cycle Tour and the Midmar Open Water Mile.

Many RSEs have been around for years in South Africa, expanding during and since the 1970s. For example, the Cape Argus Pick 'n Pay Cycle Tour started in 1977 to raise awareness of the need for cycle paths to be built in Cape Town (Saayman and Saayman, 2012). From that start the Cycle Tour has developed into an entire week of activities including the Mountain Bike Challenge, the Tricycle Tour, the Junior Cycle Tour, the Giro del Capo, the Expo, and finally the Argus Cycle Tour. By 2008 the number of entries in the event exceeded 32,000 (Saayman *et al.*, 2008). The Telkom Midmar Mile race began in 1973 when petrol restrictions limited travel to events further afield (Sookrajh, 2008; Saayman and Saayman, 2012). The Old Mutual Two Oceans Marathon, perhaps the most scenic marathon in the world, first appeared in 1970 (Saayman and Saayman, 2012). The most famous RSE, however, has a much longer pedigree. Vic Clapham, a returned soldier from World War I, initiated The Comrades Marathon in 1921 as a way to remember his fallen comrades. The race was organized over the 56 miles from Pietermaritzburg to Durban. On Empire Day, 24 May 1921, 34 runners took to the line outside the Pietermaritzburg City Hall. The race has been held every year since, with the exception of 1941–1945 during the height of World War II, alternating starting points each year between the two cities. The Comrades is now the largest ultra marathon event in the world (TKZN, 2006). More recent is the Cape Epic, which began in 2004 (Cape Epic, 2011a, b). The Epic is a mountain bike race that is becoming an iconic endurance event well known around the world and one that connects the usually remote sport of mountain biking with the urban environment of Cape Town. Participants and the community work together to coordinate events in and around the race, dramatically different from the secretive manner in which Durban organized the FIFA World Cup locally (Sole, 2010) or in which many decisions were made surrounding the organization of the 2012 London Olympics.

Case Study: Comparing the 2010 World Cup and RSEs on Tourism in Durban, South Africa

Further criticisms frequently evident in SMEs, such as the subversion of democratic practices and public transparency, were evident in South Africa in the lead up to the World Cup. In examining the 'covert management' practices in Durban, for example, it is clear the building of Moses Mabhida stadium was part of a larger and secretive plan involving Durban municipal manager Michael Sutcliffe who managed the city's 2010 build-up (Sole, 2010). Whatever the actual final economic cost, what remains is the displacement of huge quantities of scarce time, money, skills and energy for a project that amounted to little more than 'a month long television show' (Sole, 2010). In addition, while a new stadium in Durban was 'nice to have', it was not a FIFA requirement for hosting matches. The new stadium was constructed, however, with a larger purpose of becoming a place to hold large-scale events and a site for tourism, unlike the stadium in Cape Town,

which lies empty most of the year and is now seriously being considered for demolition. The new sporting arenas displaced spending useful elsewhere. More strategic spending might have been used on coastal preparations for ecological changes or on alleviation of poverty or enhancing educational opportunity. Durban's beaches in particular 'are a much more profound symbol of its enduring tourism appeal than a steel arch made in Germany' (Sole, 2010).

The Durban beachfront urban renewal has been associated with middle-class and elite opportunities for leisure and tourism rather than promoting more broad social inclusion goals throughout the municipality. Importantly, this is not to say that the new beachfront (or the stadium, which is architecturally world renowned) has been negative; on the contrary, it has greatly enhanced the image of Durban and the space is now widely used in sport/leisure activities over all its length from Moses Mabhida stadium to the area of uShaka Marine World. Figure 9.1 shows a picture of Durban beachfront leisure space with the stadium in

Fig. 9.1. Durban beachfront leisure space with the stadium in background. Photo taken by Andrea Giampiccoli.

background. Many community members have used the space, though few infrastructural investments were made to the areas where they live in the numerous impoverished areas in and around the city. Embracing an almost exclusive neo-liberal, market-orientated approach, the idea among advocates of the FIFA World Cup was to position cities like Johannesburg, Durban and Cape Town among a global hierarchy of competitive metropolitan areas (Pillay *et al.*, 2009). Yet, evidence from previous such events suggests that the results of hosting do not deliver on the promise of widespread community benefit but rather concentrate benefits in particular consumption zones of urban areas.

Comparing the impact between the World Cup and smaller localized sport events (Comrades Marathon, Dusi Canoe Marathon and Midmar Mile) within KwaZulu-Natal Province where Durban is located provides insight into differential impacts of SMEs and RSEs. The numerical comparison of economic impact shows that in a 5-year period the three local events approximately equalled the impact of the World Cup. Of the 309,554 foreign tourists coming to South Africa during the World Cup period, 83,819 visited KwaZulu-Natal Province (SAT, 2010). If we multiply the number of visitors to KwaZulu-Natal Province by the foreign tourist's average spending (R11,800) (SAT, 2010), the result indicates that approximately R989,064,200 was spent in total by foreign tourists expressly present in KwaZulu-Natal Province for the World Cup. It is

possible to discern (see Table 9.1) that in a 5-year time period these three events generate approximately the same economic impact indicated for the same province. It is worth mentioning these three events have been present in the province for many years (Comrades Marathon since 1921, Dusi Canoe Marathon since 1951, and Midmar Mile since 1973) and supposedly will continue for many years ahead, making these events sustainable, less expensive, and with vastly greater long-term economic impact within the province.

Conclusions

The 2010 FIFA World Cup provided great opportunities to advertise products to a global audience, leverage export business opportunities, generate new investment, and boost citizen morale and pride. South Africa's successful bid, FIFA and media acclaim of the 2010 World Cup raised high expectations by South Africans to shift to the next level by leveraging this once-in-a-life-time opportunity. The findings from the various reports and figures from South Africa and FIFA show that the 2010 FIFA World Cup was a short-term success as it brought a brief tourism boom to South Africa between June and July 2010 and question marks remain now that the SME show has left the continent and will not return in the near future. There is plenty of scope for a new sports development plan, focused on RSEs, that

Table 9.1. Revenue generated by three sporting events in KwaZulu-Natal Province.

	Midmar Mile[a]	Comrades Marathon[b]	Dusi Canoe Marathon[c]	Total
	Total impacts (South African Rand)			
2008	32,833,733.00	76,209,076.00	9,479,417.60	118,522,226.60
2009	42,956,157.00	118,744,282.90	2,587,461.00	164,287,900.90
2010	24,984,876.00	145,633,619.00	2,331,578.00	172,950,073.00
2011	29,249,648.00	198,251,393.00	4,696,333.00	232,197,374.00
2012	35,854,363.00	107,968,437.00[d]	4,421,050.00	148,243,850.00
Grand total for 5 years of small local events				836,201,424.50

[a]Total estimated amount spent (low estimate).
[b]Estimated economic impact – total spend (at least).
[c]Estimated total impact (at least) – for 2008 total average spend (at least).
[d]Dlamini and Kohler (2012).

can also be part of event-driven tourism development strategies.

South Africa's hosting of the 2010 World Cup poses a unique opportunity to assess the impact of an SME on tourism in a developing country, particularly an African one. South Africa invested in new and renovated stadiums expecting to continue to generate revenue after the event. However, the sport stadia and luxurious hotel rooms resulted in an oversupply within South Africa. Contrary to the hope that the 2010 World Cup could have benefited South Africa more widely, related tourism benefit has intensified only in Johannesburg, Cape Town and Durban, and the major game parks and beaches near these centres. Government agencies have done little to promote rural tourism or to spread the tourism benefits more widely.

Cornelissen (2007) argued that the greatest tourism benefit from hosting the World Cup would be improvement in the country's international image instead of pointing to numbers of tourists or jobs created. While South Africa and FIFA claim the success of re-creating South Africa's image as a tourism destination on the world stage, it is difficult to be optimistic. Based on several indicators, South Africa has not achieved the desired new image yet. Its overall competitiveness as a tourism destination remains similar to where it was before the World Cup.

Preuss (2007) argues that long-term economic growth can only be reached if an SME changes the host city or nation's tourism spaces and supporting facilities for future use, such as the upgrading of the necessary infrastructure (airports, roads, railway stations, public transport) and tourism superstructure (hotels, museums, promenades, waterfronts and restaurants). 'Legacy planning', focusing on investing heavily in supporting infrastructure rather than excessive stadiums, has not been observed. Key areas of legacy-building attributes, including transportation infrastructure, tourism and travel sector human resources, and government expenditure on tourism, have not yet improved to levels needed to be globally competitive after the extensive spending and efforts for the 2010 World Cup. As Cornelissen *et al.* (2011) argue there is lack of consensus on the meaning of 'legacy' and

consequently an assessment of legacy impacts. They suggested including event impacts in relation to the context in which they occur, and integrating systematic triple bottom-line principles into mega event planning, design and evaluation. We propose SME strategies are not surprising, as they are originated and managed within specific hegemonic neo-liberal global frameworks and discourses to assist specific political, economic and cultural interests of global elites.

The comparison of spending by visitors between the 2010 World Cup and local sport events in Durban suggests another road is possible to follow. The three events evaluated have been present in the province for decades and probably will continue for many years ahead as awareness of them beyond regional and national boundaries continues to grow. These events are more sustainable, less expensive and have much greater economic impact within the region in the long term. They are also less vulnerable to global economic crises as they attract a niche market of recurring participants and spectators drawn both locally and globally. Year-to-year fluctuations have much less long-term effect on tourism numbers or economic development. Plus, a much larger share of the wealth can remain in South Africa.

Events play a large role in sport-related tourism whether they are recurring and smaller in scale or large-scale events keenly followed globally. SMEs are high-risk, high-reward activities requiring years of planning, promoting and justification both before and after they take place. SMEs attract the largest global viewing audience of any special events only perhaps exceeded by disasters of global significance such as the attacks of 11 September 2001 in the USA. As a result, governments and business leaders are eager to utilize the global attention to promote tourism and business investment as well as deliver on the sports event itself.

To summarize our key points:

- Sporting events generate revenues beyond the sporting contests themselves.
- Sports tourism emerged as an area of study examining the impact of visitors coming to a

destination with the primary purpose of viewing the sports event and/or activities surrounding that event.

- Two main types of sports events are common: sports mega events (SMEs) and recurring sports events (RSEs).
- Both SMEs and RSEs have the potential to attract tourism and return on investment.
- While SMEs require substantial investment, most RSEs require little infrastructural investment once established.
- SMEs are high-risk, high-reward or high-failure activities; RSEs are lower-reward,

lower-risk activities yet demonstrate long-term capacity for greater economic return.
- Careful planning before, during and after sports events is crucial to success.

Questions for Students

1. In what ways are sports events 'more than just a game'?
2. Why does a country like South Africa face greater risks than France or the USA in hosting an SME?

References

Adair, D. and Ritchie, B. (eds) (2004) *Sports Tourism: Impacts, Interrelationships and Issues.* Channel View Publications, Clevedon, UK.

Baade, R.A. (1996) Professional sports as catalysts for metropolitan economic development. *Journal of Urban Affairs* 18(1), 1–17.

Baade, R.A. and Dye, R. (1990) The impact of stadiums and professional sports on metropolitan area development. *Growth and Change* (Spring), 1–14.

Baade, R. and Matheson, V. (2002) Bidding for the Olympics: fool's gold? In: Pestana Barros, C., Ibrahimo, M. and Szymanski, S. (eds) *Transatlantic Sport: the Comparative Economics of North American and European Sports.* Edward Elgar Publishing, London, pp. 127–151.

Barclay, J. (2009) Predicting the costs and benefits of mega-sporting events: misjudgment of Olympic proportions? In: Shackleton, J.R. (ed.) *Economic Affairs.* Institute of Economic Affairs. Blackwell, Oxford, pp. 62–66.

Black, D.R. and van der Westhuizen, J. (2004) The allure of global games for 'semi-peripheral' polities and spaces: a research agenda. *Third World Quarterly* 25(7), 1195–1214.

Bohlmann, H.R. (2006) Predicting the economic impact of the 2010 FIFA World Cup on South Africa. University of Pretoria, Department of Economics Working Paper 2006–11 (May 2006). Department of Economics, University of Pretoria, Pretoria, South Africa.

Cape Epic (2011a) History. Milestones. ABSA [ABSA Bank] Cape Epic Online. Available at: http://www.cape-epic.com/content.php?page_id=25&title=/Milestones/ (accessed 5 July 2011).

Cape Epic (2011b) The Next Step in Epic History. ABSA [ABSA Bank] Cape Epic Online. Available at: http://www.capeepic.com/news.php?news_id=75&title=/The_Next_Step_in_Epic_History (accessed 5 July 2011).

Chalip, L. and Leyns, A. (2002) Local business leveraging of a sport event: managing an event for economic benefit. *Journal of Sport Management* 16, 133–159.

Coates, D. and Humphreys, B.R. (1999) The growth effects of sport franchises, stadia, and arenas. *Journal of Policy Analysis and Management* 18(4), 601–624.

Cornelissen, S. (2004) Sport mega-events in Africa: processes, impacts and prospects. *Tourism and Hospitality Planning & Development* 1(1), 39–55.

Cornelissen, S. (2007) Crafting legacies: the changing political economy of global sport and the 2010 FIFA World Cup™. *Politikon* 34(3), 241–259.

Cornelissen, S. and Swart, K. (2006) The 2010 Football World Cup as a political construct: the challenge of making good on an African promise. *The Sociological Review* 54(2), 108–123.

Cornelissen, S., Bob, U. and Swart, K. (2011) Towards redefining the concept of legacy in relation to sport mega-events: insights from the 2010 FIFA World Cup. *Development Southern Africa* 28(3), 307–318.

Daniels, M.J. and Norman, W.C. (2003) Estimating the economic impacts of seven regular sport tourism events. *Journal of Sport Tourism* 8(4), 214–222.

Dlamini, Z. and Kohler, K. (2012) *Comrades 2012 Impact Assessment: Top Line Summary Report.* Tourism KwaZulu-Natal, Durban, South Africa.

FIFA (2010) Study Reveals Tourism Impact in South Africa. Available at: http://www.fifa.com/worldcup/ archive/southafrica2010/news/newsid=1347377/index.html (accessed 14 May 2012).

Giampiccoli, A. and Nauright, J. (2010) Problems and prospects for community-based tourism in the New South Africa: the 2010 FIFA World Cup and beyond. *African Historical Review* 42(1), 42–62.

Gibson, H.J., Willming, C. and Holdnak, A. (2003) Small-scale event sport tourism: fans as tourists. *Tourism Management* 24, 181–190.

Higham, J. (1999) Sport as an avenue of tourism development: an analysis of the positive and negative impacts of sport tourism. *Current Issues in Tourism* 2(1), 82–90.

Horne, W.R. (2000) Municipal economic development via hallmark tourist events. *Journal of Tourism Studies* 11(1), 30–35.

Kotze, N. (2006) Cape Town and the Two Oceans Marathon: the impact of sport tourism. *Urban Forum* 3, 282–293.

Lee, C.K. and Taylor, T. (2005) Critical reflections on the economic impact assessment of a mega-event: the case of 2002 FIFA World Cup. *Tourism Management* 26, 595–603.

Matheson, V.A. and Baade, R.A. (2004) Mega-sporting events in developing nations: playing the way to prosperity? *The South African Journal of Economics* 72(5),1085–1096.

Nauright, J. (2004) Global games: culture, political economy and sport in the globalised world of the 21st century. *Third World Quarterly* 25(7), 1325–1336.

Nauright, J. (2012) The modern Olympics and the triumph of capitalist sport. *History Workshop Online* 6 August. Available at: http://www.historyworkshop.org.uk/the-modern-olympics-and-the-triumph-of-capitalist-sport/ (accessed 4 September 2012).

Perelman, M. (2012) *Barbaric Sport: a Global Plague.* Norton, New York.

Pillay, U., Tomlinson, R. and Bass, O. (eds) (2009) *Development and Dreams. The Urban Legacy of the 2010 Football World Cup.* Human Science Research Council Press, Cape Town, South Africa.

Pomfret Pillay, U. and Bass, O. (2008) Mega-events as a response to poverty reduction: the 2010 FIFA World Cup and its urban development implications. *Urban Forum* 19, 329–346.

Porter, P. (1999) Mega-sports events as municipal investments: a critique of impact analysis. In: Fizel, J.L., Gustafson, E. and Hadley, L. (eds) *Sports Economics: Current Research.* Praeger, New York, pp. 61–73.

Preuss, H. (ed.) (2007) *The Impact and Evaluation of Major Sporting Events (Sport in the Global Society).* Routledge, London.

Ritchie, B.W. (2004) Exploring small-scale sport event tourism: the case of Rugby Union and Super 12 competitions. In: Ritchie, B.W. and Adair, D. (eds) *Sport Tourism: Interrelationships, Impacts and Issues.* Channel View Publications, Clevedon, UK, pp. 135–154.

Saayman, M. and Saayman, A. (2012) Determinants of spending: an evaluation of three major sporting events. *International Journal of Tourism Research* 14(2), 124–138.

Saayman, M., Saayman, A. and du Plessis, C. (2005) Analysis of spending patterns of visitors of three World Cup cricket matches in Potchefstroom, South Africa. *Journal of Sport Tourism* 10(3), 211–221.

Saayman, M., Rossouw, R. and Saayman, A. (2008) Economic impact of visitor spending at the Cape Argus Pick 'n Pay Cycle Tour. *Africa Insight* 38(3), 100–122.

Schulz Herzenberg, C. (2010) Introduction. In: Schulz Herzenberg, C. (ed.) *Player and Referee: Conflicting Interests and the 2010 FIFA World Cup™.* Monograph 169. Institute for Security Studies, Cape Town, South Africa, pp. 1–20.

Siegfried, J. and Zimbalist, A. (2000) The economics of sports facilities and their communities. *Journal of Economic Perspectives* 14(3), 95–114.

Sole, S. (2010) Durban's Moses Mabhida Stadium: arch of hope or yoke of debt? In: Schulz Herzenberg, C. (ed.) *Player and Referee: Conflicting Interests and the 2010 FIFA World Cup™.* Monograph 169. Institute for Security Studies, Cape Town, South Africa, pp. 169–202.

Sookrajh, R. (2008) Nature-based sport events and the physical environment: a case study of the Halfway-Telkom Midmar Mile. *Alternation: Interdisciplinary Journal for the Study of the Arts and Humanities in Southern Africa* 15(1). Available at: http://alternation.ukzn.ac.za/docs/15.1/04%20Sookrajh.pdf (accessed 22 June 2011).

South African Tourism (SAT) (2010) Impact of the 2010 FIFA World Cup. Available at: http://www.southafrica.net/sat/action/media/downloadFile?media_fileid=35419 (accessed 14 August 2012).

Standeven, J. and de Knop, P. (1998) *Sport Tourism.* Human Kinetics, Champaign, Illinois.

Todaro, M.P. (2000) *Economic Development.* Pearson Education, Edinburgh, UK.

Tomlinson, R., Bass, O. and Pillay, U. (2009) Introduction. In: Pillay, U., Tomlinson, R. and Bass, O. (eds) *Development and Dreams. The Urban Legacy of the 2010 Football World Cup.* Human Science Research Council Press, Cape Town, South Africa, pp. 3–17.

Tourism KwaZulu-Natal (TKZN) (2006) An Overview of the Impact of Sports Events in KwaZulu-Natal – January to June 2006. Tourism KwaZulu-Natal Occasional Paper No. 48. Available at: http://www.kzn. org.za/userfiles/1/file/ForIvestorandResearcher/Research/Occ%20Papers%20PDFs/Occ%20paper%20 48%20Impact%20of%20Sports%20Events%20in%20KZN.pdf (accessed 5 July 2011).

Turco, D.M., Riley, R. and Swart, K. (2002) *Sport Tourism.* Fitness Information Technology, Morgantown, West Virginia.

Turco, D.M., Swart, K., Bob, U. and Moodley, V. (2003) Socio-economic impacts of sport tourism in the Durban Unicity, South Africa. *Journal of Sport Tourism* 8(4), 223–239.

Wamsley, K.B. (2002) The global sport monopoly: a synopsis of 20th century Olympic politics. *International Journal* 57(3), 395–410.

Weed, M. and Bull, C. (2003) *Sports Tourism: Participants, Policy and Providers.* Butterworth-Heinemann, London.

Yusof, A., Omar-Fauzee, M.S., Mohd, S.P. and Kim, G.S. (2009) Exploring small-scale sport event tourism in Malaysia. *Research Journal of International Studies* 9, 47–58.

10 Events and Media Spectacle

Matthew Frew*

Bournemouth University, Poole, UK

Introduction

Under the perpetual gaze of the camera with blowing whistles and waving flags, a sea of bodies, clad in national colours, are transfixed by giant screens where their hopes and dreams are played out. Suddenly a hush; a second of magic and, as the ball hits the back of the net, the Fan Park erupts and the crowd is engulfed in a wave of euphoric emotion. Queue the replay, sync the booming back beat and off go the whistles, flags and gyrating bodies lost in the sweaty heat of a summer's evening.

This is a classic festival scene where the colour and content of charged experience is captured and mediated to a watching world. In a moment, the embodied emotions of a World Cup scene are, instantaneously, connected with a globalizing media-scape. Festivals have historically been laden with symbolic meaning and a promised reinvention of community, self and identity (Waterman, 1998; Frew and McGillivray, 2005). Even in times of global gloom, festivity exerts a seductive pull to harried and disenchanted lifestyles (Ritzer, 2008) and continues to evolve as a mode of cultural consumption with mass commercial appeal (Mintel, 2010).

This chapter, drawing upon the work of Guy Debord and Slavoj Zizek, critically interrogates events and festivals and their relationship with an increasingly sophisticated media. Through a case study of Glastonbury Music Festival, it explores the extent to which festivity, rather than representing an arena of fun and frivolity, actually operates as a site that structures the social relations of the everyday. Interestingly, it is the very casual acceptance of technological progress, global growth and 'given' nature of events that drives the need for this chapter. A casual perusal of their place in history through to their socio-economic significance, policy impact and centrality in the postmodern politics of identity (Horne, 2006; Chen, 2009) provides an unapologetic rationale here. More importantly, in a time when the explosion of the new media phenomenon globally transforms and networks modern life, it is appropriate that events and festivity are placed under the powerful gaze of Debord and Zizek and allowed an alternative voice.

Clearly the chapter title, 'Events and Media Spectacle', frames the focus from the outset. However, it is our very familiarity with media and the subduing comfort it affords that should alert us to its power and politics. Today the media brings about an almost omnipresent gaze. Its globalizing ubiquity and engrained embodiment in social life may well reflect a paradigm shift (Kuhn, 1996). Whereas parents or grandparents looked on with confused distain and dismissed the rise of computer technologies, smartphones, gaming and social media as mere fads, it is difficult to argue that we are witnessing an unprecedented revolution.

*mfrew@bournemouth.ac.uk

© CAB International 2013. *Research Themes for Events*
(eds R. Finkel *et al.*)

The distinction between the 'real' and the 'virtual' is becoming increasingly an obsolete debate (Maih, 2000). Technologies are now so embedded and integrated into the everyday that 'reality' for many is one of mediated cultural co-created convergence. This is exemplified from the moment of waking as technologies become engrained, embodied and networked, binding and bridging our physical life with one that is digitized and mediated. Cultures of co-created convergence see life, work, personal journeys, relationships and experiences constantly captured and distilled into a perpetual cycle of techno-communities or networks such as Facebook, Twitter or YouTube. This world of convergence reflects the intensifying process of 'techno-capitalism' (Wolf, 1999), an E-volution if you will, and events finds itself at the forefront of the dynamic and underlying politic of this phenomenon.

In unpacking this phenomenon, the chapter opens by contextually framing the development of events and its mediatized trajectory. The discussion focuses upon events from, predominately, the period of modernity through to its mediatized present day. Following this, the core conceptual pre-occupations are explored. Here, in highlighting some conceptual possibilities or ways of thinking about media events, the work of Debord and Zizek are developed. Finally, the case study of Glastonbury Festival of Contemporary Performing Arts provides the basis for an integrated contextual discussion.

Locating Events: A 'Spectacular' Evolution

Three aspects of coverage are included within this section, which form the foundational literature for this chapter. First, it briefly addresses the nature of definitional debates surrounding the events terrain. The rationale here is to frame events without being dragged into weighty discussion at the expense of preceding points. Following this operational brevity the second aspect focuses on a historical trajectory of events, touching on its resonance across ancient civilisations through to the transformatory impact of the

Enlightenment and Modernity. Finally, the third section takes the birth of televisual technology as the pioneering platform that, eventually, transforms events into the global phenomenon seen today. From the 1936 Berlin Olympics onwards, the modern symbiotic relationship of media and events is embedded and from here the emotive and experiential power of events is discussed, or digitally charted, through to the present time.

A casual glance across academic texts, including those on leisure, general culture or specifically events, will lead to standard definitional debates (Roberts, 2004; Rojek, 2005; Page and Connell, 2010). Events often get positioned and characterized as 'historic', 'special' and 'significant occurrences' that, while consciously constructed, operate as ephemeral markers of importance in the life course and identity of individuals, communities, cityscapes or nation states (Getz, 2012). However, the field of events is vast and researchers have developed distinct typologies such as 'special', 'community', 'hallmark', 'showcase' or 'mega' events (Roche, 2000; Getz, 2008; Walters, 2008) as a means of understanding their differences. Furthermore, Roberts (2004) prefers to think of events on the basis of scale (number of those attending) and scope (local, national, international or global). However, it is the depth, breadth, scope and embedded nature of networked media that make large-scale events central to this chapter. Networked media includes the formal macro or traditional media such as BBC TV, press such as *The Times* or *Guardian*, event producers and their sponsors and the informal, the micro and dynamic media evidenced in co-created consumer networks who mediate their stories via cyberspace and social media platforms such as Faceboook or Twitter. For this chapter 'large-scale mediatized events' of 'co-created convergence' is an apposite phrase to use as it collapses those events of mass scale, international scope, and a globally mediatized reach but, significantly, is mirrored by simultaneously mediating consumer networks.

Using this definition would include mega events – those globally mediatized, peripatetic, staged 'supernovas' (Roberts, 2004) that are won by nation states and that possess extraordinary status with 'long-lived pre- and post-event social dimensions' (Roche, 2003). Additionally, while the 'megas' represent the zenith of the field, there are other major spectaculars that, while some cross-over, go beyond the community-dependant '"local" or "regional" ... rooted in one place' (Getz, 2008) attributed to hallmark events.

The attention of this chapter is on those events that by their nature are both macro and micro, mediated, attention grabbing and seductive spectaculars. There is an array of these major events, such as the Olympics, FIFA World Cup, Rio Carnival, Formula One, Commonwealth Games, European Championships, Mardi Gras or, as highlighted in the case study later, Glastonbury. Major events can be conceived of as orchestrated storytelling spectaculars – aestheticized spaces of vibrant colour, music, pomp and ceremony where anticipation and emotion are stoked to captivate and excite (Frew and McGillivray, 2008). For centuries, events have conveyed 'stories' that, while appearing as sugar-sweet, often mask ulterior motives. Events have long been the markers of civilisations but, most importantly, they have also been used as vehicles of power (Gotham, 2011; Taylor and Toohey, 2011). Events resonate across the ages with ancient civilisations pioneering the concept of the planned and produced spectacle, veiled with power (Rojek, 1995). While Greek and Roman civilisations are credited with the origins of mass sporting spectaculars, drawing 'crowds of spectators, estimated to be up to 40,000' (Toohey and Veal, 2000) other cultures also report similar developments. The Mayans, Chinese and American Indians, among others, organized special events with religious justification involving music, dancing and feasting with central displays of sporting feats and contest (Bale, 1994). Most importantly, bolstered by religious injunction, early events overtly and symbolically ratified the established social structures and hierarchies of accepted or ordained culture (Brailsford, 1992; Toohey and Veal, 2000). Events, with their captivating (if often cruel) spectacle, rapidly became a vehicle of choice to convey the deeper stories of symbolic power

and place within the social order of ancient societies. This early development and use of events is not something unique to past ages and civilisations, as the present is shaped and resonates with echoes of the past (Foucault, 1979; Bale, 1994). Traced across the Hellenic, gladiatorial era through to medieval Europe (Bale, 1994) the trajectory, reach and power of events accelerates with the onset of modernity and the industrialization and technological sophistication it spawned across the Western world in the 18th and 19th centuries.

Modernity, that epoch marked by technological innovation, industrialization and urbanization of the British Empire, transformed the world through the division and rationalization of space, time, work and leisure (Heywood *et al.*, 1995; Hancock and Tyler, 2001). In heralding the birth of modern industrial society this process not only shaped physical and social space but also produced new subject positions that would be partitioned, named and socially ranked. Modernity is a rationalizing 'panoptical machine' where the spaces and subjects of leisure/events (e.g. sports centre/recreational assistant, theatre/conductor, festival/tour manager) follow a familiar trajectory whereby they 'resemble factories, schools, barracks, hospitals, which all resemble prisons' (Foucault, 1979). Essentially, modernity remapped the world with everyone and everything categorized in terms of space, place and time including what are now recognized as events. While the new world of industrialism and technology had emerged, it was a fragile entity in a time of revolutionary turmoil. In such a climate the public authorities and social elite were suspicious of mass gatherings and cultural hangovers associated with wakes and festivities, which were beyond their control (Coalter, 1990). However, while such events became the focus of work, religious and legislative containment, the importance and power of events was sown and demonstrated with the emergence of a series of World Fairs or 'Expos'. Reflecting the success of early modernity, Expos heralded the arrival of the mega event in the mid-19th century. The Great Exhibition of Crystal Palace in 1851 established the power and global reach of, arguably, the first mega event (Roche, 2000;

Leapman, 2001). Housed in a specially commissioned glass structure with the best of British design, manufacturing and engineering taking centre stage, the Great Exhibition was designed to showcase the British Empire as the industrial world leader (Auerbach, 1999). Moreover, with Royal patronage, and attendance by luminaries and celebrity figures of the day it purportedly drew over six million visitors, which set the Great Exhibition as the benchmark for event spectacle more than 150 years ago.

Although the Expos pioneered the mega event and became a key vehicle for the fulfilment of modernity, it was the birth of television that witnessed the Expo being usurped by the modern sporting spectaculars of the Olympic Games and future FIFA World Cups. Given their 'capacity to dramatize and globalize' sporting competition, these mega events were able to capture the imagination of new unfound audiences taking spectacular stories into the 'lives, dreams, memories and time of mass publics' (Roche, 2003). The Berlin Olympics of 1936 was at the vanguard of this new media-centred events revolution. Although often considered a propaganda vehicle for Nazi Germany, it represented the first global broadcast (Eitzen, 2000) and, under the direction of filmmaker Reni Riefenstahl, this event demonstrated the reach and power of this newfound technological medium. Moreover, the advent of this new medium highlights the early-mature-late periods of modernity, which mirrors the subsequent transformation and impact of events. Roche (2003) describes these temporal shifts with: (i) the early period concerned with industrial capitalism and nation building; (ii) the mature associated with history-making, citizenship, mass production and consumption; and (iii) late modernity characterized by globalization, mass-telecommunications media, identity fragmentation, individualism and consumerism. It is in this late period that major and mega events flourish as modern consumers show a new desire for emotive and memorable experiences.

The development and dominance of consumer capitalism was reflected in the boom-time 1960s, with the emergence of youth culture and rise of the 24 h post-industrial city (Chatterton and Hollands, 2003). More importantly, as people learned to embody or 'live capitalism through its commodities, and, by living it, we validate and invigorate it' (Fiske, 1989), new and increasingly spectacular events emerged to reinforce the power of consumer culture. In the sporting context, the 1984 Los Angeles Olympics set the trend for an integrated global media and commercial spectacular (Toohey and Veal, 2000). The fusion of action, emotion and drama with media technology made these events an ideal vehicle for commerce, allowing brand promotion to be beamed directly into the homes of willing audiences across the globe. As Horne (2006) points out, 'since the 1960s', it is this power to captivate audiences and capture markets that 'US broadcasting networks ... competed to "buy" the Olympics Games'. However, while other Olympics, such as Seoul in 1988, Barcelona in 1992, Atlanta in 1996, Sydney in 2000 were 'declared bonanzas' (Roberts, 2004) the 2008 Beijing Olympics and now London 2012 illustrate the increasing power of media events. In a changing 'digital landscape' where there is 'tablet, rapid penetration of smartphones, and growing use of connected TV' (BBC, 2012) these globally mediated spectaculars now work far beyond their immediate purpose. Mass mediation allows nation states a global promotional window to symbolically flex their economic, political and ideological muscles. Although still used for political propaganda, it is their ability to penetrate consumer consciousness and glean commercial gain that has seen them developed into a 'mixed industry' of billion dollar significance (Wolf, 1999). The 'festivalization' and 'civic boosterism' (Waitt, 2004) of events makes them a central plinth in the strategic vibrancy of most nation states and cityscapes (Chatterton and Hollands, 2003). This has made the process of securing the right to host events as fundamental and, as highlighted by the recent bids for the Olympics 2012 and World Cup 2018, turned bidding into a celebrity-fuelled spectacular in its own right (Scott-Elliot, 2010). Given that they sit at the 'apex of a multibillion dollar global political economy' (Sugden and Tomlinson, 1998) it is unsurprising that the Olympics and World Cup remain the most coveted of events. However, with the exponential development of consumerism and desire by consumers for distinctive and differential experiential products (Pine and Gilmore, 1999) the mediatized events spectacular has exploded in recent times.

In a society where 'a wealth of information creates a poverty of attention' (Herbert Simon, 2006, quoted in Aronczyk, 2008) the aesthetics, experiential displays and drama of events are becoming increasingly sophisticated. The 2007 Singapore Formula One Grand Prix, as the first night-time race designed and timed for a European audience, reflects how media spectaculars can re-imagine lagging brands while enhancing the national identity and tourism strategy of cityscapes (Foley *et al.*, 2011). Furthermore, the gregarious, colourful and often titillating carnivals in Rio and New Orleans (Mardi Gras) mediatize their core experiential elements to gain competitive advantage in place marketing or city branding (Gotham, 2005). Then there are the likes of X-Games where the adrenaline of adventure sports, energetic youth, music and a festival spirit provide an ideal media mix upon which brands can surf (Wheaton, 2004). Events have become increasingly aestheticized experiential dramas, often tinged with a touch of the taboo, which makes them the captivating stuff of media and, thus, of global gold for corporate sponsors and stakeholders (Coakley and Donnelly, 2004; Horne, 2006). However, just as events have developed a symbiotic relationship with media the technological development of media itself has added a new dimension to the events spectacular. The events spectacular, regardless of its sporting, musical or cultural core, is evidencing a new and intense transformation with the emergence of cyberspace, and ubiquitous digital and social media platforms.

Events and Digital Convergence

The digital revolution heralds a new direction in the event spectacular – one that displays a social shift in the co-creation of endless media multi-narratives. The formal mass mediatiz-ation of events is attended with a sea of informal mediatization constructed by consumers themselves. In the time of the 'screenager' where the new, youth generations 'are already the thing we must become' (Rushkoff, 1997), event spectaculars offer the promise of 'hyper-experiences' (Frew and McGillivray, 2008). The Internet is evidencing an explosion of activity and a new mode of sociability as, with over 'sixty million blogs worldwide ... one is created every second' (Elliott, 2009), consumers build online lives. With over 'five billion connections' the mobile phone is 'the most prolific consumer device on the planet' (Wood, 2010) and acts as the technological conduit of embodied and cyber existence. Armed with their mobile technologies, consumers instantaneously capture, display and circulate their images to the blogosphere or across social media platforms such as Flickr, Picasa, Pinterest or MySpace. The techno-mobility and immediacy of social media bear witness to the 'Facebook era ... [or] ... general social networking phenomenon' (Shih, 2009). Moreover, with over 600 million users Facebook 'is now the dominant social network' (Clark, 2010) and current champion of the Internet. It is here that event spectaculars are fuelled by the co-creating consumer networks who, ever keen to upload their media content to their personal digital storage 'cloud', become a vortex of voyeurs caught in the gaze of self and others: 'We've moved away from Sontag's idea of photos as being accessories to our memories, towards photos as a brag – a way of telling the world what fun we're having, and how good we look having it' (Muston, 2011).

The modern event spectacular is now globally facilitated through networks of consumers who share and integrate their physical world and experiences in a plethora of online communities. Events are now in a time of cultural co-created convergence, where techno-dependent, ocularcentric and narcissistic consumers, armed with the immediacy of mobile technologies that integrate with a multitude of social networks, endlessly capture, distil and layer their mediated experiences with that of the formal spectacle of event producers (Frew and McGillivray, 2005, 2008). This is the connected generation or 'Generation-C' where personal identity is mediated and centred on the '5 Cs of engagement: Create, Connect, Consume, Communicate and Contribute' (Solis, 2012). In the competition for consumer attention, cyberspace and these new social media networks are seen as commercial gold for, just as in the past, 'commerce can be relied upon to identify any ways of making money out of whatever technology is operative' (Roberts, 2004). In an age of the 'television [or more cyber] babies', the experiential dramas of events appear a natural progression for the mediated corporate sponsors or brand families who feed off the MTV tactic where the job is: 'to "amplify the mood" ... [make] appeals to the heart rather than the head. If you can get "their emotions going", he [Pittman, MTV executive] says, "forget their logic, you've got them"' (Auderheide, 1996, cited in Miles, 2000).

While such approaches are typically evident with the media empire of Rupert Murdoch, who openly see events as a 'battering ram and lead offering' for penetrating new markets (Mason, 2002), even the BBC has strategically targeted the mobile market claiming 2012 will be a 'digital Olympics' that will be 'accessible across all mobile devices' (BBC, 2012). Given modern events are symbiotically bound to media constructs, with all their economic power and transformational potential (Gotham, 2011) it is clear that 'new media' is 'central in the battle for control' (Horne, 2006). Mark Zuckerberg, the founder of Facebook, argues that cyberspace and social media represent a universal social shift as the 'global networking of cultural activity transformed into media experiences' (Mark Zuckerberg, 2010, quoted in Smith, 2011). Therefore, whether seen as a democratizing and liberating medium or one of ominous power and manipulation, the mobility, immediacy and interactivity of new media is a game changer for events. A media matrix has evolved where consumers are now intrinsically bound to the production, consumption and re-production of the events spectacular. Given this, it is worth considering how this media matrix phenomenon and events can be theoretically read, and seen to work, and what the critical implications are that it holds for the future.

Reading Media Spectacle: Theoretical Thoughts

Although television, digital and now social media represent new phenomena in comparison with other modes of cultural consumption, the sheer impact of media across the modern world has brought it under the critical gaze of researchers, including those interested in the field of events. Traditionally attempts to understand or unpack media forms or texts (e.g. TV programme, documentary, movie video/DVD, photo, painting and written works) come under the banner of textual analysis (Flick, 1998). Here the likes of content analysis, often a process of quantifying the frequency of images, stories, references or accounts that can be identified across a given time and genre, is used to uncover historical patterns or transitions of change within media (Berger, 1998). Narrative analysis, unlike the reductionism of content analysis, takes the whole story or picture as its text. The idea here being to discern the underlying structure of the media texts seen, heard or read (Jensen and Jankonwski, 1991). Documentary analysis is another approach that often mixes qualitative and quantitative methods, drawing across a broad sweep of materials within a given area, to uncover textual meanings (Jupp and Norris, 1993). Again media texts have been analysed to uncover the ideological role they play in supporting governments, institutions or policy direction. Here texts, be it the X Factor, Big Brother or an Olympics, are unpicked to reveal the prevailing ideological principles:

> An ideology is a system of ideas or beliefs, and all media artifacts are the products of an ideology. The ideological position being put forward may be explicitly spelled out, as it is in religious tracts or political manifestos. But more often the ideology is implicit and one has to read into the text to find the ideology at work.
>
> (Stokes, 2003)

Similarly, discourse analysis is a popular method for understanding media as a deeper and politicized cultural arena. Discourse analysis is a complex 'soup' of an approach but follows a qualitative approach focusing on uncovering how the cultural construction of texts works within socio-symbolic contexts (Gee, 1999). The intersection of how the semiotics of language, knowledge and power network to produce and regulate the meanings, practices and identities of subjects and their 'reality', often masking privileging relations (e.g. class or gender), are a key focus of this method (Foucault, 1979; Butler, 1993).

However, while resonating with discourse analysis and its ideological relation, this chapter seeks to understand media spectacle through the analytical coupling of Guy Debord and Slavoj Zizek. The rationale being that, just as there is an intensification of the relationship between events and media, as traditional or formal media culturally co-create and converge with the explosion of social media, this phenomenon requires an intensified form of analysis. In order to understand more about how media spectaculars can be viewed or seen to work, it is necessary to provide a conceptual continuation of this theme by critically underpinning this chapter through the lenses of Debord and Zizek.

With his *The Society of the Spectacle* (1999; first published in 1967) text Guy Debord provided a seminal work on the role of modern media and its effects on modern life. Drawing upon the work of the Frankfurt School, having viewed traditional Marxism as anarchistic, Debord argued that the world (in the late 1960s) had become dominated by the spectator, which epitomized an overarching modern malaise. For Debord, modern capitalism had evolved into a transactional consumer society where sophisticated cultural seduction techniques generated 'pseudo-needs' and 'false desires' to produce a passive, submissive, conforming and alienated worker and citizen. As a key figure of a movement titled the Situationists International, Debord looked to subvert the power, domination and alienating effect of modern consumer capitalism through a mass proletariat revolution that sought to attack culture at the everyday level (Bottomore, 2002). In essence, Debord revises the work of Karl Marx, highlighting how consumer capitalism moulds the consciousness at the point of consumption rather than production. A subtle inversion is effected as the reviled worker becomes the coveted consumer.

However, rather than being liberated as the new consumer king, Debord argued that alienation is deepened in the world of work and life as, in their incessant acts of consumption, they produce and perpetuate the independent and ideological power of consumer capitalism itself. In the never-ending avarice of consumption the consumer is pseudo-sovereign, a paper king ignorant of how their activities bind them to an alienating life while providing the life-force for the real King – consumer capitalism (Miles, 2001). Debord provides a powerful analysis of just how this works in modern society with the media industries being the fulcrum of the process.

For Debord (1999) consumer capitalism is sustained through the 'Society of the Spectacle', a world where all transactional relationships are dominated by and through an inescapable image-based network. 'Spectacle' is not about a 'distortion of the visual world' via technologies, 'a decorative element', but instead 'it is the very heart of society's real unreality': 'The spectacle is not a collection of images; rather, it is a social relationship between people that is mediated by images' (Debord, 1999).

Debord's spectacle is fundamentally 'a tool of pacification and depoliticization'; it is a 'permanent opium war' which stupefies social subjects and distracts them from the most urgent task of real life – 'recovering their human powers through creative practice' (Kellner, 2005). For Debord the world is caught in a perpetual gaze where the substance of human interaction is debased and converted into a totality of image relays centred on consumption. The idea of the *Society of the Spectacle* reflects the transformation of capitalism from 'commodity-producing society to an image-producing society dominated by advertising, television and mass media and other culture industries' (Gotham, 2011). Given the explosion of ubiquitous media platforms, the power and impact of spectacle is almost impossible to transcend, effecting a dazzling distracting and distorting power embedded in the very consciousness of consumers. In the spectacle-embodied reality is one so intensely mediated and networked that it effects a blinding light whereby consumers find themselves in 'the omnipresent celebration of a choice already made' (Debord, 1999). Moreover, given their engrained relation with the 'digital surface of Western culture' the events industries are the ideal sites for 'visual-based consumer images and meanings' being experiential billboards 'plastered with the signs of Coca-Cola, Nike, Google and Microsoft' (Baker, 2008).

Major events, and in particular their symbiotic relationship with media, represent the intensification of Spectacle adding to 'a world that really has been turned on its head, truth is a moment of falsehood' (Debord, 1999). In the current Facebook era (Shih, 2009) where the 'connected generation' converge (Solis, 2012) the experiential consumption of events is envisioned as a sophisticated extension of the Spectacle. As exemplars of cultures of co-created convergence, events offer another mediated route to build relationships around a staged consumer experience, which negates the prospect of uncovering the self and emotively co-creating relationships beyond spectacle. Echoing the ancient Bread and Circuses of the past (Foley *et al.*, 2011) events are an ideal conduit of Spectacle. Kellner (2005) and Gotham (2011) both highlight how the mediatized spectaculars of events feed into and layer the Spectacle. The emotive content, and the capacity to trigger fantasy and capture the imagination, make events parasitic platforms of Spectacle: 'it is the faculty of the imagination that is under the direct threat of extinction from the onslaughts of the multimedia overload ... WHOEVER CONTROLS THE METAPHOR GOVERNS THE MIND' (No, 2006, cited in Baker, 2008).

Interestingly, this concept of 'fantasy' and its relationship to events further feeds into the power of Debord's Spectacle. Fantasy positions deep within the consumer consciousness to work and shape social 'reality' and embodied actions therein. It is here that the work of Slavoj Zizek comes to the fore. Zizek provides a contemporary and sophisticated conceptual addition to the Spectacle, its inherent relationship with modern media, its outworking in popular culture and, as argued in this chapter, a novel perspective on the role of media and events.

Like others, such as Foucault or Derrida, Zizek's theoretical contribution or conceptual topography can be convoluted and a confusing mire at times. However, in wrestling with the influential and complex philosophy of Hegel and Kant, the politic of Marx or psychoanalysis of Lacan, Zizek locates and attempts to clarify his theoretical treatise through consistent recourse to popular culture. Importantly, and central to this chapter, the media is a primary target of Zizekian analysis. Whether TV, press, magazines, cinema or cyberspace, Zizek looks across the array of media platforms to view media as a 'singular collective noun' encapsulating an 'overarching media system – our newly digitized society of the spectacle' (Taylor, 2010). This reference to society of the spectacle is not coincidental. In a technodependent and ocularcentric world (Frew and McGillivray, 2005) Zizek illustrates the intensification and outworking of the Spectacle as it entertainingly dazzles and distracts, masking misery and suffocating moral judgments. The products of popular culture are not, for Zizek, to be seen as a means of escape, rather they are parts of 'the ideological dream ... a dreamlike construction hindering us from seeing the real state of things' (Zizek, 1989).

At the core of Zizek's work, his conceptual jigsaw, is the concept of fantasy. At first glance the term fantasy appears as a self-evident human ability or 'power to create fictional worlds' (Harris, 2005) and, thus, distinguish the real from the fake. However, for Zizek, fantasy is not simply to be thought of as the antithesis of the 'real' world. Although fantasy is internal, based in the id, the unconscious frames our everyday reality as 'in our everyday, wakening reality we are nothing but a consciousness of this dream' (Zizek, 1989). Moreover, while fantasy is a unique quality of subjectivity, formed within the subconscious inner landscape, it is also pliable or open to intrusion. Importantly, fantasy alongside ideology, fetishises 'things' so they become 'taken-for-granted' or individually we believe them to be 'real'. Essentially, whether Jimmy Choo shoes or, in the case of this chapter, Glastonbury Festival, commodities are sanctified, imputed with meaning and value, which sees fantasy work in unison with ideology. Ideological fantasy, or the 'fantastic supplement', plays an essential role in structuring social reality as 'it consists in overlooking the illusion which is structuring our real, effective relationship to reality' (Zizek, 1989).

Fantasy also works with the problem of the 'Real and reality'. The 'Real' reflects a Lacanian influence, which like Wittgenstein's limits of language or Derrida's notion 'trace' and the infinite regression of the sign, cannot ever be fully comprehended or actualized: '[The] distinction between the reality and the Real: we cannot ever acquire a complete, all-encompassing sense of reality – some part of it must be affected by the "loss" of reality' (Zizek, 2001).

With this ever-present barrier to the Real, this loss, we construct a symbolic order; a 'world of words' or signifiers that, working in binary black/white, man/woman or presence/absence, allow us to make and navigate a 'world of things' (Mayers, 2003). Importantly, the symbolic order that names space, place and subject is mutually conditioned in and through looping acknowledgement and reference to the 'big Other'. That is those authoritative socio-political institutions, customs and practices that we believe and trust in. Only through this looping acknowledgement, between 'signifier (the acoustic component or linguistic mark) and the signifier (the conceptual element)' (Elliott, 2009), can symbolic efficiency be produced and the various identities we inhabit be legitimated. In this way 'reality' takes form and 'works' as it 'possesses performative power – is socially operative, structures the socio-symbolic reality in which I participate' (Zizek, 1999). Most importantly, media is central in constituting our 'reality' and subjective identity. Echoing Debord's Spectacle, 'a world that really has been turned on its head, truth is a moment of falsehood' (Debord, 1999), subjectivity is constructed in a socio-symbolic void where in 'the guise of presenting reality, explicit media construct it ideologically' (Debord, 1999). 'The subject's position within the symbolic order is mediated by the fantasies ... and the media's screening adds further layers to already deeply enmeshed processes' (Taylor, 2010).

In the screen age of techno-capitalism (Kellner, 2003) the subjects find themselves caught, or digitally networked, in and through a 'deluge of pseudo-concrete images' (Zizek, 1997). However, while media is engrained in the constitutive process of 'socio-symbolic reality' and, consequentially, the subjective identities assumed, Zizek argues that the big Other is breaking down or disintegrating in a time of postmodern cynicism (Zizek, 2006a). Symbolic efficiency is failing as the vestiges of authority and sanctions of those institutional arrangements of the big Other lose their power, or better, suffer a loss of faith. Interestingly, for Zizek, rather than this being a demonstration of extra-ideological times, ideology or 'ideological fantasy' comes into its own as people reflexively engage in the fiction. A 'collective lie' takes place as we pretend to believe in the big Other. People know, like the Emperor, that the big Other has no clothes but nevertheless 'agree to the deception that he is wearing new clothes' (Mayers, 2003). Essentially, this comes full circle showing how 'ideological fantasy' works or is sustained as 'it is the unconscious recognition of a fearful Real which drives our acceptance of ideology' (Ayling, 2011).

With a bit of poetic licence the premise of the movie *The Matrix* helps to pull these concepts together. The main character, Neo, finds his life, job, network of friends, pastimes and identity, his social order and self, are not 'real' but a computer construct. The images/words/signifiers (Symbolic order) and the authoritative social and ethic-political fabric of government, police, family, company and his boss (the big Other) are a symbolically efficient fabrication. In essence, and corresponding to Debord, Neo's world, his 'truth', is a 'lie made real'. Interestingly, having been liberated or disconnected from the Matrix, Neo reconnects and returns to this, now acknowledged, fantasy construct to battle and change the symbolic order that was 'made to blind you'. Moreover, the actions of another (i.e. Cypher) liberated from the Matrix, while fully aware the 'Matrix isn't real', freely chooses to accept the lie. In this, 'ideological fantasy' is revealed as, fearful or unwilling to engage with the rawness of the 'Real', he reflexively reverts to the lie to the 'reality' of the Matrix that he knows is not real. For Zizek, this is the fate of the postmodern subject who pretending to pretend falls back into subjection and in so doing perpetuates ideology: 'There is no special ingredient. It's only you. To make something special you just have to believe it's special ... this is the most elementary formula of how ideology functions today' (Zizek, 2009).

For Zizek, popular culture such as movies, the Internet, TV, or as argued here, festivity, provides gaps or fissures that can reveal the current workings and contradictions of the symbolic order. Popular culture, and specifically the role and process of its mediation, provides an avenue to unmask the workings of fantasy; how the 'fantasmic supplement' (Zizek, 2006a) ideologically structures our 'reality' through its symbolic order. As such Zizek clearly echoes Debord:

> In our 'society of the spectacle' ... what we experience as everyday reality more and more takes the form of the lie made real ... Truth has the structure of fiction; what appears in the guise of dreaming, or even daydreaming, is sometimes the truth on whose repression social reality itself is founded ... reality is for those who cannot sustain the dream.
>
> (Zizek, 2006b, website cited in Taylor, 2010)

Again, whereas Debord looked to tactics to disrupt the Spectacle (detournement), a Zizekian analysis looks to a revolutionary politic or flow of acts that will break the dyke of the current symbolic order and usher in another. Most importantly, given the centrality media and popular culture occupy within their theoretical gaze, Debord and Zizek offer a means to critically open the field of events and the role they play in structuring our socio-symbolic reality. Therefore, festivity, and its inherent fantasy or 'fantasmic supplement', provides an ideal site to locate and operationalize this novel conceptual coupling. Glastonbury Festival of Performing Arts, with its longevity and position within global festival culture, offers a perfect festival platform within which to locate the critical contribution of Debord and Zizek.

Glastonbury as Spectacle: The Dark Fantasy of Festivity

This chapter, as with others in this book, draws upon the case study approach within which to present a narrative of depth and focus (Yin,

1994; Silverman, 2010). However, rather than follow a descriptive and linear approach, the intention here is to develop an integrated discussion of Glastonbury Festival of Performing Arts through Debord and Zizek.

Modern music festivity, in the UK and across the globe, has undergone phenomenal growth in recent times (Mintel, 2008). Although still resonating with an annual youth pilgrimage and rite of passage this global growth in music festivity is matched by a postmodern turn where youth is 'now characterized not by generational age' but by lifestyles of nostalgic reanimation where 'Youth' is simply a mode of consumption (Miles, 2000). Music festivals are key touristic attractions and economic drivers (Mintel, 2010) and have increasingly become mass, multi-staged spectaculars (Stone, 2008). This is reflected across the globe from the sun and sangria of Benicassim (Barcelona, Spain), the creative chaos of Burning Man (Nevada, USA), branded bands of V Festival (England) to the celebrity cool of Coachella (California, USA). At its heart festivity has always claimed to open a door to some other-worldly region, a place of momentary escape for the self as much as the everyday since 'festival allows us to indulge and immerse some alternative aspect of our character, and still clock on for work on Monday morning' (Armitage, 2010). However, while Glastonbury Festival of Contemporary Performing Arts arguably sits at the top the festival pyramid (McKay, 2000) this other-worldly quality had earlier roots.

Although Cambridge Folk Festival and Isle of Wight were 1960s' UK inventions (Stone, 2008) it is Woodstock festival, held in Bethel, New York in 1969, that is attributed as pioneering the modern concept of festivity (Bennett, 2004; Fornatale, 2009). Woodstock, while celebrated for its ideological counter-cultural resistance, somewhat fortuitously converged with the development and global reach of mainstream television (Landy, 2009). Woodstock's countercultural revolution faded into symbolic resistance (Hebdige, 1979; Kidd, 2000) and, ironically, offered a new cultural platform for the power of mediating technology. For the first time, legendary musical fare, sexual energy and gregarious youth became a media mix, sowing the seeds of modern festivity. With Woodstock the experiential frenzy of festivity was captured and conveyed to the watching world (Wadleigh, 2009). This historic media moment serves a dual function as it, first, establishes the modern idea of festivity but, second and more importantly, produces the split of Spectacle. Woodstock created a fissure in the 'real', a new space that differentiated the 'real world' from that of the mediated 'fantasy world' of festivity. On the one hand festivity is materially produced and located in space and time while on the other it is split from its globally mediated image. Woodstock presented a new host body for the Spectacle to inhabit, effecting the relation where 'the phenomenon of separation ... the unity of the world, of a global social praxis' splits between 'reality' and the 'image' (Debord, 1994). Moreover, following Zizek, festivity emerges as one of those cultural modes or sublime objects of ideology that present 'a dreamlike construction' (Zizek, 1989) and, thus, supports the socio-symbolic order of the everyday. Nevertheless, while Woodstock represented a chaotic and contingent mediated opportunity, Glastonbury cements the contagion of Spectacle as it harnesses and manages the media matrix to become an iconic trendsetter.

Located around Worthy Farm, and founded by farmer Michael Eavis, Glastonbury evolved from free milk with £1 entrance fee in 1970 into a sophisticatedly managed and marketed product. Today Glastonbury occupies an 800-acre site, contained by a steel super fence and secured by an army of security (Glastonbury, 2010). The transformation of Glastonbury's casual amateurism to a professional event can be attributed to securing the services of the commercial organization Mean Fiddler. Under Mean Fiddler Glastonbury has become a professional affair. Interestingly, while tripling their management fee in the process (Gray, 2002), Mean Fiddler rapidly recognized the power of media, image and representation. Although disparately mediated throughout its history, Glastonbury formally embraced mass media in the mid-1990s and, following Channel 4, the BBC and the *Guardian* are now the media mainstays and sponsors of the event (Cooper, 2011). Even since the iconic

symbols and stories, such as the pyramid stage, mystical Druid ley lines have been systematically deployed and carefully woven into the anti-nuclear, ethical and environmental countercultural fabric of Glastonbury. With Mean Fiddler Glastonbury has morphed into brand Glastonbury. Romantic or idealized traditions, mystical values, aspirations and associations are strategically and repetitively articulated, which reflects the world of strategic brand production (Moor, 2003).

Modern Glastonbury is a slick, marketed, managed and mediated experiential product. Echoing many modern festivals Glastonbury exudes an 'off-world quality' (Frew and McGillivray, 2008) creating a feeling of displaced 'playspace' that 'evokes the utopian imagination and stimulates utopian consumption experiences' (Larsen and O'Reilly, 2009). Glastonbury plays this game well by mediating mantras such as the 'wild side', 'music, mud, mayhem', titillations of 'naked mud wrestling' or 'hedonistic carnage' (Stone, 2010). Importantly, media technologies not only provide the platforms to repetitively articulate the 'powerful allure of the festival experience' but also to work that frustrated desire to 'be there next time' (J. Flinn and M. Frew, 2010, unpublished paper). This is Debord's Spectacle at its best, building a personal image-centred relationship, while, simultaneously, frustrating desire and so feeding fantasy. Glastonbury, unlike Woodstock, manages its seduction through mediated images, symbolic stories and the experiences of others. A play of signification is mediated to the watching world where, with the physical and ticket limitations of the event, the experiential promise of 'off-world' Glastonbury links to embodied desire. Mediation binds the 'fantastic supplement' to individual reality stoking desire and drives demand for that 'must-have ticket'. Hooked by this play of signifier/signified, and the possibility of missing the promised fantasy, participants perform and perpetuate ideology. As festivity works its magic the ideological taken-for-granted is overlooked, ignored, thus leaving the lie or falsehood of our illusory mediated relationship with the world to simply work (Zizek, 1989; Taylor, 2010).

Modern Glastonbury embodies the evolution of media and money and how large-scale mediatized events epitomize the current era of consumerist hyper-consumption (Stiegler, 2007). Glastonbury is also a reflection of how 'the digital world is fast becoming the cutting edge of capitalist consumer culture' (Baker, 2008) and the need to respond and adapt to the 'increasing integration and corporatization of the live music industry' (Bennett, 2004). Importantly, in tapping into the experience economy (Pine and Gilmore, 1999) Glastonbury is far more commercial and rationalized than many believe (McKay, 2000; Anderton, 2008). Once inside the steel fence this is immediately evident as Glastonbury offers a matrix of experiences. Stages, tented areas and designated sites, such as Shrangri-La, Avelon, Arcadia or the infamous Trash City, appear as self-contained experiential worlds of titillating taboo. Moreover, while mystical, countercultural and charitable signifiers remind and reinforce its ethos, Glastonbury is, paradoxically, awash with a dazzling array of brands and opportunities to consume. Glastonbury, for some time now, is not only a brand but a purveyor and promoter of brands:

> Sitting on a Rizla-branded stool, sipping a cappuccino from a Rizla-branded chapter cup, and watching a Rizla-branded table football game ... Budweiser, a mobile phone mast and recharging point courtesy of Orange, a daily newschapter from *Q* magazine, sun cream from Banta, and a Smirnoff tent named 'Experience'. Clothes stalls competing for space with vegetarian breakfast cafés and purveyors of legal highs, offer high street brands such as FCUK.
>
> (Gray, 2002)

A comfortable consumer contradiction is evident as the avarice of consumerism sits alongside charitable concerns for environmental desolation, inequity and poverty. In Glastonbury, Spectacle effectively promotes the possibilities of fantasy experiences while playing on branded dreams of 'rough comfort' lifestyles (Foley *et al.*, 2005). The Spectacle of Glastonbury is one where 'rough' echoes with a countercultural cool of 'peace, love and understanding' and mixes with appeals to the

'radical flame burning in our hearts', which makes Glastonbury 'wild and unforgettable' (Glastonbury, 2010). Festivity works and capitalizes upon this wild side (Bennett, 2004) insipidly drip feeding the 'orgastic composition' of experience, which is central to the 'resurgence of festivals' (Maffesoli, 1995). By its sheer size and scope, Glastonbury is a massive experiential canvas from which its promoters and media sponsors selectively distil and display evocative images. Trash City, with its sexualized 'naked mud wrestling' or the 'hedonistic carnage of the Dance Village' (Steele, 2010) provides an effective palate from which to paint and mediate fantasy. Nevertheless, and most importantly, images of mayhem happily mingle with an array of material 'comfort' evidenced in the five-star Yute accommodation, Welsh Oogie, Ostrich or Crocodile burgers to Caribbean food and all attended with a sea of merchandizing. Even founder, Michael Eavis, has reflected on Glastonbury's evolutionary display of branded lifestyles stating that 'it's become a bit smart now ... You only have to look in the car parks. There are even Aston Martins' (citied in Bright, 2010). The issue is not the place of profit, which is evident across festivity (Anderton, 2008). It is how Glastonbury juxtaposes mysticism, environmental ethic, radical and rough vibe with commercial and luxurious comfort.

Glastonbury's Spectacle is openly hidden; the pea in a game of shells without the shells, yet, still consumers play. With its tented areas, stages and sites of Trash City, Avalon or Greenfields, Glastonbury is a contained and controlled off-world full of other off-worlds that so dazzle and distract the fact of their rationalization and branding, which mirrors the everyday, that they are lost or ignored. Glastonbury is site of 'retailatisation' (Ritzer, 2008) where, even in their 'boutique wellies, sipping its designer lager', consumers are transported by fantasy, actually made to believe that they can, simultaneously, 'stick two fingers up at the system' (Armitage, 2010). This is Spectacle; its ideological functional power enacted and embodied through the fantastic supplement of festivity that topsy-turvy off-world whose 'truth' that is 'a moment of falsehood' (Debord, 1999). In Glastonbury,

Spectacle is so experientially layered it saturates the senses, doping the consumer with the promise, or lie, of omnipresent choice, when the only choice is to consume (Debord, 1999; Kellner, 2005). Most interestingly, in this five-senses experiential economy (Pine and Gilmore, 1999) the most important sixth sense subtly dominates, namely, media. For media is the binding and insipidly intensifying conduit that perpetuates this most political of processes.

Glastonbury's relationship with media has grown exponentially over time. Today it is a leviathan of media extravaganza with 'record audience reach in 2011' (Glastonbury Festival, 2011) and 'highlights packages' sold internationally across the 'USA, Japan, Latin America, Spain and Brazil already signed up' (Cardew, 2011). Audience reach has grown year on year with a 'record audience reach in 2011, with 18.6 million viewers' on the mainstream BBC, while 'BBC Two alone reached 15.7m' (Glastonbury Festival, 2011). Moreover, Glastonbury's mediated experience is multiplied via its official website, Facebook and Twitter updates (Glastonbury Festival, 2011). Producer platforms now network with key media sponsors who in 'offering a complete multi-platform experience' (BBC, 2011) not only integrate coverage but encourage social media interactivity (Sedghi, 2011). However, and more importantly, in the digital world of smartphones, social media or the Facebook era (Shin, 2009), Glastonbury's Spectacle, its fantastic supplement, is instantaneously and immediately replicated and rebooted by its consumers.

A casual perusal of Facebook, YouTube, Flikr or Twitter reveals a plethora of videos, pictures and posts dedicated to capturing and circulating festival experiences across ever-expanding social media networks (Muston, 2011). With developing live streaming, broadband speed and instantaneous social media linkage, media has become an embedded and embodied aspect of the Glastonbury experience. Festivity, and its fantasy, is increasingly a 'strangely vicarious affair' where the lived and live are captured and circulated in a perpetual 'loop' (McNulty, 2011).

In Glastonbury, Spectacle is more than some managed brand manipulation but pretence perpetuated by its consumers. The consumer, in believing, embodying and enacting Glastonbury's fantastic supplement, captures and digitally networks this 'other' fantasy self of festivity. The Spectacle of festivity reveals the self-delusional dynamic of ideology. Glastonbury's formally mediated sugarcoated story may be produced and planted in consumers' minds, but, by their own self-mediated performativity, consumers co-created this collective lie (Mayers, 2003). Caught in a formal and social media gaze the consumer is transfixed in a web of their own making. Given its ephemeral and episodic nature, Glastonbury is charged by a sense of tantric time, which drives desire for hyper-experiences (Frew and McGillivray, 2008). Spectacle pours petrol onto the flames of fantasy, it speaks of the chance to escape, to be 'other', to experience a new self who, like the Phoenix, will burn brightly before turning to ashes. As such the fantasy of festivity becomes a mediated mode of self-flagellation. For, while consumers engage and mediate their on-site performative frenzy, those off-site contribute to this co-created media loop and gaze and like masochistic Matchstick Girls know that in looking they will frustrate and fuel desire; but look they must. And again, as fantasy rises from the ashes, Spectacle is complete.

Conclusion: Spectacle and Structuring Seduction of Events

To conclude, this chapter has presented events as an evolving phenomenon that finds itself symbiotically welded to modern media. Moreover, given the explosion of ubiquitous digital media and the desire for experiential consumption, festivity represents an ideal site to offer a new critical take on the relationship between the mediatized world and events. Events are not to be taken lightly as they are more than 'just' events. As explored here within festivity, they are sites that mask cultural contestation. Debord and Zizek offer a new perspective or re-read events and the media. Events and Media Spectacle is an alternative view from the mountaintop. They unpack and unmask festivity as a sublime object of ideology. The fantasy of festivity, its fantastic supplement, is seen to retroactively work to co-construct its own objects, subjects and their performative experiential displays, which referentially structure our everyday, commonsense, taken-for-granted 'reality'. While festivity may dazzle as modern sites of wild 'Sodom and Gomorrah', with promises of distinctive 'othering' experiences (Armitage, 2010), they are distracting constructs of Spectacle. Glastonbury, the zenith of festivity, presents itself as an off-world escape but 'attempts to escape a socially and ecologically harmful capitalist dynamic' are often 'merely disguised forms of that very system in action' (Taylor, 2010).

Glastonbury reflects Spectacle at its most seductive, promising possibilities where the self can be deconstructed and re-constructed, liberated from the ethico-social bonds found in the everyday 'real' world. Most interestingly, it is a co-constructed delusion, one where formal and self-referential media matrix to form the glue that supports the 'big Other' and socio-structural reality of the everyday. It is this that enables Glastonbury to sustain the illusion of the mystical Scots village of Brigadoon, appearing out of the mists of time, while reflecting a metropolis of consumption. For in Glastonbury the game of 'the subject's position within the symbolic order is mediated by the fantasies' and our pretence layers these 'already deeply enmeshed processes' and so actively 'construct it ideologically' (Taylor, 2010). Festivity virally delivers the 'fantastic supple-ment' of ideology. It is a Trojan horse of Spectacle, aesthetically pleasing, experientially dizzying and distracting but always parasitically loaded with the brand militia of consumer capitalism. Festivity is a romanticized self-referential story beamed into our homes, our phones and our fantasies. This is Spectacle, a mediatized, whispering dream whose message, experiential images and sugarcoated story is a brand burned into the deepest recesses of the brain.

Further Research

This chapter has promoted the benefits of socio-cultural analysis in rethinking the complexities of cultural consumption and, in particular, the field of events. For all their global impacts, events remains at an embryonic stage in critical development. However, rather than a negative position, this is a highly positive position for academics and practitioners alike. The role and impact of media, and in particular that of the social media phenomenon, is ripe for development. The opportunity to delve into and glean mass narratives via social media should be seen as a new frontier of research. As co-created convergence develops, off- and online lifestyle behaviours are important as they reflect a transformation of sociability. This would include implications for notions of citizenship, com-munity, well-being and governance as much as the outworking of social commerce. Again, the emergence of social media platforms and communities presents a challenge to existing methodological approaches and the discourses of research itself. Interestingly, it appears most social media analytics are driven from marketing and commercial perspectives, which is itself worthy of investigation. Finally, while unapologetically a champion of socio-cultural theory, there is a need within the events field to develop academic/practitioner investigations that deliver real practical product outputs. Too often the theoretical and practical realms have been positioned as opposites. This is unfruitful for both and as augmented reality, holographic and sixth-sense technologies are currently illustrating, theoreticians and practitioners of events have a lot to gain by jointly investigating such techno-phenomena.

Questions for Students

1. As social media continues to feed cultures of co-created convergence how does this challenge the event consumer-to-producer relationship?
2. Looking at the past few decades and speed of technological change why has media become such an essential part of modern life?

Further Reading

Hartley, J. (2011) *Digital Futures for Cultural and Media Studies*. Wiley, Oxford.
Lievrouw, L.A. (2011) *Alternative and Activist New Media*. Polity Press, Cambridge.
Taylor, P.A. (2010) *Zizek and the Media*. Polity Press, Cambridge.
Virilio, P. (2010) *The Futurism of the Instant: Stop-Eject*. Polity Press, Cambridge.

References

Anderton, C. (2008) Commercializing the carnivalesque: the V Festival and image/risk management. *Event Management* 12, 39–51.
Armitage, S. (2010) Glastonbury Festival at 40. *Guardian Review*, 26 October, p. 2.
Aronczyk, M. (2008) Living the brand: nationality, globality and the identity strategies of nation branding consultants. *International Journal of Communications* 2, 41–65.
Auerbach, J.A. (1999) *The Great Exhibition of 1851: a Nation on Display*. Yale University Press, New Haven, Connecticut.
Ayling, D. (2011) Consider the Way in which Zizek's Focus on Fantasy has Helped Him to Develop the Notion of Ideology and How It Works. Available at: http://www.ayling.com/content/webpages/Academic.htm (accessed 10 April 2011).
Baker, C. (2008) *Cultural Studies: Theory and Practice*. Sage, London.
Bale, J. (1994) *Landscapes of Modern Sport*. Leicester University Press. Leicester, UK.
BBC (2011) BBC Announces Most Comprehensive Multi-platform Coverage of Glastonbury To Date. BBC Press Release. Available at: http://www.bbc.co.uk/pressoffice/pressreleases/stories/2011/06_june/07/glastonbury.shtml (accessed 15 October 2011).
BBC (2012) BBC Digital Olympics. BBC Press Release. Available at: http://www.bbc.co.uk/mediacentre/mediapacks/bbc2012/gamestime/digital.html (accessed 15 May 2012).
Bennett, A. (ed.) (2004) *Remembering Woodstock*. Ashgate Publishing, Aldershot, UK.
Berger, P.L. (1998) *The Limits of Social Cohesion: Conflict and Mediation in Pluralist Societies*. Westview Press, Boulder, Colorado.
Bottomore, T. (2002) *The Frankfurt School and its Critics*. Routledge, London.
Brailsford, D. (1992) *British Sport: a Social History*. Lutterworth Press, Cambridge.
Bright, S. (2010) Glastonbury: 40 years of mud, mayhem and, er, music! *Daily Mail*, 25 June, p. 15.
Butler, J. (1993) *Bodies That Matter*. Routledge, London.
Cardew, B. (2011) Glastonbury Traffic Drives Media Partners' Success. Available at: http://www.musicweek.com/story.asp?sectioncode=1&storycode=1045826&c=1 (accessed 5 July 2011).
Chatterton, P. and Hollands, R. (2003) *Urban Nightscapes: Youth Cultures, Pleasure Spaces and Corporate Power*. Routledge, London.
Chen, K.K. (2009) *Enabling Creative Chaos: the Organization Behind the Burning Man Event*. Chicago University Press, Chicago, Illinois.
Clark, N. (2010) Now Facebook Squares Up For Google Fight. *The Independent*. Available at: http://www.independent.co.uk/news/business/news/now-facebook-squares-up-for-google-fight-7503182.html (accessed 5 July 2011).
Coakley, J. and Donnelly, P. (2004) *Sport in Society*. McGraw-Hill Reyerson, Toronto, Canada.
Coalter, F. (1990) The 'mixed economy' of leisure: the historical background to the development of the commercial, voluntary and public sectors of the leisure industries. In: Henry, I.P. (ed.) *Management and Planning in the Leisure Industries*. MacMillan, London, pp. 3–31.
Cooper, M. (2011) Glastonbury and BBC TV: How it Works. Available at: http://www.bbc.co.uk/blogs/bbcmusic/2011/06/glastonbury_and_bbc_tv_how_it.html (accessed 25 August 2011).
Debord, G. (1999) *The Society of the Spectacle*, 5th edn. Zone Books, New York.
Eitzen, S. (2000) Social control and sport. In: Coakley, J. and Dunning, E. (eds) *Handbook of Sports Studies*. Sage, London.
Elliott, A. (2009) *Contemporary Social Theory: an Introduction*. Routledge, London.
Fiske, J. (1989) *Understanding Popular Culture*. Routledge, London.
Flick, U. (1998) *An Introduction to Qualitative Research*. Sage, London.
Foley, M., Frew, M. and McGillivray, D. (2005) Rough comfort: adventure consumption on the 'edge'. In:

Humberstone, B. (ed.) *Whose Journeys? The Outdoors and Adventure as Social and Cultural Phenomena.* Institute of Outdoor Leaders, Barrow-in-Furness, UK.

Foley, M., McGillivray, D. and McPherson, G. (2011) *Event Policy: From Theory to Strategy.* Routledge, London.

Fornatale, P. (2009) *Back to the Garden: the Story of Woodstock.* Simon & Schuster, New York.

Foucault, M. (1979) *The History of Sexuality, Volume 1: An Introduction.* Allen Lane, London.

Frew, M. and McGillivray, D. (2005) Health clubs and body politics: aesthetics and the quest for physical capital. *Leisure Studies* 24(2), 161–175.

Frew, M. and McGillivray, D. (2008) Exploring hyper-experiences: performing the fan at Germany 2006. *Journal of Sport and Tourism* 13(3), 181–198.

Gee, J.P. (1999) *An Introduction to Discourse Analysis: Theory and Method.* Routledge, London.

Getz, D. (2008) Event tourism: definition, evolution, and research. *Tourism Management* 29, 403–428.

Getz, D. (2012) *Event Studies: Theory, Research and Policy for Planned Events.* Taylor & Francis, London.

Glastonbury (2010) *Glastonbury Fine Guide 2010.* Glastonbury Festival, Salisbury, UK.

Glastonbury Festival (2011) Record Audience for the BBC. Available at: http://www.glastonburyfestivals.co.uk/news/record-audience-for-bbc-coverage-watch-it-again-online-now (accessed 23 September 2011).

Gotham, K.F. (2005) Theorizing urban spectacles. *City* 9(2), 225–246.

Gotham, K.F. (2011) Resisting urban spectacle: the 1984 Louisiana World Exposition and the contradictions of mega events. *Urban Studies* 48(1), 197–214.

Gray, C. (2002) Welcome to the world of Glastonbury. *The Independent,* 28 June, pp. 15–16.

Hancock, P. and Tyler, M. (2001) *Work, Postmodernism and Organization: a Critical Introduction.* Sage, London.

Harris, D. (2005) *Key Concepts in Leisure Studies.* Sage, London.

Hebdige, D. (1979) *Subculture: the Meaning of Style.* Routledge, London.

Heywood, L., Kew, F., Bramham, P., Spink, J., Capenerhurst, J. and Henry, I. (1995) *Understanding Leisure.* Stanley Thornes, Cheltenham, UK.

Horne, J. (2006) *Sport in Consumer Culture.* Palgrave Macmillan, New York.

Jensen, K.B. and Jankonwski, N.W. (1991) *A Handbook for Qualitative Methodologies for Mass Communication Research.* Routledge, London.

Jupp, V. and Norris, C. (1993) Traditions in documentary analysis. In: Hammersley, M. (ed.) *Social Research: Philosophy, Politics and Practice.* Sage, London.

Kellner, D. (2003) Media culture and the triumph of the spectacle. In: Kellner, D. (ed.) *Media Spectacle.* Routledge, London, pp. 1–27.

Kellner, D. (2005) *Media Spectacle.* Routledge, London.

Kidd, W. (2002) *Culture and Identity.* Palgrave, Basingstoke, UK.

Kuhn, T.S. (1996) *The Structure of Scientific Revolutions,* 3rd edn. University of Chicago Press, Chicago, Illinois.

Landy, E. (2009) *Woodstock 1969: the First Festival.* Ravette Publishing, New York.

Larsen, G. and O'Reilly, D. (2009) Festival tales: utopian tales. Working Paper Series. Academy of Marketing, Bradford University, Bradford, UK.

Leapman, M. (2001) *The World for a Shilling: How the Great Exhibition of 1851 Shaped a Nation.* Headline Books, London.

Maffesoli, M. (1995) *The Time of the Tribes.* Sage, London.

Maih, A. (2000) Virtually nothing: re-evaluating the significance of cyberspace. *Leisure Studies* 19, 211–225.

Mason, D.S. (2002) Get the puck outta here! *Journal of Sport and Social Issues* 26(2), 140–147.

Mayers, T. (2003) Slavoj Zizek: Key Ideas. Available at: http://www.lacan.com/zizekchro1.htm (accessed 15 June 2011).

McKay, G. (2000) *Glastonbury: a Very English Fair.* Victor Gollancz, London.

McNulty, B. (2011) Glastonbury 2011 View From the Sofa: Part Three. *Daily Telegraph.* Available at: http://www.telegraph.co.uk/culture/glastonbury/8600797/Glastonbury-2011-view-from-the-sofa-part-three.html (accessed 9 August 2011).

Miles, S. (2000) *Youth Lifestyles in a Changing World.* Open University Press, Oxford.

Mintel (2008) *Music Concerts and Festivals – UK.* Mintel International Group, London.

Mintel (2010) *Music Concerts and Festivals.* Mintel International Group, London.

Moor, K. (2003) Branded spaces: the scope of 'new marketing'. *Journal of Consumer Culture* 3(1), 36–60.

Muston, S. (2011) Memories destroyed in a flash. The Independent, 16 May, pp. 30–31.

Page, S.J. and Connell, J. (2010) *Leisure: an Introduction*. Prentice Hall, London.

Pine, J. and Gilmore, J. (1999) *The Experience Economy: Work is Theatre and Every Business is a Stage*. Harvard Business Press, New York.

Ritzer, G. (2008) *The McDonaldization of Society*, 5th edn. Pine Forge, London.

Roberts, K. (2004) *The Leisure Industries*. Palgrave, Basingstoke, UK.

Roche, M. (2000) *Mega Events and Modernity: Olympics and Expos in the Growth of Global Culture*. Routledge, London.

Roche, M. (2003) Mega events, time and modernity: on time structures in global society. *Time & Society* 12(1), 99–126.

Rojek, C. (1995) *Decentring Leisure*. Sage Publications, London.

Rojek, C. (2005) *Leisure Theory: Principles and Practice*. Palgrave Macmillan, Basingstoke, UK.

Rushkoff, D. (1997) *Children of Chaos: Surviving the End of the World as We Know It*. Flamingo, London.

Scott-Elliot, R. (2010) Beckham 'honoured' to deliver 2018 bid to FIFA. *The Independent*, 15 May, p. 19.

Sedghi, A. (2011) Addicted to Smartphones: the Latest Ofcom Communication Results. *The Guardian*. Available at: http://www.guardian.co.uk/news/datablog/2011/aug/04/smartphones-usage-ofcom-report?INTCMP=SRCH (accessed 23 August 2011).

Shih, C. (2009) *The Facebook Era: Tapping Online Social Networks to Build Better Products, Reach New Audiences, and Sell More Stuff*. Prentice-Hall, Boston, Massachusetts.

Silverman, D. (2010) *Doing Qualitative Research*. Sage, London.

Smith, L. (2011) Facebook tycoon tips TV, books and news to go social. *iNewschapter*, 26 May, p. 11.

Solis, B. (2012) Meet Generation C: the Connected Customer. Available at: http://pandodaily.com/2012/03/06/meet-generation-c-the-connected-customer/ (accessed 7 March 2012).

Steele, D. (2010) Glastonbury photos released to celebrate 40th anniversary. *The Metro*, 14 March, p. 12.

Stiegler, B. (2007) The true price of towering capitalism. *Queen's Quarterly* 114, 340–350.

Stokes, J. (2003) *How to Do Media and Cultural Studies*. Sage, London.

Stone, C. (2008) The British pop music phenomenon. In: Ali-Knight, J., Robertson, M., Fyall, A. and Ladkin, A. (eds) *International Perspectives of Festivals and Events: Paradigms of Analysis*. Elsevier, London, pp. 205–224.

Sugden, J. and Tomlinson, A. (1998) *FIFA and the Contest for World Football*. Polity Press, Cambridge.

Taylor, P.A. (2010) *Zizek and the Media*. Polity Press, Cambridge.

Taylor, T. and Toohey, K. (2011) Ensuring safety at Australian sport event precincts creating securitised, sanitised and stifling spaces? *Urban Studies* 48(15), 3259–3275.

Toohey, K. and Veal, A. (2000) *The Olympic Games: a Social Science Perspective*. CAB International, Wallingford, UK.

Wadleigh, M. (2009) *Three Days of Peace and Music*. Ashgate Publishing, Aldershot, UK.

Waitt, G. (2004) A critical examination of Sydney's 2000 Olympic Games. In: Yeoman, I., Robertson, M., Ali-Knight, J., Drummond, S. and McMahon-Beattie, U. (eds) *Festivals and Events Management*. Elsevier, Oxford, pp. 391–408.

Walters, G. (2008) *Bidding for Major Sporting Events: Key Issues and Challenges Faced by Sports Governing Bodies*. UK Report for the Central Council for Physical Recreation (CCPR). University of London, London.

Waterman, S. (1998) Carnivals for elites? The cultural politics of art festivals. *Progress in Human Geography* 22(1), 54–74.

Wheaton, B. (2004) *Understanding Lifestyle Sports*. Routledge, London.

Wolf, M.J. (1999) *Entertainment Economy: How Mega-Media Forces are Transforming Our Lives*. Times Books, New York.

Wood, B. (2010) Over 5 Billion Mobile Phone Connections Worldwide. Available at: http://www.bbc.co.uk/news/10569081 (accessed 15 October).

Yin, R.K. (1994) *Case Study Research*. Sage, London.

Zizek, S. (1989) *The Sublime Object of Ideology*. Verso, London.

Zizek, S. (1997) *The Plague of Fantasies*. Verso, London.

Zizek, S. (1999) *The Ticklish Subject: the Absent Centre of Political Ontology*. Verso, London.

Zizek, S. (2001) *The Fright of Real Tears: Krzysztof Kieslowski between Theory and Post-Theory*. Indiana University Press, Bloomington, Indiana.

Zizek, S. (2006a) *The Parallax View*. MIT Press, Cambridge, Massachusetts.

Zizek, S. (2009) Hollywood Today: Report from an Ideological Frontline. Available at: http://www.lacan.com/essays/?page_id=347 (accessed 15 March 2010).

11 Events and Political Agendas

Rebecca Finkel*

Queen Margaret University, Edinburgh, UK

Introduction

In the past, the majority of community arts festivals were generally regarded as self-financing exercises that occasionally relied on the help of local councils and private donors for certain events. Increasingly in the past few decades, however, more arts festivals in the UK became dependent on Arts Council and national, regional and local government funding. This has meant that external funding has become steadily more important to the survival of the majority of arts festivals. It is argued that government involvement has had a growing impact on the concerns of festival organizers and also on their programming, which has become increasingly responsive to government political agendas regarding socio-economic strategies. This raises major questions about the artistic purpose and independence of arts festivals in the future. In this chapter, arts festivals are located in the current period of British policy making, which demonstrates how cultural forms are translated in contemporary society.

Gibson and Klocker (2005, p. 93) suggest, 'Regional economic policy-makers are increasingly interested in the contribution of creativity to the economic performance of regions, and, more generally, in its power to transform the images and identities of places.' Thus, the use of cultural forms as instruments for urban regeneration, place marketing,

tourism and entrepreneurial developments can be tied to the increasing competition among places for capital, residents, tourists and resources. Moreover, place marketing through improving image, economic development and regeneration are more and more tied to national cultural policies. The arts are considered dominant factors in regional 'success' and are often introduced as solutions for places that are seeking economic development (Gibson and Klocker, 2005). As Dreher (2002, cited Peck, 2005, p. 740) described this recent urban 'imperative', 'Be creative – or die'. The socio-economic targets set out by the government have led arts organizations to spend much of their time measuring their impacts in different policy areas to justify their existences and prove they are worthy of their subsidy (Mirza, 2006). Although, as Belfiore (2006) points out, there are no longer 'subsidies' according to central government, but now these are considered 'investments'. This can be interpreted as not merely a change in language but a shift in expectations and perceptions.

Critics of government involvement in the arts argue that the quality of most cultural forms becomes mediocre at best when used primarily to support non-cultural agendas and strategies (Gibson and Klocker, 2005; Belfiore, 2006; Brighton, 2006). By implementing general arts policies that are essentially vehicles to promote socio-economic advancements, the arts involved have been criticized as being

*rfinkel@qmu.ac.uk

© CAB International 2013. *Research Themes for Events*
(eds R. Finkel *et al.*)

'either homogenising or vacuous as a result' (Brighton, 2006, p. 128). As Gibson and Klocker (2005, p. 93) put it, 'Rather than present alternative ways of imagining regional futures, what seems to be happening is that a singular interpretation of creativity is being incorporated into a rather uncreative frame-work.' The frameworks in which most publicly funded arts exist no longer take into account the differences in cultural activities, tastes of the audiences and idiosyncrasies of places in their seemingly blanket roll-out of policy objectives to be met. The assumption that the same socio-economic impacts will result in different places from the same cultural activities can be argued to be a key limitation of contemporary cultural policies (Belfiore, 2006). Yet, similar cultural endeavours can be seen to be implemented throughout the UK with varying levels of success (Evans, 2005). By using the example of arts festivals, an argument is put forward that this government-sponsored replication of cultural forms is diminishing the importance put on the uniqueness of place, which can have the adverse effects of limiting community expression and sense of identity.

This is exemplified by a case study of the Cardiff Festival in order to obtain an in-depth analysis of the relationship between the festival and city council agendas, broader cultural policies and uses of urban space. It is suggested that the Cardiff Festival typifies new con-temporary approaches to urban governance, as it incorporates a confluence of: (i) urban regeneration and place marketing strategies; (ii) entrepreneurialism of public authorities; (iii) international interurban competition; and (iv) integration of festival events into newly redeveloped urban spaces. It is argued that the outcomes of the Cardiff Festival can be viewed as a translation of contemporary urban cultural policies because of an emphasis on economic and social inclusion agendas.

Literature Review

It has been argued that public expenditure on arts festivals is becoming 'related to alien objectives' (Myerscough and Bruce, 1988, p. 8) and most national and local levels of British

government have adopted the idea that the arts are worth subsidizing because they can be used as a means for social and economic development (Griffiths, 1993). Stevenson (2004) argues that cultural planning and investment is considered by the UK government as more than a policy framework for the arts and encompasses economic objectives, which include community development and social inclusion initiatives. This strategy can be seen to be making many aspects of cultural policy into social policy, urban policy, arts policy and economic policy (Evans, 2001). It is argued that the imagining of the government's agenda in economic terms, as opposed to cultural ones, is an influential factor contributing to the commercialization in the UK of cultural forms in general and arts festivals in particular. Although this instrumental rationale for public arts funding is primarily utilized at this time, it is argued to be inadequate, as it has failed to protect the arts from imminent financial cuts and ignores their intrinsic value (Kettle, 2006).

The contemporary UK cultural policy agenda can be seen to incorporate two main objectives: (i) place marketing and economic development of place; and (ii) social inclusion for individuals and communities (Stevenson, 2004). Both of these objectives have a tenuous connection with culture and the advancement of cultural forms. Although the second objective appears to use cultural policies as a tool for achieving social benefits, social inclusion strategies can be seen to have a direct connection with economic strategies. Social inclusion differs from social justice in that the former requires people to participate in society as it is constructed. Social justice, however, requires an interventionist state with a redistributive agenda to achieve equality (Everingham, 2003). The main goal of social inclusion, it is argued, is to foster participation in the economy and, therefore, is determined by people's relationship to the marketplace (Miles and Paddison, 2005). Government policies developing cultural and creative industries and creative training skills programmes in deprived neighbourhoods are ways of fostering par-ticipation in society by the socially marginal (Stevenson, 2004). For example, the London Development Agency (2005) gave £9 million to support training and employment schemes specifically tailored for communities surrounding the main Olympic Park in East London. Through social inclusion programmes, cultural production is viewed as yielding economic rewards for many communities (Stevenson, 2004). In many respects, it can be suggested that social inclusion is synonymous with economic inclusion, which can be achieved through culture.

The co-option of culture and cultural events for urban regeneration purposes can be viewed as a response to post-Fordist industrial structuring and manufacturing decline by bolstering employment possibilities (Evans, 2005). It is also perceived to be a way for places to respond to global competition by contributing to image promotion and branding as a successful destination. It is believed by many local authorities, especially in urban areas, that such strategies lead to the attraction and retention of people and capital. Also, prestigious regeneration projects are claimed to promote civic boosterism and provide a focus around which people can rally to support local values (Boyle, 1997). However, Bassett (1993) argues that a distinction should be made between cultural and economic regeneration. As he puts it:

> Cultural regeneration is more concerned with themes such as community self-development and self-expression. Economic regeneration is more concerned with growth and property development and finds expression in prestige projects and place-marketing. The latter does not necessarily contribute to the former.
>
> (Bassett, 1993, p. 1785)

It is suggested that such a distinction is not being made in a majority of UK cities, as many cultural activities and flagships are not anchored in local community expression and involvement. It is demonstrated in the case study of Cardiff Festival that some UK cities are implementing a generic culture-led regeneration model that may entertain local residents but fails to engage with them in any meaningful way.

The following section analyses the Cardiff Festival to illustrate the effects council funding and cultural policies have on a city arts festival. It is argued that the Cardiff Festival can be seen as a fairly typical example of an urban council-funded and council-run combined arts festival based on the similarities found in a study of UK arts festivals, which included a survey and interview responses by organizers of festivals of a similar size, geography and funding situation (Finkel, 2009). It is suggested that the Cardiff Festival typifies the new approaches to urban governance, as it incorporates a confluence of: (i) urban regeneration and place marketing strategies; (ii) entrepreneurialism of public authorities; (iii) international interurban competition; and (iv) integration of festival events into newly redeveloped urban spaces.

Research Methods

This case study is part of a larger research project, which examines social, economic and political impacts of UK combined arts festivals on communities and places. Combined arts festivals are defined by the Arts Council as those containing more than one genre of artistic performance, i.e. music, drama and visual arts events, as opposed to those presenting events in only a single genre of arts, such as film festivals (Casey et al., 1996). Research methods include a 42-question mail-back survey questionnaire sent to 117 combined arts festivals in the UK to obtain festival demographics, programming history, funding and future plans. The survey sent was adapted from a survey published in a 1992 study conducted by the Policy Studies Institute concerning both single-genre and combined arts festivals in the UK (Rolfe, 1992). A listing of the 117 festivals was compiled from the Arts Council of England, Scotland, Wales and Northern Ireland arts festivals lists, as well as the British Arts Festivals Association membership list, European Festivals Association membership list, British Federation of Festivals membership list and International Festivals and Events Association membership list.

The data are based on a 56% response rate. The majority of the major cities in England (Birmingham, Liverpool, Nottingham), Scotland (Edinburgh, Glasgow), Wales (Cardiff) and Northern Ireland (Belfast) who have combined arts festivals responded to the survey. The majority of combined arts festivals in Greater

London responded; these are primarily organized by local neighbourhoods or councils, as there is no major London-wide combined arts festival. The 51 combined arts festivals that failed to respond are similar in size variation and geographical area to those who did respond.

Case studies were selected for this research because they were viewed as the best means to obtain a holistic understanding of cultural systems of action, which are sets of interrelated activities in which actors in a social situation are engaged (Tellis, 1997). The Cardiff Festival was chosen in order to discern a more in-depth understanding of the aims and goals, audiences and content influences of a combined arts festival that is primarily council organized, funded and executed. A variety of methods were implemented, including semi-structured and open-ended in-depth interviews with the Events Project Manager and the Tourist Information Officer at Cardiff Council. Informal interviews and casual conversations with festival participants, volunteers and local business people at the festival contributed to the participant and direct observation and recording of the festival experience in a personal research diary.

Cardiff Festival Case Study

The Cardiff Festival is a month-long combined arts festival that stages free events around the city of Cardiff. The festival is a council sponsored and organized event designed to make the city an appealing tourist destination and boost civic pride among residents. The events emphasize street theatre, live music, dramatic theatre, youth and children's entertainment, fun fair attractions and fireworks. Venues for the festival are scattered throughout the city centre and the redeveloped waterfront area, where people can also go into shops, bars and restaurants. In the past, the festival helped to change the image of Cardiff Bay area by drawing people to the waterfront and introducing the changes made there. The festival is part of the city centre strategy to improve the integration between the city centre and the Bay and Butetown communities and

help 'boost the economy and cultural profile of Cardiff' (Cardiff City Council, 2003, pp. 3–4).

As it is a council-run festival and social inclusion is a high priority for all council events, one of the main aims is to attract a broad audience and be, as the Events Project Manager for the Cardiff Festival put it, 'artistically accessible to anyone who happens to be passing'. The festival events reflect this goal by balancing different types of performances that could appeal to different types of audiences, including young people, families, older people and tourists. The acts can be categorized as being more 'popular' in order to be inclusive and have wider appeal. The use of outdoor venues means there is the capacity to stage famous, family-friendly artists such as Sir Cliff Richard, Tom Jones and Donny Osmond that attract larger crowds. However, diversity of content is also a priority, which makes sense as 'championing cultural diversity' has been highlighted as a key element in achieving social inclusion objectives for cultural policies (Arts Council England, 2003). There are theatre and orchestra performances, as well as world music and fringe acts. Smaller venues highlight local artists, introducing a mix and balance of local and international acts. Concurrent with the combined arts festival during the month of July are the children's festival, food and drink festival, world port festival and carnival. According to the Events Project Manager at Cardiff Council, these simultaneous festivals make the city 'a destination' and also make it a good place to live because there is 'a lot going on'. The festival programme boasts, 'Cardiff Festival demonstrates the degree of cultural vibrancy that makes Cardiff one of Europe's leading cultural centres.' This is in keeping with Cardiff Council's overall marketing to make the city 'the capital for events' (Cardiff City Council, 2006b) and fits in to the overall aim of the City Centre Strategy, which is 'to achieve a distinctive, attractive, vibrant, accessible, and well managed city centre of true international standing' (Cardiff City Council, 2003).

The festival does actively try to attract tourists and reports that of its 450,000 attendees, 79% are local, 11% are regional, 4.5% are visitors from around the UK and 4.5% are international. The Events Project Manager at Cardiff Council says the goals for the festival are twofold: (i) to put Cardiff on the map as a city culturally and promote it as a tourist destination; and (ii) to put on many different activities to make the city a better and more attractive place to live. These dual objectives stem from the overall city strategy, which emphasizes the role cultural events play in aiding regeneration and development, as well as competing internationally for status and image. The *City Centre Strategy 2003–2006* (Cardiff City Council, 2003, p. 4) states, 'With worldwide competition for financial resources, it is vital that: the city centre continues to attract investment, facilities for Cardiff residents and visitors are improved, the quality of the environment is protected and enhanced, development schemes are managed effectively.' It is proposed that such projects and initiatives need to be achieved through: (i) street enhancements; (ii) continuing to develop the potential of the Bay area; (iii) hosting sporting and cultural events; and (iv) enhancing visitor attractions (Cardiff City Council, 2003, p. 4).

This kind of entrepreneurial language and message demonstrates that the city council's approach to urban governance can be seen to be incorporating contemporary views of the cultural economy and culture-led redevelopment. Many of the sentiments expressed, such as remaining competitive, bolstering street-level entertainment and regeneration of formerly neglected areas echoes the work of Florida's (2002) theories for urban economic success based on valuing creativity. Indeed, there is some cross-over between Cardiff's urban strategy and Florida's 'Toolkit for Cities', including: (i) creating opportunities for civic involvement; (ii) promoting the city; (iii) promoting a 'young adult lifestyle'; and (iv) giving the city the 'creativity treatment', or providing more and varied cultural opportunities (cited in Peck, 2005, pp. 747, 753). The festival, then, can be viewed as an instrumental part of broader city-wide socio-economic and destination management schemes implemented by the council.

The budget for the Cardiff Festival comes from the city council's Marketing and Tourism Department, which oversees sports, tourism, marketing, public buildings and events. The Marketing and Tourism Department was established after a re-organization in 1999 in order to strategically manage and deliver the council's strategies for the arts, culture, events, sports development, sports venues and civic venues (Cardiff City Council, 2006b). In the 1990s, events were relatively small scale within the department. An increased events budget to coincide with the millennium led to many highly publicized and successful events, and, according to the Events Project Manager interviewed for this research, the councillors and chief executives decided to improve the Cardiff Festival with increased funding and promotional support. Marketing is carried out in local, regional and national newspapers, television placements and local and regional radio advertising. The festival does not make a profit or have a deficit but generates some revenue from concessions and venues.

Although the Cardiff Festival is funded, staged and managed by Cardiff Council, the programme is enhanced through the support of commercial sponsors and partners. Only certain events have individual sponsors and some one-off events are staged with individual partners. Some of the sponsors include Tesco supermarket, Boots pharmacy, Hard Rock Cafe, Red Dragon local radio station, brands with mass appeal and widespread use. They reflect the kind of general audience content of the festival. The shopkeepers and restaurant and bar managers also view the festival as being positive for business. The festival events draw more crowds than usual to the central business district (CBD) during evenings and weekends, increasing income of restaurants and bars. However, hotels do not appear to be as strongly affected by the festival. As one city hotel manager put it, many people come during the festival to visit friends and usually stay with them. Based on informal questions asked at a sample of Cardiff city centre hotels, summer backpackers and business travellers account for most hotel stays in the area.

By bringing hundreds of people to these areas for entertainment, leisure and consumption purposes, the festival helps to create a 'celebratory' environment for the regeneration projects and promotes a collective sense of belonging to these spaces for the city's residents. The locations of the venues and physical spaces used for festival events and the festival's use of fixed infrastructure can be seen to be strategic in order to correlate with the council's plans for the economic growth and promotion of the city. Indeed, the locations of the festival venues overlap the city centre regeneration areas. These 14 areas are highlighted as city centre strategy priorities (Cardiff City Council, 2003).

The Events Project Manager interviewed for this research claims that they are targeting 'all sorts with each event' and can reach a broad section of the community with the different elements of the festival. Because many of the venues are on open-air stages, he argues it is important for the acts not to offend or cause controversy, otherwise the council will then 'get flak and have to deal with it'. Because the Cardiff Festival is run by the council, it is organized to adhere to the public policies of social inclusion and the cultural strategies of marketing to tourists and aiding regeneration efforts. This is reflected in the festival programming and locales selected for festival events. For example, the big budget from the council provides the opportunity for a wide variety of international, national and local performances, such as the Welsh Proms, outdoor theatre and hip hop DJs, to interest a cross-section of different audience demographics. As the festival does not need to make a profit, it can spend on well-known artists and on promotion for these artists to attract visitors from further afield. Also, the festival's use of both the city centre and the redeveloped waterfront can be seen as a political statement that symbolically groups these two areas together as the places in Cardiff where people should go for culture and entertainment.

As the focus of the festival is reaching the largest number of people, the promotion of the Welsh language is not a key priority for the council in event planning, as very few Cardiff residents speak Welsh as a first language (particularly in poorer areas). However, the council does ensure that all signs and communication are bilingual, and the Events Project Manager says they try to book many Welsh language acts and community groups to perform throughout the year. Also, the lack of Welsh concessions may be an attempt by the city council to give the proceedings a more 'global' feel, as if one could be in any European city. This 'look to Europe' is a strategy that the council has formally implemented recently (Cardiff City Council, 2006a).

The International Street Festival changed its name in 2004 from the Shoppers International Street Festival. But the latter more accurately describes the purpose of the street festival, as it is the Cardiff City Retail Partnership who supports the event along with the council. The street performances take place for 4 days in central Cardiff from noon until 5 p.m. on Queen Street and Working Street outside some of the main stores in the city. Over 100 performers put on shows in order to create a lively atmosphere that will draw potential shoppers and diners to the area. This coalition of local government and private retail businesses aids in boosting sales, which is good for the city's short-term and long-term image, as it gives exposure to the positive aspects of the urban centre, making people want to spend time there. As the Chair of Cardiff City Retail Partnership put it, 'More retailers are recognising the contribution that Cardiff Festival ... adds to Cardiff's growing reputation for shopping' (Cardiff Festival, 2003). It appears that the festival is becoming increasingly commercialized from one year to the next.

Public entertainment is now viewed as emblematic of a lively and safe atmosphere and acts as a catalyst for consumption. The use of street arts to boost sales is a well-tested strategy that has been employed in urban sectors all over Europe, most notably in Barcelona. In fact, the 2005 *Cardiff Festival Programme* mentions this by stating, '[the street festival has a] programme that will keep Barcelona on its toes!' (Cardiff Festival, 2003). This is a competitive remark, implying that Cardiff can rival Barcelona in terms of having a buzzing cultural environment. It is also a way to put Cardiff in Barcelona's league as a globally recognized cultural city, which may or may not be true. As the Executive Member for Sport, Leisure and Culture, put it, '[street theatre] enhances our credentials as a European capital' (cited in Cardiff Festival, 2005). It may seem odd that mime artists trapped in invisible boxes and silver-painted women pretending to be statues would be prioritized by the council as a crucial evaluation metric to promote the international reputation of Cardiff, as opposed to lower crime and unemployment rates or impressive business growth; yet, it is the perception of entrepreneurial local authorities that such activities can boost visitor numbers and lead to economic development. Indeed, according to Cardiff Council, street theatre is more about image promotion and supporting local enterprises than artistic endeavour per se.

In a tented village with food stalls from all over Europe, the International Food and Drink Festival takes over Roald Dahl Plass (or public square) on the waterfront of Cardiff Bay for a weekend each year. Entry is free, which encourages people to come by to sample. Although there is some Welsh food included, the food stalls feature a mix of European delicacies and South African wines. Cooking demonstrations and instruction are also featured at the festival. Due to the location, this sub-festival was instrumental in helping to change attitudes about the Cardiff Bay complex. Bringing together food and wines from all over adds an international and sophisticated element to the locale, as if the world comes to Cardiff's door. Music and street performers help to animate the surroundings, making the area appear safe and gives the impression that this is a good location for a fun day out.

It is worth analysing why the festival takes place in both the city centre and Cardiff Bay waterfront development. The latter was the former docklands, where mostly ethnically diverse populations lived and worked. After an enormous regeneration project, it now attracts over two million visitors a year to events and leisure activities (Cardiff Festival, 2005). However, the area's reconstruction also involves a narrative of dispossession and gentrification (Cowell and Thomas, 2002). Briefly recounting the history of this area is useful for understanding the political, spatial and symbolic significance of current festival events taking place in Cardiff Bay. It is also important to keep in mind that festivals are 'constructed in a way that furthers specific interests, and, in the process, marginalises others' (Quinn, 2003, p. 345). In this instance, Cardiff is no exception.

The waterfront now called Cardiff Bay[1] was known as Butetown in the mid-19th century and was mainly used for the export of coal. It was not only physically separated from the main city but was also marginalized by city officials because the private industry did not contribute to the city's economy and was outside of municipal authority. The area was further stigmatized by city residents because the docks relied on an ethnically diverse workforce. In the 1920s, the collapse of the coal trade caused many of the enterprises to fold, and poverty plagued many of the dock's ethnic minority populations (Cowell and Thomas, 2002). From that time to the late 20th century, the city council considered the physically decaying Cardiff docklands area to be useless wetlands populated by moral deviants. The ostracization of the area and its population led to the already spatially separate area being further disconnected from the growth and development of the city centre (Cowell and Thomas, 2002).

In the late 20th century, the regional and local government decided to 'modernize' and 'reclaim' the waterfront area. The Cardiff Bay Development Corporation (CBDC) was formed in 1987 with the remit of creating a globally competitive maritime city (Imrie and Thomas, 1999), which was worthy of national and international recognition and advertised the modernization of Wales as a whole (Hague and Thomas, 1997). The regeneration of the docklands was linked to 'processes seeking to create a distinctive civic image whereby the ambience and style of the city became economic assets' (Jewson and MacGregor, 1997, p. 5). So-called 'frontier' language was used by city officials in order to justify expenditure on redevelopment. Public relations portrayed the area's environment as 'wild' and 'valueless', and populations as 'anti-social' and 'not respectable' (Cowell and Thomas, 2002, p. 1243). This helped propagate the idea that the area should be reclaimed and transformed in the name of progress to make a beneficial contribution to the city. The local media helped to extend this idea by using a more positive-sounding rhetoric of revitalization and renewal in regard to the development project (Thomas and Imrie, 1999). The physical integration of the area into mainstream Cardiff was the first step in realizing the CBDC and local council's plans to create a 'world class city'.

A global regeneration model, now standard in most cities around the world, was used for Cardiff Bay. As Evans (2005, p. 967) put it, 'Culture is a driver, a catalyst or at the very least a "key player" in the process of regeneration or renewal'. Flagship redevelopments have been used in many former industrial cities, most notably Baltimore and Barcelona. Evans (2005, p. 959) comments on the 'replication in post-industrial and developing cities world-wide' of the tendency of local governments to support culture-led regeneration projects. Cardiff City Council implemented this type of regeneration model on purpose to 'maintain Cardiff's status as a thriving European capital city' (Cardiff City Council, 2003). Moreover, a 2006 planned review of the existing City Centre Strategy by the Economic Scrutiny Committee recommended that 'Cardiff should look to neighbouring cities as well as Europe and beyond as it forms its future vision' (Cardiff City Council, 2006a). By emulating these kinds of successful flagship projects, the aspirant Cardiff city government sought to fashion a world city landscape in a local landscape (Keil and Graham, 1998) by creating an urban space in which the middle classes can consume in comfort and safety (Zukin, 1995).

As a local council funded and staged entity, it is not certain whether the Cardiff Festival was designed specifically to overcome disputed urban planning projects as one of its goals. However, the use of physical space to stage festival events is interwoven within the city's cultural policies. For example, part of the original aim for the festival was to raise the profile and footfall in the Bay area, which the council feels has largely been achieved. The festival can be seen to be aiding in the general acceptance of the Cardiff Bay redevelopment in two key ways. First, it rebrands the area. Festivals have the ability to change perceptions of place by making them appear safe and exciting by the use of visual entertainment to draw people to the area. Second, the festival is helping to reunite the waterfront area with the city centre by staging events in both areas. This is part of the council's strategy to promote Cardiff Bay as 'an integral part of the city'

(Cardiff City Council, 2003). Festival events that take place in this area are the International Food and Drink Festival, MAS Carnival and various music events.

Symbolic as well as spatial integration of the Bay area is also being achieved through the festival's carnival path, which runs throughout the previously controversial area of Butetown and finishes at the redeveloped waterfront. The MAS Carnival staged by South Wales Intercultural Community Arts (SWICA) has been instrumental in changing attitudes towards Cardiff Bay. The 2005 MAS Carnival was made even bigger with more dancers, DJs and musicians because it was the 50th anniversary of Cardiff as the Welsh capital and 100th anniversary of Cardiff as a city. Cardiff 2005 and the Millennium Commission through the Urban Cultural Fund donated additional funding towards this and the Admiral Big Weekend to celebrate these milestones. The carnival route begins in Loudon Square in the area between Cardiff city centre and Cardiff Bay, formerly perceived by the white majority as a 'no man's land', and ends at Roald Dahl Plass at the waterfront. This parade route was deliberately selected to make this area seem more friendly and safe for middle-class families by having a busy, musical, colourful, very visual event take place in a formerly desolate (or perceived as desolate) section of the city. The carnival is free and hosts workshops to get more people who are unfamiliar with carnival traditions involved.

The MAS Carnival is a larger, more visual and highly promoted version of the original community carnival that used to be held in Butetown. When the organizers sought CBDC support in the 1990s, they were told that the event had to become a bigger, more sensational event (Cowell and Thomas, 2002). This meant the carnival that celebrated a marginalized ethnic community's heritage and identity was to become a marketing vehicle to attract those outside the Butetown community, including other Cardiff city residents and visitors, to the now regenerated area. The CBDC view on what constitutes an appropriate carnival is in keeping with its visions for Cardiff Bay: safe, vibrant and sanitized to be appropriate for mainstream audiences. The CBDC felt 'no carnival was better than a local carnival' if it did not fit in to the image of the new Cardiff Bay setting (Cowell and Thomas, 2002, p. 1252). This is not simply a case of Cardiff being precious about its regeneration agenda. Many regeneration schemes worldwide favour 'the visible over the informal and community-based culture' (Evans, 2005, p. 977). However, in attempting to benefit the community, the council ended up marginalizing a group of them. In many respects, the residents of Butetown were dispossessed for a second time with the co-option of their carnival by the council. The first time was a physical dispossession of the docklands area in which they lived; and the second time was a cultural dispossession of their traditional celebration. It has been evinced that social groups who perceive themselves to be marginalized have engaged in festivals to assert identity and lay claim to space (Quinn, 2003). The origins of the Notting Hill Carnival are a perfect example of the use of cultural festivity as a platform to achieve such ends. However, the Butetown residents were disempowered in both instances and further segregated from mainstream society in daily life and symbolic celebration.

By receiving municipal support, the former Butetown carnival is now under jurisdiction to be policed and, in many respects, controlled. As Boyle (1997, p. 1994) put it, 'Groups that otherwise might have constituted a threat are rendered silent by virtue of their participation in the event.' It can be argued that this so-called cultural carnival is not cultural at all but a state-sponsored co-opted event that exercises control over marginalized populations in order to sell the city to visitors and mainstream audiences. This is another example of how Cardiff Council is trying to enhance the city's national and international profile by hosting a similar activity in a similar style to carnivals held in other global maritime cities, such as Buenos Aires, Venice and Sydney, among others. Unfortunately, it can be seen to be doing so to the detriment of a section of its local community.

With the Cardiff Festival, the council aims to create a month-long spectacle to bring tourists and city residents to enjoy the city centre and waterfront areas of the city. This means the festival does not take too many risks

or innovations with programming and features mainly general entertainment with some well-known artists to attract crowds. This regard for style over substance in arts provision for the expressed purpose of 'branding the city through cultural flagships and festivals' can be seen to be an example of 'karaoke architecture, where it is not important how well you sing, but that you do it with verve and gusto' (Evans, 2003, p. 417). Indeed, the Cardiff Festival can largely be understood as a commercial entity that exists to benefit the city. This influx of people during the month helps to boost spending in the restaurants and shops in the event areas, thus also helping the city's businesses to prosper. It is these image marketing and economic development goals that drive the festival, which is understandable given the way in which local authorities view and co-opt cultural events to further their civic agendas and interests.

Conclusions

Changes in central and local government's approach to arts festivals can be attributed to many factors, perhaps one of the most important of which is the growing emphasis on entrepreneurialism in governance. This focuses on ways for public authorities to foster growth and boost the image of a city. As more cities transform their physical spaces with fixed infrastructure ranging from retail areas to parks to cultural centres, arts festivals are increasingly on the front lines of urban development strategies because of their low production costs and entertaining and animating properties. It is argued that, in the UK, the government has focused attention on arts festivals because they have the potential to assist in the promotion and support of cultural agendas, urban regeneration, tourism, place marketing and image promotion. As more cities compete for people, capital and status, the role of arts festivals becomes increasingly important in conveying positive messages about the liveability and viability of a place. This instrumental approach can be seen to be having direct and indirect effects on the programming and organization of arts festivals.

The case study of the Cardiff Festival highlights these main issues in contemporary urban governance and the roles that arts festivals play in facilitating place marketing, regeneration and development agendas. Paradoxically, Cardiff Council is trying to 'sell' the city through the festival, but it has been found that the organizers are making no attempt to differentiate the programming or brand the festival as distinctly pertaining to Cardiff or Wales. The lack of Welsh identity and heritage signs and symbols on display during the Cardiff Festival makes it appear generic and does not anchor the festival to the city. It can be argued that once a festival loses its connection to place and people, it loses its originality and meaning, thus becoming predictable and unimportant to people's lives and a greater sense of self. Also, the year-long programme of events and activities held in the city centre and Cardiff Bay area has increased the number of festival-like occurrences in the city. It is suggested that if there is always something spectacle-related happening, then the festival no longer can be considered special in providing a clear break from everyday life. This begs the question, if festivals are becoming routine, what provides a break from the festivals?

Questions for Students

1. In what ways can public policies affect the content, atmosphere and experiences of festivals?
2. In the case study of Cardiff, how could the council further bridge the divide between political agendas and local communities' interests?

Note

[1] This area was not always called Cardiff Bay. In fact, this is a title devised from a public relations department rather than a name based on cartography or history. It was known as Tiger Bay, but this had negative connotations relating to the poverty and dereliction of the area. Cardiff Bay is supposed to represent a new beginning for the area and also emphasize Cardiff as a maritime city (Imrie and Thomas, 1999).

References

Arts Council England (2003) *Ambitions for the Arts 2003–2006.* Arts Council England, London.
Bassett, K. (1993) Urban cultural strategies and urban regeneration: a case study and critique. *Environment and Planning A* 25(12), 1773–1789.
Belfiore, E. (2006) The social impacts of the arts – myth or reality? In: Mirza, M. (ed.) *Culture Vultures: Is UK Arts Policy Damaging the Arts?* Policy Exchange, London, pp. 20–37.
Boyle, M. (1997) Civic boosterism in the politics of local eceonomic development – 'institutional positions' and 'strategic orientations' in the consumption of hallmark events. *Environment and Planning A* 29, 1975–1997.
Brighton, A. (2006) Consumed by the political: the ruination of the Arts Council. In: Mirza, M. (ed.) *Culture Vultures: Is UK Arts Policy Damaging the Arts?* Policy Exchange, London, pp. 111–129.
Cardiff City Council (2003) *City Centre Strategy 2003–2006.* Cardiff City Council, Cardiff, UK.
Cardiff City Council (2006a) *Look to Europe for City Centre Strategy.* Cardiff City Council, Cardiff. Available at: www.cardiff.gov.uk/content.asp?nav=&id=1228&Positioning_Article_ID=&Language=&d1=0 (accessed 25 November 2012).
Cardiff City Council (2006b) Cardiff City Council website. Available at: www.cardiff.gov.uk (accessed 25 November 2012).
Cardiff Festival (2003) *Cardiff Festival Programme.* Cardiff Festival, Cardiff.
Cardiff Festival (2005) *Cardiff Festival Programme.* Cardiff Festival, Cardiff.
Casey, B., Dunlop, R. and Selwood, S. (1996) *Culture as Commodity? The Economics of the Arts and Built Heritage in the UK.* Policy Studies Institute, London.
Cowell, R. and Thomas, H. (2002) Managing nature and narratives of dispossession: reclaiming territory in Cardiff Bay. *Urban Studies* 39(7), 1241–1260.
Dreher, C. (2002) Be creative – or die. *Salon*, 6 June. Available at: www.salon.com (accessed 25 November 2012).

Evans, G. (2001) *Cultural Planning: an Urban Renaissance?* Routledge, London.

Evans, G. (2003) Hard-branding the cultural city – from Prado to Prada. *International Journal of Urban and Regional Research* 27(2), 417–440.

Evans, G. (2005) Measure for measure: evaluating the evidence of culture's contribution to regeneration. *Urban Studies* 42(5/6), 959–983.

Everingham, C. (2003) *Social Justice and the Politics of Community.* Ashgate, London.

Finkel, R. (2009) A picture of the contemporary combined arts festival landscape. *Cultural Trends* 18(1), 3–21.

Florida, R. (2002) *The Rise of the Creative Class: and How It's Transforming Work, Leisure, Community and Everyday Life.* Perseus Books Group, New York.

Gibson, C. and Klocker, N. (2005) The 'cultural turn' in Australian regional economic development discourse: neoliberalising creativity? *Geographical Research* 43(1), 93–102.

Griffiths, R. (1993) The politics of cultural policy in urban regeneration strategies. *Policy and Politics* 21(1), 39–46.

Hague, C. and Thomas, H. (1997) Capital city planning: Cardiff and Edinburgh compared. In: MacDonald, R. and Thomas, H. (eds) *Nationality and Planning in Scotland and Wales.* University of Wales Press, Cardiff.

Imrie, R. and Thomas, H. (eds) (1999) *British Urban Policy.* Sage Publications, London.

Jewson, N. and MacGregor, S. (1997) *Transforming Cities: Contested Governance and New Spatial Divisions.* Routledge, London.

Keil, R. and Graham, J. (1998) Reasserting nature: constructing urban environments after Fordism. In: Braun, B. and Castree, N. (eds) *Remaking Reality: Nature and the Millennium.* Routledge, London, pp. 100–125.

Kettle, M. (2006) The gulf between the arts and New Labour is growing wider. *Guardian*, 20 May, p. 35.

London Development Agency (2005) £9 Million Funding to Boost 2012 Training and Job Opportunities. Available at: www.lda.org.uk/server/show/ConWebDoc.1301 (accessed 25 November 2012).

Miles, S. and Paddison, R. (2005) Introduction: the rise and rise of culture-led urban regeneration. *Urban Studies* 42 (5/6), 833–839.

Mirza, M. (ed.) (2006) *Culture Vultures: Is UK Arts Policy Damaging the Arts?* Policy Exchange, London.

Myerscough, J. and Bruce, A. (1988) *The Economic Importance of the Arts in Britain.* Policy Studies Institute, London.

Peck, J. (2005) Struggling with the creative class. *International Journal of Urban and Regional Research* 29(4), 740–770.

Quinn, B. (2003) Symbols, practices and myth-making: cultural perspectives on the Wexford Festival Opera. *Tourism Geographies* 5(3), 329–349.

Rolfe, H. (1992) *Arts Festivals in the UK.* Policy Studies Institute, London.

Stevenson, D. (2004) 'Civic gold' rush: cultural planning and the politics of the Third Way. *International Journal of Cultural Policy* 10, 119–131.

Tellis, W. (1997) Introduction to case study. *The Qualitative Report* 3(2). Available from: www.nova.edu/ssss/QR/QR3-2/tellis1.html (accessed 25 November 2012).

Thomas, H. and Imrie, R. (1999) Urban policy, modernisation, and the regeneration of Cardiff Bay. In: Imrie, R. and Thomas, H. (eds) *British Urban Policy.* Sage Publications, London, pp. 106–127.

Zukin, S. (1995) *The Culture of Cities.* Blackwell, Cambridge, Massachusetts.

12 Events and Resistance

David McGillivray* and Jennifer Jones
University of the West of Scotland, Paisley, UK

Introduction

Before exploring the main theories of resistance and their relevance to the events terrain, it is pertinent to expand upon the rationale for writing a chapter on events and resistance in the first place. Why is it relevant to talk about resistance in a textbook about research themes in events? There are three principal reasons worth rehearsing here. First, as Foley *et al.* (2011) argue, mega sporting and cultural events are subject to growing criticism over the manner in which their purpose has been narrowly channelled to the achievement of political and economic outcomes even although a significant body of evidence suggests that these overly 'governed' and 'managed' events do not produce the planned benefits that organizers desire. The presence of over-estimated benefits and underestimated costs (Whitson and Horne, 2006) has focused attention (in practice and in academia) on the claims made by proponents, leading to greater scrutiny over so-called return on investment (ROI) or return on objectives (ROO). A second, related, reason why resistance is important is because events are also said to have become too distant to the interests of their professed beneficiaries (e.g. 'citizens'), diluting their legitimacy as an effective policy lever. In the context of major events, legitimacy is closely related to sustainability and legacy and if they fail to deliver benefits for the communities they serve then the longer-term aspirations of their

hosts are likely to remain unattainable. The presence of a legitimacy deficit operates as a source of motivation for those individuals and groups who wish to offer alternative versions of the value accruable from investment in major events – whether through dissent, protest or resistance.

Finally, alongside the increased interest in resistance, born as a result of the perceived inequities of mega sporting and cultural events, come new methods of coordinating and organising resistance, which can now be considered as events in themselves. As a range of stakeholder groups seek to hold politicians and growth coalition partners to account through raising awareness of alternative discourses and narratives there is evidence of renewed interest in the effective mobilization of citizen and community action to secure social change. New techniques available through the emergence of the new media (Levinson, 2009) are proving useful to those interested in coordinating and mobilizing discontent and resistance around major sporting and cultural events as they enable large audiences to be reached and information to be shared in real-time to facilitate greater organizational effectiveness. There is evidence of collectives – often ephemeral and temporary – forming and making use of readily available digital technologies to challenge and contest the existing power structures that mega events are accused of reinforcing. That does not mean that organized resistance to mega sporting or

*david.mcgillivray@uws.ac.uk

cultural events, via the digital medium, represents a panacea of protest. Instead, as this chapter illustrates, there are significant difficulties in spreading a legacy of protest and organized resistance between host cities because of the specific local and national issues that define each one. For this introduction, it is sufficient to say that there is a growing thirst, globally, to subject the state-corporate nexus at the heart of sponsoring major sporting and cultural events, to account.

That an 'Events and Resistance' chapter is necessary in a text of this sort also owes much to sheer popularity and global profile that major events now attract. From the 19th century onwards, World Fairs, International Expos and, latterly, the Olympic Games, were utilized for the global circulation of political, economic and cultural ideologies (Roche, 2000), but advances in information and communication technologies in the last two decades have transformed the landscape, providing those on the periphery with an opportunity to have their message transported to the mainstream like never before. A diverse range of interest groups ranging from anti-capitalist protestors, environmental campaigners and human rights activists now regularly use the spectacle (Debord, 1973) of major events to promote their own agendas. It is, therefore, worth considering how these groups organize themselves, which techniques they use to secure the stage for their own messages and the ways in which dominant narratives seek to re-establish primacy for their ideas. This chapter, first, introduces the main conceptual issues (resistance and its digital expression), then outlines the primary contextual agenda of major sporting and cultural events, before integrating these through the vehicle of a dedicated case study of the Olympic Games and new media activism.

Theorising Resistance (In a Digital Age)

This section provides a brief exploration of the academic literature around resistance, refracted through the lens of cultural studies, leisure studies, event studies (Getz, 2007) and, latterly, digital culture theory. Over the last 30 years, in the realm of cultural and, to a lesser extent, leisure studies, the theoretical landscape occupied by the Birmingham Centre for Contemporary Cultural Studies (CCCS) has been particularly influential in articulating a neo-Marxist perspective on resistance. Focusing on the realm of mass communications, the Birmingham School, as it was commonly known, considered how leisure practices could be employed effectively to develop oppositional identities for the disenfranchised and dis-empowered masses. As Rojek (2005, p. 108) suggests, 'by developing leisure and play forms that, so to speak, are inscribed over the requirements of consumer culture, individuals and groups position themselves in alternative or oppositional space that challenge the rule of capital and the state'. The play forms that CCCS scholars referred to included music, fashion and literature and they were particularly interested in the 'positioning' of certain segments of society, achieved through a 'war of man-oeuvre', whereby the dominant economic and political groups attempted to incorporate protest and resistance to further tie individuals into the desired social order. The CCCS (e.g. Hall, 1980) focused their critique on those techniques of media amplification and media spiral used by the state apparatus to generate anxiety about threats to the status quo – an analysis that remains pertinent to the moral media panics created around young people's use of technologically-mediated communication channels in the current period (e.g. Twitter and Facebook). However, while the CCCS provided a powerful critique of the capitalist system and the opportunity that play forms presented for symbolic forms of resistance, its continuing focus on class relations as a determining focus came under increasing scrutiny from emerging feminist, post-structural and postmodern perspectives from the late 1980s.

Feminist accounts, for example, while sharing a concern with the universally oppressed subject, suggested that women rather than the proletariat occupy this subservient position. Yet, even within the field of feminism, over the last two decades, foundational thinking has been challenged by the emergence of post-feminist perspectives, which contest the notion of a singular concept of 'woman' that can simply be freed from patriarchal conditions. Rather, led by Butler (1993, 1999), the concern of post-feminists has been with how the subject position of woman comes into being, is regulated and can be governed.

Whatever the conceptual differences between these schools of thought, each theory of resistance shares a concern with the extent of constraint (and, by definition, freedom) available to individuals and groups and their capacity to resist or subvert aspects of dominant culture(s). For example, scholars in the postmodern tradition, popularized in the 1980s and early 1990s (e.g. Lyotard, 1984; Featherstone, 1991) are criticized for suggesting that power can be 'too easily opposed, countered and thrown off by so-called active agents' (McRobbie, 1995, p. 86). As McRobbie goes on to argue, 'it is quite something else to posit a kind of free-floating freedom and agency on the part of consumers of mass culture to construct their own "subversive readings" and thus undermine the power of the media'. McRobbie's concern is that it can appear that those promoting liberating possibilities in a world of fluid identities are refusing to acknowledge the continuing effectiveness of power and authority to constrain the life chances of some, while enhancing those of others. In other words, while there may well be evidence of 'momentary or fleeting transgressions' (McRobbie, 1995, p. 87) as evidence of the effective expression of resistance this does not equate to successful (or sustainable) agential action. Rather, drawing on Butler's post-structural analysis, the 'dominant order constrains such "reiterations" and provides the conditions of existence for evasions of dis-placements so that the hegemonic normativity is renewed' (McRobbie, 1995, p. 87). This influential post-structural analysis posits that power is multidimensional, not simply a possession deployed by the powerful against the powerless but rather a force that conditions what is possible, permitting certain actions, behaviours and subject positions to operate while, at the same time, disqualifying others. To understand this perspective further it is necessary to rehearse the work of Michel Foucault, one of the foremost theorists of resistance over the last three decades.

Foucault argued that 'resistance is never in a position of exteriority in relation to power' (Foucault, 1978, p. 95) and is, in fact, a prerequisite for the existence of power itself (Burrell, 1988). In this sense, Foucault's conception of power stresses the 'multiplicity of points of resistance which play the role of adversary, target, support or handle within power relations' (Burrell, 1988, p. 228). So, rather than view individuals as docile subjects, trapped within a web of disciplinary power, unable to find an escape route (which Foucault's earlier writings seem to imply), a more nuanced analysis of Foucault's writings is his conviction that contestation, conflict and resistance were a constant force, operating at the everyday (micro) level, reflecting the imperfections of power. His *Discipline and Punish* writings have been criticized for (apparently) suggesting that human beings are simply the product of some 'coherent regime of domination that produces persons in the form of which it dreams' (du Gay, 2000, p. 181). However, Foucault's self-reflexive ethos is more accurately portrayed in the view that 'individuals constantly escape, evade, and subvert the functioning of discipline' (Miller, 1987, p. 196) rather than engage in obedient conformity to the demands place upon them. In this sense, Foucault's later writings on governmentality are of value to this discussion because he argues that local resistances, 'fragile relays' and 'contested locales' are a features of any governance relationship (Rose, 1999, p. 51). Governmentality 'allows one to acknowledge the complexities, subtleties and micro negotiations of relations of power ... and involves recognition that any project of governance is always incomplete and partial in respect to the objects and practices it governs' (Petersen, 1997, p. 203). In this interpretation of the workings of power, competing claims and affirmations that unsettle, subvert and make uncomfortable its deployment are an ever-present feature. This is even more marked in an age defined by the presence of online spaces, which destabilize the conventional archi-tectures, infrastructures and institutional environments where resistance has been most obviously manifest (e.g. buildings and cities). So, Foucault's analysis of power as multi-dimensional and always incomplete provides this chapter with a conceptual direction that also helps explain the potential impact and influence of digital cultures on the landscape of major sporting and cultural events.

There are plentiful examples of the digital medium being employed to escape, evade and subvert the functioning of discipline. New forms of e-activism, for example, utilize the Internet and its numerous channels to generate collectivities and amplify protest, dissent and resistance (Hands, 2011). However, it is also important to cast a critical eye over the spaces made possible by the proliferation of new digital forms and to assess their effectiveness as a means of promoting opposing claims and affirmations. There can be little doubt that, at the very least, the greater availability of digital technologies provides the marginalized or unvoiced with a powerful weapon to use against the object of their displeasure. One useful contemporary example is the use of user-generated video content as a means of challenging the dominant discourse around protest. As Elmer and Opel (2008, p. 54) suggest: 'The ability to produce, edit, and distribute digital video is a radical challenge to a logic predicated on image control. This proliferation of digital media tools complicates the potential for images of resistance and dissent.' Here, a readily available domestic technology (e.g. the smartphone) is utilized to create a competing version of events that would otherwise have been reported in a one-dimensional manner.

The potential of digital tools to decentralize, empower, mobil(e)ize (Hands, 2011) and organize (Rheingold, 2002) is well rehearsed, but there are also many sceptical voices cautioning proponents about the limits of so-called cyber utopianism. At the forefront of recent critiques is Morozov's (2011) text The Net Delusion, which offers a stinging riposte to those commentators optimistic about the potential of information freedoms promised by the Internet. While a supporter of the democratizing potential of new media, Morozov is critical of the over-stated emancipatory potential of the Internet and of an Internet-centrism, which frames every important question about politics and society as a problem that the Internet can solve. He is particularly critical of the 'slaktavism' that new media

platforms can encourage – whereby the Internet contributes to a consumerist protest mentality, devoid of risk and commitment on behalf of participants. Morozov (2011) argues that it is just as likely that authoritarian regimes will use the self-same technological tools to close down Internet freedoms as open them up in response to cyber-protest movements. Morozov also calls for a degree of cyber-realism, arguing that the Internet and its digital variants can only be effective when looking to achieve specific political agendas. He suggests that information, organization and leverage are the counter-pillars of authoritarianism and posits that the Internet represents the most effective vehicle for strengthening these. While a withering and sometime cynical analysis of the liberatory potential of cyberspace, many of Morozov's concerns are important in understanding the potential of the digital medium to provide a new space for meaningful contestation and resistance – and also the limits of that aspiration.

Goode (2009) also warns that it is too tempting to conceive of alternative media as a purely radical 'movement' that exists to oppose and challenge the mainstream, corporate media. For example, the political economy of the 'citizen journalism' sector is one of commerce and advertising with a growing relationship to existing media corporations (Goode, 2009). It is not surprising that existing media would adopt and present the citizen media rhetoric as a style of broadcast as it allows a response to the 'new' in new media and provides 'different perspectives, modes of address and story selection' (Goode, 2009, p. 1289). The appropriation of citizen media stylistic practices is now apparent in sections of broadcast and newspaper media where the reader is invited to contribute stories, content and opinion in return for the promise of potentially being printed – an incentive for participation and a method of enfolding the alterity back into the dominant frame.

This is not to say that all radical, alternative media activism will eventually end up being consumed by the forces that it wished to challenge, nor does the use of commercial, free-to-use platforms restrict the validity of the alternative narratives presented. The presumed horizontal and interactive nature of new media situates it as a potential remedy to the one-to-many, broadcast model of the mainstream media (Holmes, 1997), whose programming is treated as the dominant narrative. More specifically, alternative media, citizen journalism or community media act as quite deliberate interventions within the existing media landscape. The alternative media is often defined by its mode of production and distribution, the form of content, aesthetic quality and how it interacts with its audiences and often the focus is to challenge the dominant narratives of the mainstream media, to provide a voice to marginal communities or to build networks between other groups of similar focus (Downing, 2001; Atton, 2002).

However, there is an interesting interplay at work whereby the forces of new and 'old' media are coexisting and colonizing each others' spaces and using each others' newsgathering and distribution techniques. And, of interest in the remainder of this chapter, is the way that digital technologies are employed before, during and after mega events to capture, distribute and challenge the dominant narratives at play – creating an alternative media context in its own right.

Events and Resistance: From Carnival to the Olympic Games

Having presented a review of some important theories of resistance in the preceding section, it is now necessary to reflect upon some of the myriad ways that cultural and sporting events have been used to present dominant narratives about nation, identity, politics and economy while also being the focal point for resistance to these motives. This section, therefore, provides the context to support the preceding discussion of concepts. Events (cultural, sporting and political) have, historically, served a dual purpose – as a means for governing authorities to extend social control while, at the same time, operating as the vehicle for resistance or protest to the dominant elite. The Nazi's use of the 1936 Olympic Games to 'aggrandize National Socialism both in the sight of the domestic population and in the eyes of the world' (Rojek,

2005, p. 95) is an oft-used example of the manipulation of an event for political ends. However, cultural festivity has also played an important historical function for securing social order through offering temporary carnivalesque spaces of liminality in which political, social and cultural agendas are played out. From Mardi Gras, New Orleans (see Gotham, 2005) to the numerous European Carnivals (Gilmore, 1998), people have been encouraged to take to the streets *en masse* for a time-bound period to celebrate inverted hierarchies, life's fertile possibilities and 'official culture's claims to authority, stability, sobriety, immutability and immortality' (Schechner, 1995, p. 46). However, as Schechner (1995) stresses, while the impression given is of unbounded freedom, these events remain scheduled, using fixed parading routes, and are easily managed by elite groups, 'official culture smiles as it asks ordinary people to confirm the existing power structures' (Schechner, 1995, p. 83). By offering bread and circuses (Veyne, 1990), the submissive and grateful population conforms to the conventional social order, having enjoyed their extraordinary liberties, or 'temporary disruptions of an underlying order' (Schechner, 1995, p. 86).

The notion that festivals and events represent a mechanism for contestation between the governers and the governed has a long history. Rojek (2005) argues (as do others) that one of the primary functions of leisure is 'control' and that leisure, while associated with freedom, self-determination and choice, has many restraints upon it, including in the realm of assembly, which is relevant to the field of events, 'public assembly, for play or protest is subject to notification and policing. Spontaneous public assembly and "loitering" are categorized as a threat to the peace' (Rojek, 2005, p. 93). The civil unrest in the City of London in August 2011 brought the apparent 'threat' created by collective assembly into sharp focus, but managing planned festivals and events and public gatherings has been the source of much consternation historically – and this is merely amplified in the 21st century because of the wall-to-wall rolling news coverage available globally. Official culture seeks to produce and control public celebrations, ensuring their orderly passage, 'moving in one direction and proceeding from a known beginning to a known end in time as well as space' (Schechner, 1995, p. 82). Fears over disorganized, chaotic (Edensor, 1998) and overly distributed movements generate a regulatory impulse on behalf of organizers, but the emergence of neo-liberal economic policies around the globe in the 1980s and 1990s also necessitated (and justified) the introduction of tightened regulations, a clearer separation of spectator and participant (in the name of safety) and the open co-option of commercial forces to 'sponsor' festivities. A good example of the increasing prevalence of staged events is the public viewing areas now commonplace around major sporting spectacles. The 2006 FIFA World Cup held in Germany was the first to systematically create 'Fan Parks' at each of the ten host cities as a means of housing travelling ticketless fans and to allow corporate sponsors to generate increased returns on their investment with respect to merchandising sales and brand exposure (Frew and McGillivray, 2008). These staged events align with the trend towards preemptive action on behalf of the governing authorities to segregate people in the name of 'securing' commercial space. In the name of creating managed brand environments, official (FIFA-endorsed) Fan Parks became privatized spaces excluding not only the marginalized but also 'local' producers and associated business interests not part of the FIFA commercial sponsor family. In recent years this trend towards staging public viewing areas (officially sanctioned and controlled) has only intensified in number and in scale. The provision of spaces for Live Sites in Olympic Host Cities is now contractually binding and represents an effective method of managing potentially problematic large public assemblies around Games time.

However, despite the apparent temporary and illusory opportunity for resistance provided by the carnival, festival, or public viewing experience at major sports events, the emergence of an accessible digital medium provides an additional space where alternative modes of resistance around major events can be imagined. While the history of resistance at major sporting spectacles is punctuated with tales of terrorism (i.e. Munich Olympics 1972), and boycotts (i.e. Moscow 1980 and Los Angeles 1984) techniques of resistance have also moved on significantly since the birth of the Internet two decades ago. Ambush marketing, social media campaigns and citizen journalism are now commonly used to disrupt the established order. Paraphrasing Foucault, these approaches represent micro-level strategies and tactics, providing revised claims and affirmations about the desirability of the spectacle effect of the Olympics, for example.

Fluidity, multiple meanings and creative uses of public space are possible in the conceptualization of resistance provided by Foucault. In the urban studies tradition, for example, Stevenson (2003, p. 42) argues that people frequently create alternative 'narratives' of their engagement with, and use of, public spaces that cannot be easily read off from objective, structural analyses, meaning that people are 'not necessarily the passive victims or recipients of dominant ideologies and oppressive power relations' (Stevenson, 2003). De Certeau (1988) also suggests that dominant power relations are 'incomplete', and meaningful practices can be enacted in urban spaces to avoid the nets of surveillance, policing and discipline indicative of the late capitalist city. What he calls 'tactical resistance' is possible, where space can be reclaimed, reinterpreted and shaped and identities can be reworked against prescribed or imposed meanings. The urban environment is a dynamic, lived space open to 'unofficial' representations as well as the official approach. Despite attempts to fix meanings undertaken by the cultural intermediaries of entrepreneurial governance (Foley *et al.*, 2011), urban space remains an arena for social action to take place where negotiation is part of everyday life.

This analysis of negotiated social space between official culture and the activities of social actors is especially pertinent when consideration is given to the role of digital platforms and techniques. The governing authorities no longer have sole rights to control the narrative with the presence of 'YouTube politics and other forms of user-generated media – technologies that have afforded a degree of counter surveillance' (Elmer and

Opel, 2008, p. 53). So, while organized resistance at events continues to require the mainstream media to amplify its messages, it is now also the case that media content can come from within-event audiences, using the freely available digital tools and ubiquity of user-generated content (UGC).

New Media Activism: Vancouver 2010 and London 2012

The illustrative case study for this chapter is the Olympic Games, specifically the Winter Olympics in Vancouver 2010 and the Summer Olympics of London in 2012. The case study is a particularly appropriate method of illustration for this topic because it can help to demonstrate the presence of 'ideas of local resistance in specific empirical contexts' (Alvesson and Deetz, 2000, p. 110), which aligns well with Foucault's conceptualization of resistance. The case study method is also an apposite means of illustrating power play and resistance in action around a major sporting event. Both the Vancouver 2010 Winter Olympics and the London 2012 Summer Olympics represent a watershed in the theory and practice of event resistance because of the utilization of new media (and social media) tools to mobilize resistance to the excesses associated with this sporting mega event. In exploring the Olympics and new media activism, two guiding principles must be established. First, it is necessary to explore how those within the case networks identity themselves and with each other, either through the content that they have produced for an online audience or the ways in which they use media rhetoric to strengthen the authority of their reporting and of their position. Second, it is important to assess what opportunities arise through participation in an organized citizen media network, and how this may have an effect on their ability to analyse or critique narratives and events. This is especially important, as in return for access to central activities, existing broadcasters and journalists at the Games are already suspended in their critical presence (Dayan and Katz, 1994).

The major events terrain provides a rich tapestry of examples pertaining to the utilization of new media as a force for dissent, protest and resistance. A cursory glance at the most popular new media platforms (e.g. Twitter, Facebook and blogs) attests to the explosion of information circulating about protest, dissent and resistance relating to the Olympic Games (e.g. Games Monitor, Around the Rings, #media2012, SochiReporter). Organization is improving and political leverage is evident, though always partial and contested. The Internet represents the amplification of everyday community conversations and this is perhaps one of the web's greatest strengths, especially when applied to the practices of resistance around mega events. Issues that would have previously passed below the radar because space (physical and media) was completely controlled by the political-corporate-media complex, now produce a cacophony of voices. New media activism around these events creates its own airtime and develops its own means of distributing that content without having to engage with the power brokers that have cornered the official media narrative. For example, the volume of activity from the unaccredited media around the 2008 Summer Olympic Games in Beijing and the 2010 Winter Olympics in Vancouver was unprecedented. The now ubiquitous social media channels enable vast networks to be activated in a manner unheard of before and with great immediacy. That, in itself, holds the authorities to account as they find it more difficult to control the media message with such diversity of platforms available and distributed so widely.

Speed, of communication and representation (Virilio, 2000), is creating challenges of control and management for mega event owners and corporate sponsors alike. The levelling of publishing also opens up the door for new political agencies (including the strengthening of existing agendas). However, the de-rationalizing of media relations, which new media forms promised, is increasingly being followed by techniques to re-rationalize content as social technologies are appropriated to extend the corporate reach to new markets and commercializing them for pecuniary gain. This represents continuity with the history of consumer culture, 'commodifying rebellion' (Sanjek and Sanjek, 1996). This is a counter argument to the cyber-optimism of an Internet-centric worldview – that perhaps independent new media sites (e.g. blogs) remain unable to compete with the established industry models because the mainstream media uses the easily availability of digital tools to direct traffic to their content, 'borrowing' principles of UGC and participatory media cultures. The threat of such corporate appropriation is well put by Real (2007, p. 182) who argues that:

> Given the trends towards convergences and consolidation of ownership, the likelihood of a spiral of silence emerges, in which fringe minority voices get less hearing and are gradually brought into conformity ... the hegemony of the privileged over web content and values will marginalize less powerful groups as it has in other media.

Issues relating to commoditization and conformity arise when the 'end product' – the content – is traded as a commodity, perhaps by the platform itself, or by an individual, group or organization on behalf of those who created it. Here, the citizen media producer is removed from the value chain, and 'rewarded' in some other way. According to Terranova (2000), it may not be the 'bad boys of capitalism' that move in to neutralize and 'incorporate' alternative media production into its food chain but instead it is the product of a more 'immanent process of channeling collective labor (even as cultural labor) into monetary flows and its structuration within capitalist business practices' (Terranova, 2000, p. 104).

However, at the same time, there are much more optimistic voices stressing the potential for, at least, localized and particularistic forms of protest and resistance enacted through new media around the Olympic Games. Because of the philosophy of Olympism, its international reach, avowed apolitical aims and (relatively) recent commercial success, the Olympic Games is a site of contestation over media. Media rights value has grown exponentially over the last decades, though accompanied by concerns over politics, values, engagement, ownership and control. As communication technologies have been transformed, the media population during Games time has also diversified. For example, since the Sydney 2000 Olympic Games, host-city sponsored, non-accredited media centres

have emerged, providing facilities and access to visiting journalists and/or bloggers without International Olympic Committee (IOC) media accreditation (Miah *et al.*, 2008). More recently during the Vancouver Winter Olympics, as well as a British Columbia government-hosted centre, there were at least three declared independent centres that were acknowledged and formalized prior to the Games, to report stories from within Vancouver and the surrounding region. Overall, there were at least six types of media venue in operation during the Games time period, illustrating the increased plurality of the Olympic Games' media landscape. The Vancouver Organizing Committee (VANOC) provided at least two of these venues, namely the Main Press Centre (MPC) and the International Broadcast Centre (IBC), which had several built-for-purpose facilities across the geographical locations of the events (such as in downtown Vancouver and the winter sports resort of Whistler). Further to these facilities, there was also a host-province-led non-accredited media centre, British Columbia International Media Centre (BCIMC), which provided a space and a set of resources for visiting international journalists who may or may not have received IOC official accreditation for the official media venues. In addition, there was also a substantial and independent social or citizen media presence within these Games time spaces. Indeed, the Olympic Review, which followed the Vancouver Games, cited them as being 'The First Social Media Olympics' (IOC, 2010, p. 10). However, the IOC's official articulation of this phenomenon concerned the use of UGC within extremely controlled and organized circumstances, including IOC 'official' Flickr (a photo-sharing website), Facebook and Twitter sites that selected particular threads and narratives, which suited the dominant messages that the Vancouver Games wished to be represented by. This example illustrates, in microscope, the disciplining power of governing agencies as they attempt to capture the tools of the citizen media activist and use them for official (and often corporate) ends.

Yet, at one and the same time, the presence of at least three pre-confirmed independent media centres or organizations in Vancouver with no formal IOC, VANOC or host-province accreditation provides evidence of localized points of resistance. These venues provided locational support and a form of accreditation for journalists or citizen reporters to act as media workers 'on the ground' during this transformative time. Two of the most influential were the W2 Arts and Culture House, a community media centre that was situated in the Downtown Eastside of Vancouver, often referred to as 'Canada's poorest postcode' (Lenskyj, 2008) and True North Media House (TNMH), an entirely online self-accredited media centre, that provided media pass templates for anyone to print and laminate, in order to access stories and activities that could be shared and uploaded via personal websites and blogging platforms. What BCIMC, W2 and TNMH had in common was the intention to cover alternative stories that emerged during Games time, which official journalists and media reporters might not have the motivation or ability to cover due to their roles relating to sports-only access. Furthermore, the low cost of energy to self-publish through the use of digital and mobile technologies afforded the ability for those who may not be identified as 'official' journalists to capture, upload and share content that rarely gets covered during the Olympic Games (Tapscott and Williams, 2008). Like VANOC, W2 also used Twitter, Facebook, Flickr and YouTube to capture and share content relating to their interpretation of the Games time period. One notable example was that of Fearless City Mobile, a grassroots collective of those who resided in the Downtown East Side, who used 40 donated mobile phones with video and data sharing capacity to capture their own perspectives of the Vancouver Games, while acting as 'human rights documenters' (Fearless City Mobile, 2010). These outputs were screened in eight live public spaces across the city, turning the spectacle into another venue. The stories captured by those within and connected to W2 served to generate a searchable database of geo-locative content that could be accessed by the local and international community online.

The TNMH was an online project designed to grow an Olympic media centre using only social media platforms. Participants signed up using a web form and then produced their own pre-designed media pass, finishing the process of accreditation. That pass linked to a set of guidelines and objectives, focusing on the requirement to: (i) create and publish content that would be useful to international 'media creators'; (ii) offer a platform for lesser-known athletes; (iii) promote the Cultural Olympiad and community groups; and (iv) showcase Vancouver as a 'new media innovator and entrepreneurial hub', setting the ground work towards future Olympic Games (TNMH, 2010). The group supplemented their online interaction with a range of self-governing activities including 'tweetups', photo-walks, field trips and outings with international journalists. Additionally, some TNMH participants managed to gain accreditation to the BCIMC, allowing them to pull in additional content from the press streams generated by the non-accredited centre. During the course of the games, TNMH moved from a social media experience to a full-blown media outlet, at least when it came to gaining access to particular areas. The blurring between the 'official' and the blogger was maintained through the way in which content was shared and posted. Published materials on individual websites and social media profiles were aggregated into a page using a syndication protocol, which TNMH called a 'firehose' of content. What the activities of W2 and TNMH did was raised questions about what exactly is required from an individual in order to be considered as 'media' during an intense period of activity such as that generated at an Olympic Games, within an Olympic City. The Vancouver experience demonstrated that citizen media networks could be created globally and that there was a place for their alternative narratives within a more democratized media landscape.

With reference to London 2012, Caplan (2010) argues that the battle of the narrative and legacy for these Games began early online, through the use of web and mobile protocols by individuals and the official London Organizing Committee of the Olympic and Paralympic Games (LOCOG). By accessing photography around the event locations, Caplan looks at how formal, informal and protest movements around the Olympic Games use the visual medium of photography to represent their viewpoints. These are not just staged and prepared photographs but include mobile snapshots, equipped with geographical data, which have been 'shot from the hip' and shared quickly across social media platforms. He also argues that the act of rebellion or narrative hijacking, which the democratization of communication technologies enables, cannot happen with just one or two objects, such as the casual image. There needs to be a 'mobbing' effect to facilitate change in the existing dialogue around the mega event. So, while the informal capturing of images and wider digital content from citizens is rarely going to have an effect on the wider Games communication framework, it does, at least, generate a wider set of messages, from different parties affected by the Olympic Games. From this starting point, messages (visual and auditory) can be spread in a multitude of ways, to multiple individuals and groups, both online and offline. Using the online sphere to promote more participatory media cultures around the Olympic Games adheres to Caplan's (2010) view that this space is becoming important in the construction of a mega event and how pro- and anti-groups communicate their messages.

The digital medium has also facilitated the development of a new entrant to the existing media marketplace around Olympic Games titled #media2012 (www.media2012.org). The #media2012 initiative was inspired by both academic research and cultural activity and represented a community-led response to the radical (new) media change proposed by the IOC at the 2009 Olympic congress – and to be first delivered during the London 2012 Olympiad. The #media2012 blueprint (Miah, 2010) explicitly asked UK citizens to consider the Olympics as more than a mediated global sports event and instead to consider the Games as a participatory media festival. The network was founded on the principles of 'open media' based on the promotion of peer-to-peer conversations, across local, national and international boundaries, through the production and distribution of citizen-generated content. Through this activity at London 2012 it was the first Olympic Games to promote a community legacy with digital media as its interface.

Of course, in pursuing a commitment to open media, it could be argued that the nature, style and focus of the outputs are not as 'important' as the process of participation itself. That is, as there are no limits on what is considered 'acceptable' material, then there is the opportunity to create media that differs considerably to the dominant narrative of the London 2012 Games. By documenting, archiving and curating the 'alternative' stories rather than prescribed activities and capturing action that is often omitted from mainstream broadcast the co-production of a de-centralized legacy (and therefore, strands of history) can be achieved. This could, theoretically, be amplified and aggregated across a constantly widening network with shared aims and online through social media platforms such as Twitter and Facebook. Extended international networks are already forming between host cities across international boundaries providing the hope that micro-level strategies in open media can be aggregated to create greater impacts.

Conclusion

This chapter has explored an increasingly important research theme within the events terrain. Because of their sheer size and scale, mega sporting events are invariably a target for a myriad of individuals and groups seeking to vocalize their discontent through an expression of dissent, protest or active resistance. The ready availability of domesticated digital tools helps to organize and mobilize resistance in a way that aligns closely with Foucault's conception of resistance as ever present, employing a multitude of micro-strategies to escape, evade and subvert the functioning of discipline. Mega event owners and the official media landscape tend to narrowly define the narrative around how the Olympic Games can be represented. However, developments in open (and new) media around the Olympic Games increasingly blurs the boundaries between the producers and the consumers of content, drawing attention to competing claims and affirmations and acting to unsettle the unchallenged deployment of power that has previously existed. Controlling the mega event message is increasingly difficult as established broadcast media strategies collide with the networking capacity of web 2.0 and the popularity of social software to communicate alternative readings of events instantaneously and across the globe. Initiatives like #media2012 provide an alternative 'space' (and platform) to report mega events, free of imposed guidelines and restricted editorial control – a potentially enriching source of participatory media within which resistance can be democratized.

Future Research Directions

This chapter focused specifically on resistance around major sporting and cultural events. There remains a need for more research into the power of the new media narrative in shaping the 'story' of major events. The focus of future work needs to be less on volume of activity (quantitative) and more on the quality and impact of participatory media cultures in influencing the narrative of mega events (qualititative). Only then is it possible to more fully understand whether the power relations

between official and alternative narratives are shifting and if so, how this is being achieved.

In looking to the future, there is also a greater need to study the dynamics of unplanned events – those that perhaps arise out of political or economic concerns but which utilize digital platforms effectively to organize, mobilize and communicate their cause to mass audiences. The riots that occurred in London in August 2011 are likely to lead to more authoritarian, pre-emptive approaches to the management of public assembly and this area, in its own right, is in need of further critical investigation.

Questions for Students

1. Why have sporting and cultural events historically been the site of protest and resistance?
2. Why have the techniques used for protest and resistance changed over the last decade and to what extent has the emergence of the Internet and new media led to more effective resistance movements?

Further Reading

Caplan, P. (2010) London 2012: distributed imag(in)ings and exploiting protocol. *PLATFORM: Journal of Media and Communication* 2(2), 24–39.
Morozov, E. (2011) *The Net Delusion*. Penguin Books, London.
Schechner, R. (1995) *The Future of Ritual: Writings on Culture and Performance*. Routledge, London.

References

Alvesson, M. and Deetz, S. (2000). *Doing Critical Management Research*. Sage, London.
Atton, C. (2002) *Alternative Media*. Sage, London.
Burrell, G. (1988) Modernism, postmodernism and organizational analysis 2: the contribution of Michel Foucault. *Organization Studies* 9(2), 221–235.
Butler, J. (1993) *Bodies That Matter: On the Discursive Limits of Sex*. Routledge, New York.
Butler, J. (1999) *Gender Trouble: Feminism and the Subversion of Identity*, 2nd edn. Routledge, New York.
Caplan, P. (2010) London 2012: distributed imag(in)ings and exploiting protocol. *PLATFORM: Journal of Media and Communication* 2(2), 24–39.
Dayan, D. and Katz, E. (1994) *Media Events: the Live Broadcasting of History*. Harvard University Press, Cambridge, Massachusetts.
Debord, G. (1973) *The Society of the Spectacle*. Zone Books, New York.
De Certeau, M. (1988) *The Practice of Everyday Life*. Translated by S. Rendall. University of New York Press, New York.

Downing, J. (2001) *Radical Media: Rebellious Communication and Social Movements.* Sage, London.

du Gay, P. (2000) Enterprise and its futures: a response to Fournier and Grey. *Organization* 7(1), 165–183.

Edensor, T. (1998) The culture of the Indian street. In: Fyfe, N. (ed.) *Images of the Street: Planning, Identity and Control in Public Space.* Routledge, London, pp. 201–219.

Elmer, G. and Opel, A. (2008) *Preempting Dissent: the Politics of an Inevitable Future.* Arbeiter Ring Publishing, Winnipeg, Manitoba, Canada.

Fearless City Mobile (2010) Available at: http://ahamedia.ca/category/fearless-city-mobile-project/ (accessed 14 May 2013).

Featherstone, M. (1991) *Consumer Culture and Postmodernism.* Sage, London.

Foley, M., McGillivray, D. and McPherson, G. (2011) *Event Policy: From Theory to Strategy.* Routledge, London.

Foucault, M. (1978). *The History of Sexuality, Volume 1: An Introduction.* Pantheon Books, New York.

Frew, M. and McGillivray, D. (2008) Exploring hyper-experiences: performing the fan at Germany 2006. *Journal of Sport & Tourism* 13(3), 181–198.

Getz, D. (2007) *Event Studies: Theory, Research and Policy for Planned Events.* Elsevier, Oxford.

Gilmore, D.D. (1998) *Carnival and Culture.* Yale University Press, London.

Goode, L. (2009) Social news, citizen journalism and democracy. *New Media and Society* 11(8), 1287–1305.

Gotham, K.F. (2005) Tourism gentrification: the case of New Orleans' Vieux Carre (French Quarter). *Urban Studies* 42(7), 1099–1121.

Hall, S. (1980) Cultural studies: two paradigms. *Media, Culture and Society* 2, 57–72.

Hands, J. (2011) *@ is for Activism.* Pluto Press, London.

Holmes, D. (1997) Virtual identity: communities of broadcast, communities of interactivity. In: Holmes, D. (ed.) *Virtual Politics.* Sage, London, pp. 26–45.

International Olympic Committee (IOC) (2010) Olympic Review. No. 74. Available at: http://view.digipage.net/?id=olympicreview74 (accessed 16 August 2011).

Lenskyj, H. (2008) *Olympic Industry Resistance: Challenging Olympic Power and Propaganda.* SUNY Press, New York.

Levinson, P. (2009) *New New Media.* Allyn & Bacon, Boston, Massachusetts.

Lyotard, J.-F. (1984) *The Postmodern Condition: a Report on Knowledge.* Translated by G. Bennignton and B. Massumi. University of Minnesota, St Paul, Minnesota.

McRobbie, A. (1995) *The Uses of Cultural Studies.* Sage, London.

Miah, A. (2010) #media2012: Media Blueprint for London 2012. *Culture @ the Olympics* 12. Available at: http://www.culturalolympics.org.uk/2010/07/media-blueprint-for-the-london-2012-games/ (accessed 11 September 2011).

Miah, A., Gracia, B. and Zhihui, T. (2008) We are the media: non-accredited media centres. In Price, E.M. and Dayan, P. (2008) *Owning the Olympics: Narratives of the New China.* University of Michigan Press, Ann Arbor, Michigan, pp. 452–488.

Miller, P. (1987) *Domination and Power.* Routledge and Kegan Paul, London.

Morozov, E. (2011) *The Net Delusion.* Penguin Books, London.

Petersen, A. (1997) Risk, governance and the new public health. In: Petersen, A. and Bunton, R. (eds) *Foucault, Health and Medicine.* Routledge, London, pp. 189–206.

Real, M. (2007) Sports online: the newest player in media sport. In: Raney, A. and Bryant, J. (eds) *Handbook of Sports and Media.* Lawrence Erlbaum/Routledge, Mahwah, New Jersey, pp. 171–184.

Rheingold, H. (2002) *Smart Mobs: the Next Social Revolution.* Perseus Publishing, Cambridge, Massachusetts.

Roche, M. (2000) *Mega-events and Modernity: Olympics and Expos in the Growth of Global Culture.* Routledge, London.

Rojek, C. (2005) *Leisure Theory: Principles and Practice.* Palgrave Macmillan, Basingstoke, UK.

Rose, N. (1999) *Powers of Freedom.* Cambridge University Press, Cambridge.

Sanjek, D. and Sanjek, R. (1996) *Pennies from Heaven: the American Popular Music Business in the Twentieth Century.* Da Capo Press, New York.

Schechner, R. (1995) *The Future of Ritual: Writings on Culture and Performance.* Routledge, London.

Stevenson, D. (2003) *Cities and Urban Cultures.* Open University Press, Maidenhead, UK.

Tapscott, D. and Williams, A. (2008) *Wikinomics: How Mass Collaboration Changes Everything.* Atlantic, London.

Terranova, T. (2000) Free labor: producing culture for the digital economy. *Social Text* 63, 18(2), 33–58.

True North Media House (TNMH) (2010) Available at: http://web.archive.org/web/20100609183620/http://truenorthmediahouse.com/ (accessed 14 May 2005).

Veyne, P. (1990) *Bread and Circuses: Historical Sociology and Political Pluralism.* Translated by B. Pearce. Penguin, London.

Virilio, P. (2000) *A Landscape of Events.* MIT Press, Cambridge, Massachusetts.

Whitson, D. and Horne, J. (2006) Underestimated costs and overestimated benefits? Comparing the outcomes of sports mega-events in Canada and Japan. *Sociological Review* 54(2), 71–89.

13 Events and Environmental Awareness

Anna Borley,[1]* Debra Wale[2] and Peter Robinson[2]

[1]University of Northampton, Northampton, UK; [2]University of Wolverhampton, Walsall, UK

Introduction

This chapter considers the growth of the sustainability agenda within the events industry, and outlines the change and development in festival ethos towards a 'greener' approach. It argues that festival organizers in the UK are increasingly seeking approaches to engage audiences in sustainable and ethical behaviour, to ensure that the negative impacts of such events are minimized in line with social and political debate of recent years.

It considers that Glastonbury Festival is keen to maintain its green roots and is using green messages to educate a new generation of festival goers in sustainable practices such as recycling. A case study details the results of a semiotic study of Glastonbury's green campaign and its impact upon audience behaviour, providing evidence that, while festivals are effective forums for short-term change in behaviour through green education, securing a legacy of green cultural behaviour is problematic and needs further consideration and ongoing educational initiatives.

The Growth of Environmental Awareness and Sustainability

The last 5 years has seen considerable growth in the number and variety of music festivals in the UK, increasing from 300 in 2007 (Ali-Knight *et al.*, 2008) to an estimated 700 in 2012 (Wood, 2012). Contributing factors to this have been: (i) creation of a festival culture heightened by the change in festival ethos; (ii) changes within the music industry; and (iii) increased audience awareness of festivals due to commercialization and media attention (Long and Robinson, 2004). Modern music festivals can range in typology and genre, from commercial pop festivals like the iTunes Festival, niche festivals such as Cropredy, to family oriented events such as Womad Festival (Ali-Knight *et al.*, 2008).

Due to the growing scale of music festivals, it is vital to recognize the increasing impacts that such events impose on the macro- and micro-environment, and indeed, the pressures of hosting such pivotal events. Music festivals, which attract audiences of any scale, inevitably produce negative environmental impacts, particularly major and mega events where 'the environmental impacts produced by large numbers of people cohabiting in a restricted space become very obvious very quickly' (Ali-Knight *et al.*, 2008).

Until recently, the environmental impacts of events have been ignored, and while the concept of sustainable events is a relatively new concept, authors such as Bowdin *et al.* (2011), Getz (2012) and Goldblatt (2012) trace its history to the original concept of global

*anna.borley@northampton.ac.uk

© CAB International 2013. *Research Themes for Events*
(eds R. Finkel *et al.*)

sustainability, which was developed by the World Commission on Environment and Development (WCED) in 1987. The issue of sustainability has been brought to the forefront of social recognition through government policy, which has derived from the development of the Agenda 21 framework (Getz, 2009). While the concept of 'green issues' is a growing global trend in all aspects of business and day-to-day life, it is only recently that brands have started to take them seriously (Arnold, 2009). According to research published by A Greener Festival (2008), the average festival goer has an increased awareness of the negative impact festivals have on the environment, with 48% of people surveyed in 2008 stating that they would pay more for a greener festival. Therefore, the need for festivals to become more sustainable or even carbon neutral is more important than ever.

Bowdin *et al.* (2011) defines the concept of 'green' or sustainable events as: 'Events that refer to the minimization of negative environmental impacts of their activity, including carbon reduction, waste reduction, recycling and other initiatives that event managers can implement.'

Organizers of music festivals on every scale have recognized the need to develop and implement such activities in the form of sustainability strategies, in order to secure the future of the festival, which will be explored in detail later on in the chapter. In particular, Glastonbury Festival has recognized the need to promote its historic 'green' ethos, and to comply with current sustainability standards (Bowdin *et al.*, 2006). In 2009, 5572 tents were left behind at Glastonbury Festival, along with 2220 camping chairs, 3321 airbeds, 400 gazebos and 6538 sleeping bags, all of which had to be transported to a landfill, at the expense of the festival organizer (A Greener Festival, 2008). In an effort to combat this waste issue, Glastonbury Festival has developed several marketing campaigns over the years, which incorporate 'green' messaging in various guises, in an attempt to influence 'green' behaviour.

Jones (2009) has analysed the changing role that events play within society, and states that 'events need to minimize their environmental impacts and maximize any benefits they can offer to the community and the planet', which supports the ideology that the adoption of sustainability principles can have a wide internal and external impact. Music festivals have, on the whole, acted positively to address the growing pressures of sustainability. Ali-Knight *et al.* (2008) support this in their discussion of new market trends that are evident in the industry at present, some of which suggest that the role of sustainability at music festivals is perhaps more important than profit making, particularly for those festivals who claim to be carbon neutral, or have very minimal negative impacts upon the environment (for example, Shambala Festival). Most UK festivals are adopting a 'green' policy, and some have won awards for their contributions to 'green' practice, with the help of organizations such as A Greener Festival and Julie's Bicycle (Jones, 2009), and some have taken on the responsible role of communicating 'green' messages throughout the whole ethos of their organization, for example, the Big Green Gathering who claim that the festival 'is a celebration of our natural world and our place within it. As such, it is a place for enjoyment, learning and fun' (Big Green Gathering, 2012). In addition to this, Jones (2009) discusses the idea that as a result of adopting a sustainability focus as a festival organizer, ongoing behaviour and attitudes of the audience, contractors, suppliers and the industry as a whole can be influenced. Therefore, the creation of a 'short-term mini-utopia' (Jones, 2009) can leave a lasting legacy and give participants the aspiration to live more sustainably.

Consumerism and Trends in Sustainability

Arnold (2009) has outlined the key trends in consumption of goods and services over recent years, which are key to understanding patterns in ethical behaviour, such as recycling and green travel. While the recent recession has brought about a more frugal attitude in spending, which has been compared to the post-war period, the concepts of 'churn' or 'hyper consumerism' are spreading through the

Western world. Arnold (2009) goes on to state that churn has created a demand for cheap and disposable products, particularly within the retail industry, and raises the question: 'it's all very well having recycling bins, but the question is why we are throwing things away in the first place?' Furthermore, Goldblatt (2012) indicates that cheap tents marketed as 'festival tents' were creating issues for music festivals, as festival goers can afford to leave them behind, creating a huge waste issue. While the government is continually attempting to improve recycling and waste disposal efforts, a change in consumer attitude and behaviour is needed to fully address the issue. Arnold (2009) highlights the use of gestures as an emotional marketing tool to encourage a change in behaviour and engage event audiences with sustainability, such as organizations truthfully demonstrating that they are willing to engage in ethical practice, in order to show the customer the direction to follow.

Greening events

Festivals staged in semi-rural and rural locations may have positive impacts upon the environment by means of raising the awareness and appreciation of the natural landscape. Festival organizers have the ongoing challenge of creating events that meet the needs of the audience, yet embrace sustainability. The biggest contributor to carbon dioxide emissions from a festival is the audience; festivals with large numbers of people cohabiting in a restricted space produce negative environmental impacts very quickly (Ali-Knight et al., 2008). Until recently, the environmental impacts of events have been largely ignored.

It is the negative impacts that are mainly the current focus of research. For example, Allen et al. (2005), Yeoman et al. (2009) and Bowdin et al. (2011) have identified that transport to and from festivals is a major contributor to carbon emissions, especially car travel. Perhaps the most pressing issue for festival organizers is that of transportation to and from the event. Research conducted by the Latitude Festival demonstrates that if festival goers travel alone by car, they are emitting ten

times more carbon than if they travelled to the festival by coach and three-and-a-half times as much carbon as if they travelled by train (Latitude Festival, 2011). The carriage of equipment to and from the festival site is also a large contributor to carbon emissions, which raises the question of whether festival organizers should use local suppliers and locally available equipment.

The Latitude Festival promotes sustainable travel options through: (i) the use of rail networks; (ii) encouraging lift shares; and (iii) promoting bike travel by providing safer bike racks onsite at the festival. Many other festivals now encourage coach travel, and actively encourage festival goers to purchase coach travel packages. In 2006, Glastonbury Festival extended its coach package options by 10,000 to stimulate coach travel to the site (Glastonbury Festival, 2011a), and in 2011, expanded its green travel options to include a package for 'green travellers' who chose to travel via train or coach. Incentives include the exclusive use of solar showers, separate camping areas and food tokens. Festivals based within city locations, such as Summer Sundae, may have found it easier to encourage the use of public transport, due to the infrastructure already being in place. However, festival organizers at greenfield sites may find it more of a challenge to encourage their audiences to use public transport.

Litter and waste are also large contributors to environmental damage from festivals, and large festivals such as Glastonbury will generate significant amounts of litter (Bowdin et al., 2006; Robinson et al., 2010). Onsite litter is not only unsightly but may pose a health hazard to visitors and locals. The challenge that festival organizers face is the method of waste disposal, which is often a major expense (Bowdin et al., 2006; Robinson et al., 2010). Furthermore, festivals like Glastonbury may encounter waste management issues due to tents being left on site after the festival. Greenfield festival sites may also encounter problems with water pollution from waste disposal and carbon emissions from tankers transporting waste water from festival sites (Bowdin et al., 2006). Energy usage may also be seen to be a major concern at festivals owing to the large amount of electricity consumed from musical equipment and lighting. To add to the already expanding list of negative impacts of festivals, physical environmental damage to greenfield sites, particularly land that may be used for farming after the event, and noise pollution are also concerns (Jones, 2009). To address the issues of water pollution, festivals have committed to transporting sewage and waste water offsite, using lagoons as temporary holding facilities, and protecting natural watercourses.

Promoting a culture of environmental awareness

With the ever-growing presence of sustainability and corporate social responsibility (CSR) at the forefront of social and political debate, it can be seen that in addition to providing a platform for social change and education, the role of the festival organizer is to increasingly embrace and promote sustainable practice. Bowdin *et al.* (2006) and Yeoman *et al.* (2009) have suggested that events have been targeted by governments to help promote 'green values', as a way to reach the public and influence attitudes (A Greener Festival, 2008), and, subsequently in recent years, festival organizers have realized the pressures of incorporating such practice into the planning and operational aspects of their events. While legislation did not traditionally require an event to consider such factors, the BS 8901 standard, introduced in November 2007, offers a framework that can be used by event managers to plan for the sustainable outcomes of their event (Jones, 2009).

The Institute of Energy and Sustainable Development (IESD) at De Montfort University has recently recognized that festivals can be an ideal place to educate young people about the effects of climate change and has developed 'Face Your Elephant', which is a research project that aims to measure the impacts of education on people's motivations to become 'greener' (Face Your Elephant, 2011). Many music festivals (such as the Big Green Gathering, as previously discussed) have developed their ethos and culture around the need to provide eco-education and bring about change, and have subsequently created green brands or themes to 'wave the green flag' – thus recognizing the opportunity they can provide to achieve this, both at the event and through its legacy.

The increasing use of green messages at events, in particular music festivals, can be seen to provide a catalyst for events to meet their sustainability agendas and to engage positively with their audiences. Such communication can attempt to change or influence audience behaviour, for example, encouraging the festival goer to recycle or take their camping equipment home with them, and can also arguably influence their behaviour and perceptions of sustainability in the longer term. Jones (2009) supports the idea that festivals play an essential role in fostering change, particularly when it concerns the sustainability agenda, and states that: 'the role of a music festival is a change agent. Knowledge, inspiration and conversation are the most powerful tools.' Therefore, this role should be nurtured by the event organizer to ensure maximum impact and success in engaging audiences and promoting environmental awareness.

While environmental, political and social values are perhaps only a few of the main focuses at modern music festivals, the huge arena of potential engagement that music festivals create, partnered with the growing sustainability agenda, should give festival organizers the motivation to use the opportunities wisely to change audience behaviour and attitudes, as evidenced throughout the chapter.

Case Study: Developing a 'Green Awareness' Culture at Events

The following case study discusses the use of 'green' messages used throughout media campaigns at Glastonbury Music Festival in 2010 and 2011, evaluating the audience's reaction to such messages, and therefore making an assessment as to whether the organizers were successful in developing an awareness of 'green' issues such as recycling and removal of waste.

A semiotic content analysis of the green initiatives and campaigns used by Glastonbury Festival was carried out in 2011 to enable the messages used by festival organizers to be decoded. The study of semiotics is commonly used within mass communications research to analyse and interrogate visual images (Hansen *et al.*, 1998). A series of objective 'signs' were interpreted by the researcher in order to establish the true meaning of images and messages used within the campaigns.

It was noted earlier in the chapter that the effective communication of sustainability initiatives and campaigns is key when attempting to change or influence audience behaviour and perceptions. According to Jones (2009), a combination of marketing theory and consumer psychology should be used by music festival organizers to fully assess the 'personality' of the audience and to thus design the 'green' messages and sustainability initiatives to fit and make the maximum impact.

The case study examines the use of traditional marketing communications models examined by Masterman and Wood (2005) and Pickton and Broderick (2005). More specifically, hierarchy of effects concepts, which outline the 'journey' that the consumer takes in order for an action to be provoked, were applied to the decision-making processes of the festival audience. AIDA and DAGMAR models specifically refer to a call to 'action' rather than intent to purchase a good or service and are therefore most relevant to the study that examines behaviour rather than consumption of a product.

Glastonbury Festival, established in the early 1970s, has grown from a small, free, hippie festival with 12,000 attendees (Glastonbury Festival, 2011b) to a festival that attracts a mass audience of over 170,000 attendees (Richards and Palmer, 2011). Glastonbury is keen to promote its historic green roots (Bowdin *et al.*, 2011), which are reflected in its core values (see Box 13.1). Now it is using marketing methods to comply with new and existing environmental standards and entrench sustainability within the cultural core of the festival, as owing to its expansion it recognizes the significant impact that it has upon the physical environment (Bowdin *et al.*, 2011).

> **Box 13.1.** Glastonbury core values (Glastonbury Festival, 2011c).
>
> The Festival is committed to support environmental and humanitarian charities and projects, and to assist local causes and groups. This commitment is central to the culture and values of the festival.

In the effort to combat waste issues, Glastonbury Festival organizers have developed marketing campaigns incorporating 'green messages'. These are expected to influence subsequent behaviour, while at the festival and beyond, and to enforce the branding of Glastonbury as a green festival.

As Glastonbury Festival is still one of the UK's largest and most renowned music events, the organizers have taken on an increasing responsibility to lead the way in issues of sustainability, and cannot assume that their audience will automatically share the same levels of environmental concern. While Glastonbury Festival does not endorse commercial sponsorship, the organizers have increasingly recognized that the event itself provides an ideal opportunity to promote its charitable causes, such as Oxfam and WaterAid, and in recent years, have used similar platforms to promote sustainability initiatives that have been adopted by the festival. Advertising, promotional campaigns, initiatives and branding are being used to encourage a change in audience behaviour, and to promote a greener, sustainable approach to festival participation.

Green campaigns

Two green campaigns were identified as the focus for the 2011 festival, which took place in June. The first campaign was predominantly film-based and had been running in the same guise since 2010. Short films were produced to communicate the issue of taking camping waste home. They included a logo depicting the key message 'Please take it home again' (see Fig. 13.1) to ensure that the key messages were memorable and had an impact on the audience.

Fig. 13.1. 'Please take it home again' logo: Glastonbury Green Campaign 2011.

They were shared with the festival audience using the official Glastonbury Festival website and were transmitted during music intervals on the main stages and on social networking sites across the duration of the festival. The motivation for the campaign stemmed from 2009 when the festival organizers battled with record amounts of campsite waste left behind by festival goers, including tents, airbeds and gazebos. It was hoped that displaying images of the 2009 event would highlight the increasing cost of landfill tax and its environmental implications (Julie's Bicycle, 2011). Findings revealed a year-on-year difference in the use of the logo and the message in the green 'signals' communicated to the audience via the films.

In 2010, the film used more elements in its production, including: (i) moving images of abandoned camping equipment such as tents and gazebos; (ii) a 'child-like' limerick (used in humour but with a serious message about consequences); (iii) powerful backing music; and (iv) text displaying a series of 'waste facts' from the 2009 festival. Overall, the film appeared to display a complex series of 'signs', including: (i) notions of destroying the natural landscape; (ii) the importance of preserving the environment for future generations; and (iii) feelings of guilt, abandonment and disrespect for the festival site and surrounding environment. The impact of the overall message was achieved through the use of the key 'strap-line': 'Please take it home'.

The film produced for the 2011 festival contained fewer visual elements and had a slightly less hard-hitting tone. This could have been a result of the fact that the 2010 waste audit demonstrated an improvement in camping waste left behind from 2009. The use of the same logo, which signifies connotations of nature, wilderness and even heritage, is in tune with the overall ethos and culture of the festival; therefore, subtleties of language and imagery could have a positive effect on the audience (Jones, 2009).

Analysis of the message portrayed in both films supports traditional marketing communications models and reveals how Glastonbury Festival organizers entice their audience to 'think, feel and do', which are common outputs of the implementation of hierarchy of effects models such as DAGMAR, whereby the aims of the campaign are to remind the audience of the negative environmental impacts to invoke feelings of guilt and responsibility. In terms of encouraging an 'action' from the audience, which could relate to individuals taking part in recycling, taking their tent home with them, or travelling to the festival using public transport, findings from an interview with festival organizers revealed that incentives to reward the audience are being developed. Therefore, while the organizers have not set out to develop their campaign aim and objectives through the use of such conceptual models, their ideas bear the characteristics of a campaign that has made use of a typical hierarchy of effects model to ensure the consumer is taken through the various emotive stages to reach an action.

The second campaign used by the festival focused on green travel to and from the festival site, which was communicated to the audience via the official website, and via a leaflet sent to all ticket holders. Festival goers were encouraged to participate in green travel by using public transport or a bicycle scheme and were given incentives, which included: (i) sole use of solar showers for green travellers; (ii) access to compost toilets; and (iii) discounts on food and festival merchandise.

Most communications campaigns are undertaken in the hope that action will be invoked (Habermas, 1990, cited in Hansen, 1993) and, therefore, research conducted to examine the type of actions undertaken was able to determine the approach that the festival organization adopted to reach their audience and to encourage them to use green transport methods. Findings demonstrated that while the green traveller information revealed a small number of characteristics of communicative action, the majority of characteristics of the campaign resembled a strategic action campaign, which commonly uses influence and manipulation to achieve goals. This is evidenced through the indicative content of the leaflet, which focused on providing incentives for the green traveller rather than working to reach a joint consensus on how greener travel can be achieved. While it is evident that the festival organizers made some attempt to understand the inconvenience of using public transport to reach a greenfield festival site, their main focus was to incentivize the action to make it more appealing.

In comparison, the two campaigns used very different methods of audience communication. While the campaign to encourage festival goers to take their camping waste home used a progression of shock tactics, empathy and 'hard-hitting' facts, the green traveller initiative focused on incentives and making the act of green travel look more appealing to the audience. This demonstrates that a range of green messages, initiatives and campaigns, from basic marketing theory to consumer behaviour psychology, can be used in a variety of ways in order to provoke action and attempt to change or influence the way in which the audience behaves during the festival (Jones, 2009).

It has been demonstrated so far that music festivals such as Glastonbury are increasingly using 'green messages' to promote sustainable behaviour through the implementation of a variety of initiatives and campaigns, from recycling, to green travel to and from the festival site. While the 'encoding' of messages used to encourage this type of behaviour at a major UK music festival has been analysed, it is important to also assess the audience reaction to the messages in order to establish whether the audience 'de-codes' the messages effectively and whether this has an impact on their behaviour during the festival.

Audience behaviour and attitude towards green travel and recycling

Research was conducted with a representative sample of the audience of Glastonbury Festival in June 2011 to determine attitudes and behaviour towards recycling and green travel. Several questions in the online survey focused on the assessment of current behaviour and attitudes towards green travel and recycling in order to assess whether the audience were already receptive to 'green messages' and to consider whether the festival was already 'preaching to the converted'.

In terms of recycling behaviour, the majority of respondents revealed that they always recycled, and when asked about their 'normal' attitude to travelling via 'green means' (public transport), the majority of respondents 'sometimes' travelled via public transport. Therefore, findings demonstrate that 'normal' audience behaviour and attitude towards recycling is reasonably responsible, which is reinforced by recent strategies to increase household, corporate and city-wide recycling. In comparison to recycling behaviour, respondents did not seem to be as committed to green travel, which could be linked to the perceived benefits, costs and availability of green travel options, compared with widely available recycling options. Further questions assessing audience attitude towards recycling and green travel indicated that the 'normal day-to-day' behaviour of the surveyed festival goers was already accepting of green practices, and, in most cases, festival goers were recycling and travelling in a 'green manner' wherever possible.

Audience green behaviour while at the festival

Respondents were asked a series of questions related to their 'green' behaviour while at the music festival. It was revealed that 38% of the sample travelled to the festival by car with three or more passengers, and 29% travelled by car with two or fewer passengers. The 'travel by car' category represented the majority of respondents with 20% travelling by public transport (coach, lift share or train). Therefore, findings demonstrate that there is still a long way to go when encouraging festival goers to adopt a greener attitude towards travel, which raises the same concerns that Allen *et al.* (2005), Yeoman *et al.* (2009) and Bowdin *et al.*

(2011) have regarding transport (especially car travel) to and from festivals as a major contributor to carbon emissions.

In terms of the audience's intention to recycle and take their camping equipment home with them, compared with their actual action, the majority of respondents did fulfil their intentions. Of the 96% of respondents who intended taking their camping equipment home with them, 87% did; and of the 87% of respondents who intended to recycle during the festival, 67% did. Respondents who did not recycle or take their camping equipment home stated various reasons for not doing so, including: (i) reducing the amount they needed to carry from the festival site; (ii) difficult weather conditions; (iii) unusable camping equipment; (iv) lack of supply of recycling bags; and (v) over-flowing recycling bins. This perhaps indicates that self-convenience may be the key consideration for a small minority of festival goers, who may make the decision not to recycle and take camping equipment home as it is an inconvenience to them.

Furthermore, secondary research findings indicated that in order for individuals to feel motivated to take action, they must have a 'transforming experience' (Hover and Van Mierlo, 2006, cited in Getz, 2009), which is gained from an emotional reaction to stimulus and a recall of the emotion. As earlier findings indicated, the 2010 campaign provoked a more emotive reaction resulting in feelings of guilt. This may have influenced a positive reaction to the campaign, resulting in a more successful waste audit than 2011 results. In contrast to this, motivation to recycle and take waste and camping equipment home may have been severely affected by the bad weather conditions at the 2011 festival, as opposed to the hot weather experienced for the duration of the 2010 event.

Audience interpretation of green messages and campaigns

When examining audience awareness of the green campaigns, initiatives and messages in the earlier part of the case study, 82% of respondents had been made aware of the 'take it home again' campaign before the festival, and 85% on average were made aware of green travel schemes before the festival, demonstrating a successful and effective campaign in terms of awareness. A further 12% were made aware of the 'take it home again' campaign during the festival, and, on average, 7% were made aware of the green travel schemes during the course of the festival. It can be seen that the festival organizers were more effective in raising awareness before the festival, which is essential in terms of encouraging green travellers to make their purchase decisions before they buy their tickets. In terms of raising awareness of the importance of taking camping equipment home again after the festival, the festival should be able to maintain, if not increase, the amount of people who are made aware of the initiative over the duration of the festival, as the behavioural change will take place after the festival rather than beforehand.

Respondents who had been made aware of green travel initiatives and the 'Please take it home again' campaign were asked to comment on how they were made aware of the campaigns and their perceived effectiveness. The festival's official website was responsible for raising the majority of awareness. Social media was also responsible for raising awareness of both initiatives with other communication methods such as e-mail, websites and leaflets sent with tickets playing a small part in raising awareness. While the audience were made aware of such campaigns, it was important to investigate whether the initiatives had achieved attitude and behavioural change.

Findings demonstrate the majority of respondents (72%) did not believe that the green travel campaign changed their attitude and behaviour. Furthermore, survey questions investigating the audience opinion of the incentives used to reward green travel demonstrated that they were predominantly ineffective. The use of incentives may be appealing to one segment of the audience, perhaps those seeking value for money or those who do not have any other means of transport. However, those who normally travel to the festival by car (67% of those surveyed) may see such incentives as inadequate when compared with the benefits of travelling by car.

Considerations should also be made to the barriers to communication that may have affected the festival audience, thus influencing the overall effectiveness of the key messages. Utilizing the model of the communication process (Pickton and Broderick, 2005; Dibb and Simkin, 2010), 'noise' or interruptions from stimuli such as bands and other forms of entertainment formed a communication barrier, having an impact upon the communication of messages at the festival; for example, the 'Please take it home again' film did not have a huge impact. However, the same cannot be said for stimulus when browsing the web and in particular, social networking sites, which were found to be successful in communicating key messages. Therefore, it may be concluded that stimulus or 'noise' itself is not the sole barrier. Festival audiences may be more receptive to messages before the event due to the fact that they are not yet fully immersed in the festival experience until they arrive at the festival.

The respondents who were aware of the 'Please take it home again' campaign were asked to give their opinions on whether the messages in the film footage were effective in changing audience behaviour. Findings demonstrated that the majority of respondents felt shocked by the footage but believed that they would have taken their equipment home with them anyway. These findings demonstrate and confirm that the majority of respondents were already practising 'green' behaviour and would have acted responsibly even if they had not seen the film footage. It could then be argued that the festival organizers do not necessarily need to promote this type of behaviour, as their audiences are already acting responsibly. However, as there is still a percentage of the audience who do not take their camping equipment home with them, it is still deemed to be the responsibility of the festival organizers to ensure they are attempting to reach the types of people who do not already practise such behaviour. Therefore, 34% of people who were willing to change their behaviour after seeing the film footage compared with 9% who would not change should be deemed a successful campaign.

Findings from the qualitative content analysis indicated that the key message of the 2011 film footage was to motivate and empower the audience to take responsibility for their actions. The majority of respondents, who were asked to interpret the key message in the film, agreed that the film was promoting and communicating a need for the audience to take responsibility for taking their camping equipment home with them, demonstrating that the audience decoded the messages effectively. Of the respondents, 33% also felt that the film was focusing on the negative environmental impacts, which was evident from the encoded images and sounds from the content analysis.

Effectiveness of communication

The final questions in the online survey focused on the overall effectiveness of green messages that were communicated to the audience. The majority of respondents felt that the overall communication of green messages was effective, compared with a small proportion who thought they were ineffective. That 23% of respondents were unsure perhaps indicates that some methods of communication did not promote messages effectively.

When asked what would convince the audience to recycle, travel in a green manner to the festival and take their camping equipment home with them, incentives were the most popular choice, followed by social media campaigns and the continued use of film footage. As these types of communication are already being used before and during the festival, it can only be assumed that continued use and perhaps improvement of the initiatives (for example more appealing incentives) could all be used to try and influence audience behaviour.

In conclusion, the festival appears to be successful in engaging with its audience through the use of the official website, social media and onsite film footage, all of which have had varying degrees of success in terms of making the audience aware of green messages and actually changing their behaviour.

Recycling behaviour already seems to be practised by the festival audience, and the festival organizers should ensure that they are facilitating the engagement in green behaviour. The challenging aspects of sustainability for the festival organizers include convincing their audience to move away from 'convenient' behaviour such as car travel and leaving cheap camping equipment behind due to walking distances or the condition of equipment after it has endured weather conditions. Therefore, festival organizers should perhaps turn their attention to ensuring that green messages address such issues not only before but also during the festival to gain maximum impact and remind the audience that such initiatives are in place. Such measures may include incentives for participation in schemes to ensure no camping equipment is left behind, better incentives to entice car users to give up their 'privileges' and ensuring festival goers do not have to endure lengthy journeys while carrying all of their camping equipment. Hover and Van Mierlo (2006, cited in Getz, 2009) indicate that a 'transforming experience' inevitably leads to a long-term change in attitude and behaviour. Findings for the majority of the campaigns indicate that the festival 'experience' was not 'transforming' enough to provoke short-term action; therefore, a legacy of green behaviour will require alternative strategies.

Conclusion

The UK festival industry has undergone rapid growth with the number of festivals increasing by 133% in the last 5 years. This has inevitably led to an increase in audience size, coupled with the negative environmental impacts associated with their attendance behaviour, such as transportation – a major contributor to carbon emissions. UK festivals such as Glastonbury, Latitude, Big Green Gathering and Bestival have all recognized the need to be 'green', to minimize negative environmental impacts, and to address the sustainability agenda – corporate sustainability policies detail their intentions to fulfil their commitment to social responsibility and sustainability in event management. Some festivals are actively implementing these policies.

Festivals have attempted to engage festival goers in the concept of sustainability by communicating 'green' values and educating audiences in 'green' practices such as introducing campaigns with a series of 'green messages', which have become entrenched within the culture and ethos of the festival, for example, the famous 'Love the Farm, Leave no Trace' campaign at Glastonbury Festival. Many other major UK music festivals have followed suit by providing 'green messengers' to work on site at the event to promote the message and ethos.

Research into audience behaviour investigated the impact that marketing campaigns have had upon festival goers, providing behavioural insight for the future marketing and management of festivals. Furthermore, research and research findings will continue to evolve as the culture of festival goers, and event audiences more widely, are changed through communication by the event organizers and as a result of the changing norms, values and beliefs of the audience community through education.

Research among festival audiences will always be challenging, not least because it is hard to attain a representative sample from such large audience numbers, but a number of studies have made an attempt to establish baseline data for future studies. It is noted in Chapter 5 that greater research is needed around behaviours, motivations and audience attendance at festivals and at many other events. This is equally true of issues around culture and the ethical positions of audience members. The need to institutionalize the 'green' paradigm is frequently highlighted by theorists, which can perhaps enforce festival organizers and others in the event sector, into taking sustainability issues seriously. Allied to this is the need to understand how much this view on sustainability is embodied by different event audiences and how short-term behaviour can become a legacy of action, therefore supporting the need for continued research to study cultural change at events.

There is a clear culture of environmental awareness in the festival sector, which is yet to be transferred to other sectors of the events industry. It is perhaps important to recognize that the biggest issue concerning sustainability is overcoming the social barriers that are created when people think of climate change, simply owing to a lack of understanding of the issues or the science behind it.

Questions for Students

1. Critically analyse the methods used in the case study to manage environmental issues.
2. Critically evaluate the research findings outlined in the case study. How else can festival organizers seek to influence awareness and adoption of 'green' behaviour?

Further Reading

Getz, D. (2009) Policy for sustainable and responsible events: institutionalisation of a new paradigm. *Journal of Policy Research in Tourism, Leisure and Events* 1, 61–78.
Robinson, P., Wale, D. and Dickson, G. (eds) (2010) *Event Management*. CAB International, Wallingford, UK.
Robinson, P., Heitmann, S. and Dieke, P. (eds) (2011) *Research Themes in Tourism*. CAB International, Wallingford, UK.

References

A Greener Festival (2008) 2008 Summary of Research Headlines. Available at: http://www.agreenerfestival.com/2011/12/new-website-for-agreenerfestival-dot-com/ (accessed 3 February 2012).
Ali-Knight, J., Robertson, M., Fyall, A. and Ladkin, A. (2008) *International Perspectives of Festivals and Events: Paradigms of Analysis*. Elsevier, London.
Allen, J., O'Toole, W., McDonnell, I. and Harris, R. (2005) *Festival and Special Event Management*. Wiley, Chichester, UK.
Arnold, C. (2009) *Ethical Marketing and the New Consumer*. Wiley, Chichester, UK.
Big Green Gathering (2012) Available at: http://www.big-green-gathering.com/ (accessed 3 February 2012).
Bowdin, G., Allen, J., O'Toole, W., Harris, R. and McDonnell, I. (2006) *Events Management*, 2nd edn. Elsevier, Oxford.
Bowdin, G., Allen, J., O'Toole, W., Harris, R. and McDonnell, I. (2011) *Events Management*, 3rd edn. Elsevier, Oxford.
Dibb, S. and Simkin, L. (2010) *Marketing Essentials*. Cengage Learning EMEA, Andover, UK.
Face your Elephant (2011) What We Do/Society. Available at: http://faceyourelephant.org/explore/society (accessed 27 September 2011).
Getz, D. (2009) Policy for sustainable and responsible events: institutionalisation of a new paradigm. *Journal of Policy Research in Tourism, Leisure and Events* 1, 61–78.
Getz, D. (2012) *Event Studies: Theory, Research and Policy for Planned Events*, 2nd edn. Butterworth-Heinemann, Oxford.
Glastonbury Festival (2011a) Green Traveller Initiative. Glastonbury Festival, Glastonbury. Available at: http://www.glastonburyfestivals.co.uk/information/green-glastonbury/green-traveller-initiative (accessed 27 September 2011).
Glastonbury Festival (2011b) History. Glastonbury: Glastonbury Festival. Available at: http://www.glastonburyfestivals.co.uk/history/1971/ (accessed 27 September 2011).
Glastonbury Festival (2011c) Involvement with Charities and Local Organisations. Glastonbury Festival, Glastonbury. Available at: http://www.glastonburyfestivals.co.uk/_assets/pdf/educational-resources/28BeneficiaryCharities.pdf (accessed 20 September 2011).
Goldblatt, S. (2012) *The Complete Guide to Greener Meetings and Events*. Wiley, Hoboken, New Jersey.
Hansen, A. (1993) *The Mass Media and Environmental Issues*. Leicester University Press, Leicester, UK.
Hansen, A., Cottle, S., Negrine, R. and Newbold, C. (1998) *Mass Communications Research Methods*. Palgrave Macmillon, Basingstoke, UK.

Jones, M. (2009) *Sustainable Event Management: a Practical Guide*. Earthscan, London.

Julie's Bicycle (2011) Julie's Bicycle. Available at: http://www.juliesbicycle.com/resources/case-studies/festivals/glastonbury (accessed 27 September 2011).

Latitude Festival (2011) Latitude Green. Southwold: The Latitude Festival. Available at: http://www.latitudefestival.com/information/travel (accessed 27 September 2011).

Long, P. and Robinson, M. (2004) *Festivals and Tourism: Marketing, Management and Evaluation*. Business Education Publishers, Sunderland, UK.

Masterman, G. and Wood, E. (2005) *Innovative Marketing Communications for the Events Industry*. Butterworth-Heinemann, Oxford.

Pickton, D. and Broderick, A. (2005) *Integrated Marketing Communications*. Prentice Hall, Upper Saddle River, New Jersey.

Richards, G. and Palmer, R. (2010) *Eventful Cities*. Butterworth-Heinemann, Oxford.

Robinson, P., Wale, D. and Dickson, G. (eds) (2010) *Event Management*. CAB International, Wallingford, UK.

Wood, Z. (2012) Vince Power's Music Festivals Company Prepares to Call in Administrators. Available at: http://www.guardian.co.uk/business/2012/sep/24/vince-power-music-festivals-administrators (accessed 17 May 2013).

Yeoman, I., Robertson, M., Ali-Knight, J., Drummond, S. and McMahon-Beattie, U. (2009) *Festivals and Event Management: an International Arts and Culture Perspective*. Butterworth-Heinemann, Oxford.

14 Events and Technology

Malcolm Foley* and Gordon Hunt

University of the West of Scotland, Paisley, UK

Introduction

This chapter considers the relationships between events and technology and the research implications of conceptualizing these within actor-network theory (ANT). As part of the act of problematizing themes in events research, this approach requires a reconsideration of what is to be considered to be knowledge about events that can be legitimately pursued as well as the process of this pursuit and the outcomes of these acts. The approach brings human and technology interactions to the fore in the delivery of an event, or a series, such as the Formula One championships, and focuses upon the isolation and description of the various elements and their relationships in a network. It recognizes that these are neither static, nor limited in either time or space. The chapter offers its case study, the Formula One championships, as an extension of the ontological and epistemological implications of the approach taken to events and technologies.

Research on the role, purpose and impact of various technologies on the events and festivities sector of local, national and international economies tends to envisage relationships that privilege the 'human' but simultaneously display technological determinism. In these accounts, technologies have often been said to drive, lead or cause changes to delivery, consumption and regulation of events. There is a tendency for people to be seen as

either small in number, as active innovators and inventors of technologies, or a much larger mass of passive consumers who are relatively docile in their acceptance of their changing technological environment at events – and of the concomitant implications upon other aspects of their exposure. These, relatively functional, considerations of events and festivity have had significant impact upon analyses and understandings of 'events management', 'events policy' or 'events studies' within specific ontological and epistemological paradigms. Of course, such analyses are often presented as the dominant (and 'common sense') preoccupations of government and, unsurprisingly then, of academics and policy makers working to meet governments' information needs and investment decisions. Understandings of economic impacts, community developments or state intervention strategies are regularly the information outcomes of these types of studies.

While research and published work in these traditions do not ignore globalization and other international strategic considerations in their analysis, these are often 'peripheral' to the main preoccupations of the work. They can be extrinsic pressures bearing upon events and festivals (e.g. in the form of potential reductions in ideas and practices of community, or in user expectations of mediatisation, which sit uncomfortably alongside desires for authenticity), or pressures to increase throughputs of (usually non-local)

*malcolm.foley@uws.ac.uk

© CAB International 2013. *Research Themes for Events*
(eds R. Finkel *et al.*)

consumers towards broadly economic touristic 'benefits' for cities and regions (with further implications for community, authenticity or communications mechanisms). Yet the technologies that appear to have the most significant impacts upon the experience of contemporary events and festivity are: (i) global in their gestation and reach; (ii) unavoidable for many users and organizers; and (iii) increasingly central to the meanings and purposes of events. Further, technologies from outside the specific moments of event delivery can have implications for everything from the possibility of bringing an international audience to an event, to the actualities of what is to count as the event (and in the eyes of some, what it should be).

Thus, in addressing the task of preparing a chapter entitled 'Events and Technology' for a book entitled *Research Themes for Events*, we were conscious of the need to consider the relationships between events and technologies in a way that privileged neither element of the title (titles of, say, 'technology in events' or 'event technologies' could have produced a radically different chapter) and problematized the sets of relationships between, and among, each. Essentially, posing questions about the connections between events (perceived as predominantly social constructions) and technology (perceived as predominantly a by-product of scientific inquiry) raises more fundamental issues about the separation of 'science' and 'society'. This conceptual discontinuity, 'the idea that there is a special scientific method, a realm where truth prospers in the absence of power, is a myth' (Callon *et al.*, 1986) is especially problematical in a book about research, some of which elevates the 'scientific' method. These authors continue by adding that, for too long, scholars have 'been content to simplify the heterogeneous links that tie the "scientific" and the "technological" to the rest of the social world.'

For us, this required a different way of theorizing about essentiality of events, about the research questions that might be asked, and about the kinds of outcomes that a research project might elicit – that is, there are ontological and epistemological considerations that often remain unexplored. We have attempted to resolve this by adapting ANT to the field, encouraging a re-conceptualization of events and technology as one in which these relationships are centred as the locus of inquiry and the focus of research questions and outcomes. This view was given added impetus by the requirement to produce a 'case study' as part of the chapter; the case study commonly being both an approach and an outcome, of ANT.

Re-conceptualizing Events and Technology

To a large extent, events comprise a series of habits and procedures that are self-sustaining and that involve clusters of human and non-human (including technological) actors (more correctly, *actants*) performing sets of relations. In turn, while they continue to be performed, these relations will create both actual and symbolic meaning. Both users and generators of events and festivities have long networked with technologies to create and recreate meanings that can be characterized as 'events' or 'festivity'. In describing the connections between the mediators of an event, the actants crucial to its performance, we seek to describe the social situations that can comprise individual events and locate those that appear to be the most prominent within the network.

In researching an object such as Formula One, we are conscious that it appears as a single entity, a 'black box', which embodies both unity and complexity. The first of these is apparent in the naming of a what comprises a network of motor races, circuits, drivers, cars, teams, sponsors, mediated spectacles, advertising, prizes and all of the relationships between them as a single element – Formula One. The second is apparent in the 'unpacking' of the box when opened into the elements cited in the previous sentence (and more) and exposing each individually as well as the networks between them. We have chosen to consider Formula One because of the evident role of technology in its formation and development as a sporting, a consumer and a media spectacle, characterized by 'events' called Grands Prix. Cars, circuits, drivers, communications and competition each act as powerful transmitters of technologies and then interact with themselves and with other actants, such as spectators, television (TV) viewers, commentators and enhanced local communications from remote parts of the circuits to perform the events. The relationships between the elements isolated above and the further networks of Grands Prix deliver together the Drivers' and the Constructors' Championships that are the essential elements that become the focus of those networks throughout the Formula One season. Each race meeting, each racing team, each season and each championship are repeatedly performed and then dismantled on an apparently endless (and sometimes contradictory) continuation of shifting rules, attempts to improve safety, higher speed in lap times, handling and comfort enhancements and heightened experiences for all involved. There is a persistent and almost inevitable expectation of 'progress' in each of these elements, and in many other aspects of Formula One, which serves to sustain a viable market for continued investment, highly lucrative sponsorship, periodic selling of media rights and frenzied spectator and viewer expectations. So the networks of material items (largely technologies) integrate with the symbolic environment (meanings attributed by people to, for example, the events; the branding of the cars, the teams, the drivers; the keenness of competition) to simultaneously become the single 'black box' of 'Formula One'. The spectator, whether at the circuit or beyond it, may be easily marginalized from many of these elements of Formula One. The complex network, when seen as Formula One, becomes more than the sum of each of its (invisible) parts – it is punctualized and the 'visibility' of the network is reduced to a seemingly simple action. It is suggested that only when punctualization breaks down does the actor-network become obvious, visible or even relevant. A car, which is a complex actor network, is very little understood by the average driver until it ceases to function. At that point, the driver becomes only too well aware of the performance of the actor-network via its many separate components and their interactions – for example the engine, the maker's warranty, the promise of reliability embodied in the brand,

etc. A Grand Prix event can be most easily punctualized (and turned into a case study) analytically when it is not performed precisely as it is expected that it will be by its 'fans' (who themselves are part of the actor-network, of course). But Grands Prix (like many events that repeat over space and time within a brand framework) are relatively easily punctualized and can be replicated across the globe as part of a wider network consisting of the Formula One franchise and its various championships.

Actors and Actants

Before turning to a consideration of Formula One as a case study, it may be useful to consider how a vocabulary of events and technology within the network of actors and actants may be proposed. How can an event or a festival be researched from the perspective of a series of connections? Knowledge production in the post-Enlightenment orthodoxy tends to view dichotomies between people and physical objects, to distinguish between the natural world and the realm of human-produced culture. In viewing the object of inquiry as 'merely' a series of associations that are constantly being re-engineered and in which none is privileged over another is to see it as a set of relationships between participants – some human, others not. A phenomenon such as Formula One comes into being in the various and continuous interplay between the actors and actants and that network is itself also an actor in the process. Human agency is seen as greater than that which can be ascribed to any individual entities (actor or actant) – the source of agency is the relationship between them.

Voicing meanings as defined by the actors (and the spokespeople for actants) through case study

In attempting to construct a case study based upon these theoretical positions, it becomes imperative to identify the actors (which will be used from now onwards to indicate both actors and actants). In our analysis, it is clear that there are a number of factors that lead to the kind of apparent 'breakdown' that can enable punctualization, for example: (i) increasing interest, but simultaneous reductions, in local spectatorship; (ii) crises of legitimacy for some race circuits – whether 'traditional' but unable to meet financial demands, or 'recent' and unable to generate democratic local interest; (iii) continued questions about ownership of the franchise of Formula One itself; and (iv) races that are 'processional' with very few winning teams. That is not to say that Formula One is 'broken' – merely that current circumstances present opportunities for analysis and evaluation. It is acknowledged, of course, that the context of the circumstances will have a significant bearing upon the analysis.

Central to the meaning of Formula One are the *drivers* (for whom there is a championship based upon individual performance in races) and the *constructors* (i.e. the teams, for which there is also a championship) of the cars, who could be said to 'voice' the *cars*. The technological and cultural significance of the cars continues to preoccupy a number of commentators, with elements such as the aesthetics of the vehicles, their safety, comfort and performance features and their relationships with particular drivers through the *history of the sport* (e.g. from Lotus and Jim Clark in the 1960s through Ayrton Senna at McLaren in the 1980s to Ferrari and Michael Schumacher in the 2000s) playing greater or lesser significance at certain times. Features such as the onset of *sponsorship* of the teams (starting in the late 1960s with a cigarette manufacturer sponsoring the, then, successful Lotus team) and the regulation of that sponsorship in some nation states (the initial 'banning' of tobacco sponsorship by the UK). All of these operate within a highly regulated *network of governance* (the Fédération Internationale de l'Automobile, FIA), covering both *championships* and in which each of the above has a role, but for which there are key spokespeople and/or 'owners' of the franchise. Grands Prix races take place on *circuits*, the number, ownership and geographical spread of which has shifted over time, perhaps reflecting a combination of political and market forces and the growth of interest in the championships.

That growth of interest has coincided with significant *media* coverage, which has, itself, grown in scale, scope and penetration – particularly with the advent of technologies and *devices* that close the gap between consumers/spectators/fans and the event itself. Global communications organizations bid for the TV rights to screen Formula One and there are several magazines, many with online content, devoted almost entirely to Formula One. *Spectatorship* has declined in some localities, sometimes associated with changes in circuits or the onset of newer, safer but, allegedly, less 'exciting' races. Nevertheless, local circuit owners and stakeholders have an obvious, vested interest in managing and delivering a live experience that ranks with other national sporting occasions. Enhancing technologies available at (and beyond) circuits can help them achieve this. Developers and manufacturers of games (from Waddington's board game 'Formula One' offering cardboard dashboards and circuits in the 1960s to current offerings on several platforms giving extremely life-like visual experiences via TV) have long seen the attraction of Formula One and have exploited opportunities to replicate the Formula One experience in the homes of their consumers across various technologies. Finally, each Grand Prix has a '*heritage*' of varying *provenance*. Some stretch unbroken into a distant past in the early to mid-20th century, others have disappeared and re-appeared, while yet more are of very recent vintage. Sometimes, but not always, this has to do with particular circuits (e.g. Silverstone in Britain, Spa in Belgium, Monza in Italy, Nürburgring in Germany, the streets of Monaco) and the attachment of spectator-fans to the heritage of these places – largely a matter of authenticity. Clearly, some circuits built more recently, and in nation states where the heritage of Grand Prix racing is less of a factor in national consciousness, have less of a fan base upon which to build local loyalties or touristic experiences for spectators. However, the totality of the network of 'heritage' and recently designed circuits of city streets (Singapore now offers a 'night' Grand Prix through its city streets, almost echoing some films and video games) presents a series of challenges that test the relationships and distances between fans, technologies, the drivers and those presenting coverage of the events.

Thus, a viable case study would need to validate the elements and demonstrate the relationships of, at least, the following: (i) the drivers; (ii) the constructors; (iii) the cars; (iv) governance and regulation; (v) the championships; (vi) the sponsors; (vii) the circuits; (viii) 'live' spectators and their changing experiences; (ix) media and games interests and representations of the sport; (x) 'fans' of the sport who connect via a plurality of live and media opportunities and devices; (xi) the heritage of all of the above; and (xii) the known history of the sport in the context of the geopolitics of nation states in the mid- to late 20th century onwards. The influence and actions within these networks of key individuals and institutions would also be an important element to consider. Critical is the demonstration that these are not a simply a series of individual, structural factors but that they are networked as a consequence of their actions and interactions into an inescapable 'black box' that can be characterized as the contemporary phenomenon that is Formula One. When that box is opened and the elements and networks exposed, what ensues, what predominates?

Case Study – Formula One

The Formula One World Championship began in 1950. The initial championship consisted of seven races compared with the 20 scheduled races of the 2012 championship. In the early years races were predominantly in Europe with a single race in North America. In the 21st century races are held worldwide with a growing emphasis on emerging economies and the Middle East, although the fan base remains predominantly European. The immense financial demands involved in building a circuit and paying the fees for holding the race have favoured countries with significant government funding available or where finance is available from emerging business sectors even when these countries tend to have a limited local fan base.

Perhaps more so than other sports, the Formula One fan base in Britain tends to separate into two main groups: (i) long-term fans with an interest in all aspects of the sport; and (ii) fans attracted by the success of a particular driver. Thus, in the UK, the popularity of the sport has increased in phases, often related to the success of British drivers, in particular James Hunt's victory in the 1976 championship, the 'Mansell mania' of the early 1990s culminating in his 1992 championship victory and the subsequent career of Damon Hill who was champion in 1996. A further surge of interest was heralded by Lewis Hamilton's entry into the sport in 2007, followed by his 2008 championship victory. Long-term fans divide into groups more interested in the technical engineering aspects of the sport and those more interested in the racing itself, although these groups overlap. In essence fans combine an appreciation for the technical innovation of the cars and the skill of the drivers with a visceral pleasure in the speed and spectacle of the races themselves. The 'fan experience' of Formula One has changed radically in the last decade as a result of technological developments. This falls into two main areas: (i) the experience at the event; and (ii) the experiencing of the event through the media.

Event structure

A Formula One event takes place across a 3-day period, comprising a day of 'practice', a day of 'qualifying' and the day of the race itself. Fans may attend for all 3 days or, more commonly, for the qualifying and race days which take place on a Saturday and Sunday, respectively. Fans may pay for grandstand tickets or 'general admission', which is considerably cheaper but involves finding a suitable vantage point around the circuit. In addition to the Formula One activity a range of 'support races' are staged. Some of these are local to the circuit and some travel with the Formula One package to some or all of the events in a season. In recent years it has become common at some races to hold associated events such as rock concerts on the evening after the race, either at the circuit itself or at a nearby venue.

The live experience

From the early years of Formula One to relatively recent times the sole source of information for a spectator at the track was the public address (PA) system, through which the circuit's own commentator would provide a description of the race. For some parts of the circuit this commentary would be drowned out by the noise of the cars. Experienced spectators would also keep their own 'lap charts' noting the position of the cars on each lap, and a lap chart template was usually provided in the printed race programme. The advent of large-scale video screens allowed the TV feed to be broadcast around the circuit and many of the grandstands would have a screen within sight of them to augment the PA system.

In 2003 a Canadian company created Kangaroo TV (Autosport, 2006), renamed FanVision in 2010. This provided a handset for spectators containing live timing screens, video feed, in-car video footage and the BBC's radio commentary feed, allowing spectators to be fully informed throughout the event with real-time information wherever they were on the circuit. These handsets could be hired for the event or bought outright by regular attenders. They were also used by the teams and their sponsors as 'extras' for their guests (Autosport, 2007). The information feed for these devices was restricted to the circuit area and they could not be used remotely. In an interesting external issue, FanVision ceased to be available at Formula One events at the end of 2012 after the company failed to agree new licensing terms with the commercial rights holder (Bernie Ecclestone) (Autosport, 2013).

All of these technologies were provided by the race organizers or their supporting companies. However, the advent of smartphones and social media channels (see below) also enables spectators to monitor other information flows during an event, assuming appropriate access to network or wireless coverage.

The live experience of Formula One is primarily based on the impact of the speed, smell and noise of the cars and the skill of the drivers. The ability of spectators to view the action on the circuit varies according to the circuit layout and the position of the grandstands and other spectator areas. In many cases spectators will choose to watch at a position overlooking a corner, chicane or other challenging part of the circuit where the speed and driver skill will be most on display and action such as overtaking is likely. At many circuits this may be combined with a wider view of part of the circuit allowing a range of action to be viewed. While viewing at the start/finish line area may seem a logical choice, in practice action at this point of the circuit is likely to be limited although this is often compensated by a view of the pits area where there is considerable activity at various points in the race. The key point in relation to live spectating is that the choice has to be made of which area of the circuit upon which the spectator will focus. This contrasts with sports such as football and rugby where a spectator will reasonably expect to have at least some view of the whole playing area. A Formula One spectator is at a single point on the circuit and their experience of action elsewhere will be dependent on access to a large screen, the circuit commentary via the PA system, a radio commentary or a FanVision device. In this sense they are in the same position as a TV viewer in relation to all the action taking place away from their specific point on the circuit, which will need to be delivered to them through some form of media or they will be unlikely to be able to interpret the action they are seeing in terms of the whole race. It also means that TV has the potential to add considerably to the apparent competitiveness of the race through judicious editing, statistical information and commentator skills.

A Formula One circuit may have a limited relationship to its geographical location. Where earlier 20th century circuits, some of which are still in use, are a product of their surroundings, many more recent circuits represent a 'new build' approach on a cleared site rather than an adaptation of existing features. The Spa Francorchamps circuit in Belgium (which remained on the Formula One calendar in 2011 but was under threat for financial reasons) was created in 1921 using public roads, which were closed for the race. The original circuit was 14 miles in length and was used in this form until 1970 when the permanent circuit was established. The permanent circuit is only 4.5 miles in length but is still based on the shape and contours of the public road network. For this reason the circuit is rooted in its landscape and its challenges are determined by that landscape in terms of gradients, corners and weather conditions (it is located in a forested area notorious for its wet weather). In contrast the recent Yeongam circuit in South Korea (Autosport Plus, 2010) has been laid out on a cleared site. Many of the newer circuits feature corners copied from other famous circuits. While this may lead to a challenging circuit it is decontextualized from the geography or history of the area. There is an inevitable distinction between historic circuits that are rooted in the culture of their areas and used by generations of Formula One participants and the newer circuits that have been created purely as commercial facilities. The growth of Formula One as a global business has, however, meant that more and more of the historic circuits are being dropped, and while fans may value the history of the sport, it is clear that the commercial rights holders will not maintain any race that cannot meet their financial demands, regardless of its cultural significance. For the purposes of this case study the main impact of this development will be that, for a spectator, the live experience will lack context and they may be less likely to spend significant amounts on travelling long distance to a circuit that is no different to one closer to home. This is being reflected in spectator numbers at some of the new circuits and, therefore, in their ability to maintain their financial commitments. As a result of this fans may continue to visit Spa Francorchamps or Silverstone for the British Grand Prix but consider the TV experience to be preferable for other races. For the live experience to continue to be meaningful it may need to incorporate elements of the TV and social media experience while maintaining the visceral thrill of the live action and the sense of being in a meaningful location.

A related element in the development of the live experience has been the reduction in direct access to the participants (drivers, constructors, cars) for the general spectator. In the early days of Formula One the paddock (the area where the teams are based) and pit lane (the area containing the garages and the access to the track) were generally open to spectators except during the race itself. From the 1980s onwards this access has steadily declined until the present day when only the rich are able to buy access to the Paddock Club, while a small number of spectators are able to undertake a 'pit walk' at specific times and under close supervision while the teams attempt to hide their cars and technologies from the cameras to protect their technological advantage. In part this is an inevitable response to modern security issues, but in reality it is related to maximizing the earning potential of the sport and maintaining its elitist feel. It has resulted in a sense of separation between the teams and drivers and the spectators, who rely on the media coverage to provide them with insight into what is happening within the paddock. This is another example of the inability of the live experience to provide the same depth of engagement with the event as the media experience in the modern sport. As noted below, recent TV coverage has aimed to recreate a sense of the spectator being inside rather than outside the action and the advent of Internet and social media channels have the potential to develop this even further. While the visceral experience of live Formula One will undoubtedly remain a thrill for many spectators, the total immersion experience is increasingly not about being at the circuit but being immersed in the media channels that are available to communicate the complete event to the fan wherever they are.

TV coverage

Early TV coverage of Formula One consisted of short highlights programmes of prominent events such as the Monaco and British races. Systematic live coverage began in the mid-1980s and has developed into almost blanket coverage of race weekends. Up to 2002 each event had a 'host broadcaster', usually one of the main networks of that country, and the race feed from this broadcaster was used by all other broadcasters. From 1996 to 2002 a pay-per-view feed from F1 Digital (nicknamed 'BernieVision') was available to supplement the standard coverage under the aegis of Formula One Management, the company that ran the commercial side of the sport. Although this service ended in 2002, it resulted in Formula One Management gradually taking control of broadcasting from each circuit through the use of a permanent production team generating the 'world feed' taken by all broadcasters. This feed includes the availability of 'in car' footage and team radio broadcasts (released on a time-shift basis a few minutes after they are sent), both innovations pioneered by F1 Digital. All of this has a tendency to increase the sense of similarity between Grands Prix, as the aesthetics of coverage from different localities converge.

The structure of the event and the range of participants also create a challenge for broadcasters. In 2012 Formula One comprised 12 teams each fielding two cars. The teams have differing levels of resources, drivers of varying levels of skill and experience and differing technical approaches within the fixed set of regulations. In practical terms this means that in any given season a small number of teams will finish in the top places at each race, the bulk of teams will find themselves running in the middle of the field and a small number of teams will be at the rear of the field. The emphasis is, naturally, on the teams and, more importantly for fans, the drivers at the front of the field. Coverage of other teams on TV will in general take place either when the race is uneventful at the front of the field, when the lead drivers are lapping the other cars in the field or when a specific incident occurs which affects the race as a whole (an accident, a car failure or an incident involving a lead car and a 'back marker'). Each team, however, has its dedicated fans who wish to be informed about its progress and, while not of direct concern to the fans, each team has sponsors who invest in a team in return for publicity and wish to see their brand exposed to the TV audience. Broadcasters attempt to ensure that some coverage is given to all teams. This often takes the form of dedicated features on specific teams which may highlight a particular aspect of the technical or sporting regulations common to all teams, providing general background as well as highlighting the particular team. Beyond the TV audience, the wider social media environment has allowed teams to expand their engagement with fans and this is covered in the following sections.

The advent of digital TV has allowed for a greater degree of flexibility in catering to the different requirements of Formula One viewers. For example, the BBC has made extensive use of its 'red button' service to provide extended analysis after a race. Sky has extended this concept with its dedicated Formula One channel, which allows for uninterrupted coverage. This has generally taken the form of interviews and discussions with a wide range of team personnel as well as race organizers and other officials. The relaxed style of this approach (the presenters are usually based in one of the team hospitality units or roam the pit lane area acquiring people to interview in an apparently ad hoc fashion) results in the ability to reveal a deeper level of information about the events of the race and any underlying issues, adding to the viewer's understanding. It is this ability of technology to bring the spectator inside the event that is a primary feature of the modern Formula One fan experience.

Web-based coverage: official information flows

Formula One is a technical sport, where the ability to view and analyse a data flow can add significantly to the spectator's appreciation of the action. For the casual spectator this means principally access to timing and positional information including: (i) lap times; (ii) time gaps between cars; (iii) car positions on the track; and (iv) the placing and timing of pit stops.

While on-track action is the core of Formula One, significant portions of a race can be what Formula One journalists call 'processional', where the cars are sufficiently spaced on the track that they are not attempting to overtake or defend from another car. In these circumstances the ability to view and analyse the timing data becomes important in allowing the spectator to see which car may be catching another or where the faster cars are on the track. In recent years the governing body of the sport has made basic timing information freely available to fans via its website (Formula 1, 2012; www.formula1.com). With the advent of smartphones and tablets it has added to this with the provision of a timing app that provides real-time lap-timing information and a driver tracker giving positions on the circuit and allowing fans to follow a favourite driver. While this is only a small subset of the data available to the teams themselves and the media at the track, it significantly enhances the spectator experience. The availability of the data flow allows the spectator to immerse themselves in the event in a manner not possible simply from visual information. The real potential for developing this relationship between the spectator and the event, however, comes from the development of Web 2.0 technologies as part of the immersive technology environment in which the spectator exists.

Web-based coverage: the potential of Web 2.0

The explosion of activity on the Internet made possible by Web 2.0 technologies and platforms has had a significant impact for Formula One. The ability of anyone with an Internet connection or a smartphone to post and interact with content about Formula One has transformed the fan experience and increased the options for fans. This sense of active engagement is the key to the potential of Web 2.0, and in particular social media, to transform the fan experience. Essential to this development is the ready availability of devices on which the services can be accessed. Laptop and desktop computers allow access but are limited in portability and in ease of use. The combination of greater information availability, social media channels that allow interaction and flexible handheld devices has the potential to significantly increase the immersive experience for Formula One spectators.

A key feature of the Web 2.0 environment has been the removal of the need for technical expertise in the creation of web content. While early web forums allowed fans to discuss the sport, engagement was restricted largely to moderated discussion groups from central

providers in the mainstream media. Actual content still came from the main media outlets. As Web 2.0 made it easier to create web content and data became more readily available, the potential for individuals to re-package and enhance that content increased. The essential democratization of the Web 2.0 environment has created the potential for individuals to contribute to the interpretation of and engagement with the sport and the potential for fans to access the content in ways that best suit them.

Sidepodcast.com was founded in 2006 with the mission 'to create, maintain, and further conversation about Formula 1' (Sidepodcast.com, 2012). This initially took the form of regular podcasts about Formula One events and has expanded to include a range of podcasts on Formula One-related topics and live online commentary on the races via the website's 'dashboard' page. The site also uses social media feeds such as Twitter to push content to fans, including the 'factbyte factbox' feed, which replicates the 'dashboard' content during races. The Sidepodcast Twitter feed mentioned above has just under 7000 followers at the time of writing. While this is a relatively modest number in terms of the web as a whole, for a private individual to reach that number of people on a regular basis with their views on a sport would not be possible in any other environment.

More formal media outlets also use social media to provide commentary on races. The magazine *Autosport* has been in existence for over 60 years and is a journal of record for Formula One. In addition to Twitter feeds for its journalists and an official magazine feed it uses the 'autosportlive' feed to provide play-by-play commentary on the races. At the time of writing 'autosportlive' has 30,000 followers. While this commentary essentially replicates what can be obtained from the TV feed or from other outlets, it provides a choice for fans on how they wish to engage with the event. It also creates a more dynamic relationship with the magazine, which would have been limited in the past to the weekly publication. The news feeds from the magazine website (Twitter is used to provide publication alerts) allow it to stay current in comparison with the days when a significant event occurring after a publication deadline would result in a week's delay before reporting and often inaccurate information in the current issue. The use of the live commentary service also maintains the relationship between magazine and reader during the event itself, so that the reader does not simply experience the magazine as a commentary after the event but as an integral part of the event itself, providing both instant reaction and more considered reaction later.

A further facet of the social media environment is the use by the Formula One teams themselves of services such as Twitter. Most teams have long-standing fan clubs and websites that carry team information and post-race reports and comments. Some have even hosted discussion groups in the past. Social media channels have enabled them to develop this into a more dynamic relationship with fans. Most teams have an official Twitter feed that will post before, during and after a race with information about the progress of the drivers and comments on events in the race. Some teams also allow individual team members to tweet, although the top teams do not appear to have allowed this to the same degree as the less successful teams, presumably to avoid giving away what they consider to be sensitive information. Many drivers have their own personal Twitter feeds although the demands of sponsors and their teams tend to result in their comments being relatively bland. This is not always the case, however, as demonstrated by Lewis Hamilton's tweeting of confidential data from his and his team mate Jenson Button's cars at the 2012 Belgian Grand Prix (Autosport, 2012). The developing expectation that teams will be more open to using these channels is likely to transform the sport in the coming decade. An example of the potential of this is the Twitter account of former Lotus Racing technical director Mike Gascoigne who made extensive use of his Twitter feed to comment on the progress of his drivers during a race and report on issues such as track conditions (Mike Gascoyne, 2012). The owner of Caterham (formerly Lotus) Racing, Tony Fernandes, is also an extensive Twitter user (Tony Fernandes, 2012). Caterham Racing is an example of one of the new Formula One teams using the social media environment to build a fan base and project a particular team image (MyCaterhamF1, 2012).

Conclusion

One of the key issues facing Formula One in the 21st century is the danger that many races can be seen as boring by casual spectators. In part, this is because of the advances in aerodynamics that have made cars very difficult to overtake, leading to so-called 'processional' races. This has been compounded by the fact that, in any era, only two or three teams produce a car capable of winning consistently and at times a single team has gained such superiority that few other teams are able to challenge them (for example, Ferrari's domination with Michael Schumacher between 2000 and 2004). Formula One has always been a multi-faceted sport that operates on a number of levels and, even in eras of domination, there are technical, tactical and political issues that interest fans, though the fact remains that close racing is the desire of most fans. Max Mosley's famous 1999 assertion that fans should view the race as a chess match with a number of complex strategic elements produced widespread derision but does contain a fundamental issue about the complexity of the sport and the need to understand it in its totality. Even in competitive periods races are not composed of non-stop activity and the nature of a 90-min event of this kind allows the fan time to explore the different layers of the action.

The selling of terrestrial TV rights in the UK to Sky for 2012 raises a further question for the fan experience. Non-Sky customers are able to see half of the season's events live on the BBC. It is possible to use the other media described in this study to follow the live event without the benefit of the video feed and while this is clearly far from ideal a combination of radio commentary and other resources still provide a rich fan experience. Waiting for the BBC's later repeat of the action allows a fan to watch the visual action but not to access the real-time delivery of data and information from other sources described here. The question is whether fans will choose to experience the live action through the resources available to them even without a video feed rather than forgo them in favour of a delayed visual experience where the result is not already known. The nature of fan choices made in this area will tell us much about the ultimate value of the additional elements in the experience of the Formula One fan. (This will of course apply only to fans who choose not to pay for access to Sky, but it is anticipated that there will be a significant minority of fans for whom this is a financial or technical decision and the live audience in the UK is likely to reduce as a result.)

The technical developments described above that have enhanced and developed the fan experience are beginning to enable spectators to make the most of these different layers to create and personalize an immersive experience of the sport. During a race a Formula One fan with the appropriate access to TV, mobile devices and networks can follow the action through the TV coverage while monitoring official timing feeds and viewing comments from teams and Formula One commentators as the race happens. They can find details on specific events in the race interpreted almost as they happen and post their own comments in real time as well as responding to requests for comments from others. Many of these options are also available to fans at the circuit, again given access to appropriate devices and network connectivity. Their experience of the race is shaped by all these inputs and by their ability to make their own contribution to the conversation. This experience extends beyond the boundaries of the race itself to pre- and post-race comment and analysis, allowing fans to consider events in a deeper way. There is clearly the potential for a more meaningful fan experience using these technologies as the event expands not only beyond the venue itself but beyond its limited time frame. A Formula One race takes place in a physical circuit in a particular place at a specific time, but this now bears little relation to the manner in which fans will engage with it. While the live experience will continue to be a major element, the changing nature of circuits and their locations must lead us to question how important the physical fan experience of this sport will be in a social media environment.

In the context of this book, the case study presented above demonstrates the indivisibility of the technologies from the event itself. In a technology redolent environment such as Formula One where the technologies of the races are crucial to the outcomes, it is not difficult to see that fans may become alienated from the experience of viewing or spectatorship where their access is limited by physical space, secrecy of the teams, personal technical knowledge or the editorial judgements of media organizations. Emerging themes in Formula One suggest that the availability of some data upon performance and context and the networking of these data before, during and after the Grands Prix are being combined at the level of the individual consumer to construct their own actor-network tailored to meet personal needs while serving to deepen, elongate and intensify the Formula One phenomenon. Further research upon the provenance, use and outcomes of these usages will surely be a by-product of the technologies themselves – essentially the research, and the researchers, will become part of the actor-network.

Research Directions

As noted earlier in this chapter, the main tendencies in the researching of events have been towards estimating the volume and value of festivity, partly as a means of understanding the 'benefits' of bidding for, mounting and continuing to deliver them. Of comparable interest have been studies of the impacts of festivity upon environments, local communities and economic activity, including the 'regeneration' of place as a viable economic entity. All of these types of research represent a fairly well-trodden path of work that fits largely within paradigms associated with 'policy' or 'management' or 'marketing' and have a strong association with leisure and tourism studies/ management. These studies are often, but not always, associated with a positivist research paradigm.

Consideration of technology as a significant part of the events experience has often been a mechanism whereby it is at the forefront of research activity. A common way in which to problematize technology in an events and festivals environment is to see it as an opportunity to 'enhance' the experience of an event or the reach of its 'audience'. In this kind of research, technology is often a silent and deterministic element of the events experience, 'designed-in' as a means of heightening some aspect of the event. Such research is often, but not always, associated with humanistic approaches and paradigms of research practice. Using case study analysis as part of a research study where ANT is at the fore is a relatively unusual way to pursue understandings of events, their dynamics and their key constituent elements, although ANT is relatively common in other research contexts.

Questions for Students

1. Develop an ANT case study by punctualizing a local event with which you are familiar.
2. Critically review the ways in which technology is represented in research about events and festivities published for, or by, your government tourism agency.

Further Reading

For those interested in gaining a better understanding of the range of research conducted within this field, we recommend the coverage and analyses of Don Getz (2007) *Event Studies: Theory, Research and Policy for Planned Events* and Foley *et al.*'s (2012) *Event Policy: From Theory to Strategy*. Those wishing to explore the possibilities of ANT are directed towards the excellent resource provided by Lancaster University's Department of Sociology (Lancaster University, 2004; available at: http://www.lancs.ac.uk/fass/centres/css/ant/ant-a.htm), which provides an annotated list of significant publications devoted to ANT. In exploring perspectives on technology and its social and cultural significance, readers are directed towards the field of sociology of science and sociology of technology if they wish to further explore the origins of relationships and networks covered in this chapter.

References

Autosport (2006) Kangaroo TV on Course for 2007 Roll Out. Available at: http://www.autosport.com/news/report.php/id/53012/ (accessed 15 May 2013).

Autosport (2007) Kangaroo TV Joins Forces with McLaren. Available at: http://www.autosport.com/news/report.php/id/58628/ (accessed 14 May 2013).

Autosport (2012) McLaren says Lewis Hamilton's Telemetry Tweet 'an error of judgement'. Available at: http://www.autosport.com/news/report.php/id/102214/ (accessed 15 May 2013).

Autosport (2013) FanVision Absent from Formula 1 in 2013. Available at: http://www.autosport.com/news/report.php/id/105060/ (accessed 10 January 2013).

Autosport Plus (2010) The Challenges Ahead for the Korean GP. Dieter Rencken. Available at: http://plus.autosport.com/premium/feature/3157/ (accessed 3 November 2010).

Callon, M., Law, J. and Ripp, A. (eds) (1986) *Mapping the Dynamics of Science and Technology: Sociology of Science in the Real World.* Macmillan, London.

Foley, M., McGillivray, D. and McPherson, G. (2011) *Event Policy: From Theory to Strategy.* Routledge, Abingdon, UK.

Formula 1 (2012) Available at: www.formula1.com (accessed 15 May 2013).

Getz, D. (2007) *Event Studies: Theory, Research and Policy for Planned Events.* Elsevier, Oxford.

Lancaster University (2004) ANT Resource Aphabetical List, version2.2. Available at: http://www.lancs.ac.uk/fass/centres/css/ant/ant-a.htm (accessed 14 May 2013).

Mike Gascoyne (2012) Available at: https://twitter.com/MikeGascoyne (accessed 15 May 2013).

MyCaterhamF1 (2012) Available at: https://twitter.com/MyCaterhamF1 (accessed 15 May 2013).

Sidepodcast.com (2012) Available at: https://twitter.com/sidepodcast (accessed 15 May 2013).

Tony Fernandes (2012) Available at: https://twitter.com/tonyfernandes (accessed 15 May 2013).

15 Conclusion

Rebecca Finkel,[1]* David McGillivray,[2] Gayle McPherson[2] and Peter Robinson[3]

[1]Queen Margaret University, Edinburgh, UK; [2]University of the West of Scotland, Paisley, UK; [3]University of Wolverhampton, Walsall, UK

This book was conceived to fill a gap in the study of events and festivity with a research-oriented events management text. The book has focused on exposing underpinning theoretical frameworks and draws upon international case studies to help explain various event phenomena. It has intentionally considered events from a research perspective, generating insights into the principal methodological approaches employed to produce empirical data while drawing attention to the future research needs of the field of event management.

Some topics contained within the text were already linked to a well-established body of work, such as the economics of events (Jago and Dwyer, Chapter 7) or event motivations (Gelder and Robinson, Chapter 5), but these contributing authors have successfully generated new insights, proposed alternative research questions or outlined new research directions. Other chapters have introduced relatively new or unexplored areas of study, such as the influence of digital and social media on the production and consumption of events (McGillivray and Jones, Chapter 12; Foley and Hunt, Chapter 14), environmental awareness and events (Borley et al., Chapter 13) and the role of festivals in wider community development processes (Jepson and Clarke, Chapter 2). We also set out to ensure that the book was

truly international in its reach and this has been achieved with case studies including the volunteer experience of the Commonwealth Games in Delhi, India, to the Sydney Gay and Lesbian Mardi Gras in Australia. We were also keen to include contributions that encourage critical thought on behalf of the undergraduate and postgraduate students and researchers interacting with the text. The discussion of media spectacle by Frew (Chapter 10) and Finkel's political agendas chapter (Chapter 11) provide excellent examples of authors challenging conventional wisdom in the events field. In this short concluding chapter, we want to pull together just a few of the research insights emerging from the text and propose some early future research directions offered by our contributing authors.

Research Insights

The contents of this book evidence the diverse purpose, functions and forms of events in the early 21st century. Some well-developed themes, such as the economics of events (Jago and Dwyer, Chapter 7), the management of events (Goldblatt, Chapter 8), the relationship between events and tourism (Nauright et al., Chapter 9) and the mediatization of events (Frew, Chapter

*rfinkel@qmu.ac.uk

© CAB International 2013. *Research Themes for Events*
(eds R. Finkel *et al.*)

10) have been updated to reflect the state of play in these areas of investigation. Illuminating insights have been provided into other, more recent, threads within the events literature: (i) how events are increasingly understood to have a social and community development dimension (Jepson and Clarke, Chapter 2; Misener, Chapter 3; McGillivray *et al.*, Chapter 4); (ii) how personal and psychological factors impinge upon the consumption of events (Gelder and Robinson, Chapter 5); (iii) how sexual and gendered identities are both reflected in events and provide the content for them (Markwell and Waitt, Chapter 6); and (iv) how digital and social media environments transform the production and consumption modalities for events (Foley and Hunt, Chapter 14). Finally, we have also been able to reflect on the increasingly politicized event terrain with contributions on: (i) the political agendas that underpin event strategies (Finkel, Chapter 11); (ii) the presence of resistance in its multivariate form within events (McGillivray and Jones, Chapter 12); and (iii) the impact of a powerful environmental awareness on the future of events (Borley *et al.*, Chapter 13).

There are a number of important conceptual threads that can be pulled out from the contributing chapters. First, it is noticeable how varied the field of event management is and how eclectic (and rich) its theoretical underpinning has become. For example, Jago and Dwyer (Chapter 7) emphasize the importance of economic theory in understanding the impact of events for governments, host cities, local councils and commercial interests. In contrast, Misener (Chapter 3) draws on leveraging theory to situate her discussion of the positive potential for the events process to build social capital. In a similar vein, McGillivray *et al.* (Chapter 4) draw on social capital theory to emphasize how volunteering at major sporting events can contribute to meaningful trust-based and reciprocal arrangements.

Other contributors draw more heavily on social and cultural theory to underpin their work. McGillivray and Jones (Chapter 12) draw on cultural studies and the digital humanities to understand how resistance is being re-shaped in the digital age and Frew (Chapter 10) takes his

lead from post-structural theory to stress the dark side of the media spectacle that dominates so many events. Markwell and Waitt (Chapter 6) also draw on post-structural perspectives to conceptualize Sydney's Mardi Gras as a site where sexualities are negotiated, performed and felt rather than prescribed.

Finally, a number of contributors draw on theories of community to explain the significance of varied event phenomena. For example, McGillivray *et al.* (Chapter 4) talk about volunteering communities, an increasingly prominent element in the planning and delivery of large-scale sport events. McGillivray and Jones (Chapter 12) emphasize communities of resistance – the disenfranchised who now frequently use online environments to promote their messages, organize and mobilize their disagreements around mega events. Misener, in her exploration of social capital around two large-scale events in North America (Chapter 3), explores the sustainability of community involvement and the beneficiaries of these. Jepson and Clarke (Chapter 2) argue for a definition of community festivals that is more inclusive, 'created as the result of an inclusive community planning process to celebrate the particular way of life of people and groups in the local community'. They also draw on theories of power to explain the decision-making processes that govern community festival planning processes.

The diverse theoretical traditions represented in this text point towards two principal research insights. First, the notion of an events management discipline is, as yet, unfulfilled. This text includes contributors with a diverse range of academic backgrounds including psychology, sociology, political economy, economics, cultural geography, philosophy, leisure studies and management. While this eclecticism generates much gnashing of teeth within the event management field (see debates about the events body of knowledge as an example), it is our view that the plurality of perspectives adds to its dynamism – offering new insights that would otherwise be contained within strict disciplinary boundaries. Our second insight relates to the need to form more extensive research communities of practice focused on the conceptual development of the events field. This may come under the banner of a centre for event studies or equivalent and should be a space for critical dialogue on the ontological and epistemological base for the events field.

Future Directions in Event Research

Another common feature of the chapters contained within this book is their call to arms for further research into various event phenomena so that those responsible for policy, bidding, delivery and evaluation are more fully informed, drawing on evidence emanating from a number of disciplines and fields. There are important insights to draw from the contributing chapters that need to be summarized briefly here.

Over the last two or three decades, economic analyses of the 'value' of events have dominated event research. Within that context, is it perhaps surprising (but welcome) to hear Jago and Dwyer (Chapter 7) criticize an obsession with the economic dimension in event evaluation, arguing that is to the detriment of the very important social and environmental costs and benefits. They propose that, in order for government funding to be more comprehensively appraised, event assessments need to be broadened to take, where practicable, a more comprehensive approach embracing not only economic but social and environmental factors. They suggest the need for more research into cost–benefit analysis (CBA) to determine the extent (if any) of government assistance to be provided for events.

In contrast, those sympathetic to the wider social, cultural, political and environmental outcomes of events find support in this text for further research into non-economic values. As Misener (Chapter 3) suggests with respect to leveraging theory, 'there is a lack of understanding about the effects of leveraging tactics on local and regional development strategies and thus future research must take an interdisciplinary approach to understanding event-related outcomes'. McGillivray *et al.* (Chapter 4) also stress the need for more longitudinal research in the study of major

event volunteers so that our limited understanding about longer-term legacies in communities can be strengthened. In line with the view of Misener, McGillivray *et al.* also urge event researchers to take greater cognisance of research being conducted in other disciplines and fields of study, especially around social capital (and its complexities) so that the event volunteer policies and practices developed are informed by the most robust research evidence available.

Beyond the relative 'value' of event research, McGillivray and Jones (Chapter 12) and Misener (Chapter 3) also propose that to make a difference in the lives of those affected by events from local communities, participants must be involved in the design and process of *doing* research. The turn towards co-creation is apparent in a number of academic fields and McGillivray and Jones call for more research into the power of new media narratives in shaping the story of major events. They stress the need for research focused on the quality and impact of participatory media cultures in influencing the narrative of mega events as 'only then is it possible to more fully understand whether the power relations between official and alternative narratives are shifting and if so, how this is being achieved'. In line with Foley and Hunt (Chapter 14), they also propose research into the dynamics of unplanned events – those that arise out of political or economic concerns but which utilize digital platforms effectively to organize, mobilize and communicate their cause.

In this text, Frew (Chapter 10) calls for a greater focus on a socio-cultural analysis of event phenomena, particularly in relation to media and its variants (new and social). He suggests that 'the opportunity to delve into and glean mass narratives via social media should be seen as a new frontier of research'. There is certainly a rich thread of work in exploring how new media facilitates the co-creation of events and the implications for established understandings of citizenship, community, well-being, governance and the outworking of social commerce. As Frew suggests, and others in this volume have alluded to, the emergence of social media platforms presents a challenge to existing methodological approaches and the dominant discourses of research itself.

Jepson and Clarke (Chapter 2) suggest we need to focus more on practical guidelines for monitoring best practice and community inclusion within the planning process and request that we test multi-methodological approaches within community festival research. They also call for a less detached academic-practitioner perspective and this view is echoed by Frew, who suggests that, 'too often the theoretical and practical realms have been positioned as opposites'.

At the 2012 Global Events Congress in Stavanger there was a call for a research group in Event Policy and Professor Donald Getz, University of Queensland, has proposed an Event Studies approach. Internationally, there exists an ATLAS (Association for Tourism and Leisure Education) Events Special Interest Group, established in 2010 to act as a focus for events research and scholarship. This group is currently coordinating a comparative research project to facilitate the identification of trends and developments in events internationally. Progressing further research into the conceptual, methodological and contextual issues brought forth in this text depends upon these embryonic collectives establishing a critical mass of event-related scholars working to collaboratively agreed research agendas. The generation of collaborative analyses of event processes and outcomes will be particularly useful for those teaching and researching across international borders.

Index

Page numbers in **bold** type refer to figures, tables and boxes